Desperate Passage

ETHAN RARICK

DESPERATE PASSAGE

The Donner Party's
Perilous Journey West

OXFORD
UNIVERSITY PRESS

OXFORD
UNIVERSITY PRESS

Oxford University Press, Inc., publishes works that further
Oxford University's objective of excellence
in research, scholarship, and education.

Oxford   New York
Auckland   Cape Town   Dar es Salaam   Hong Kong   Karachi
Kuala Lumpur   Madrid   Melbourne   Mexico City   Nairobi
New Delhi   Shanghai   Taipei   Toronto

With offices in
Argentina   Austria   Brazil   Chile   Czech Republic   France   Greece
Guatemala   Hungary   Italy   Japan   Poland   Portugal   Singapore
South Korea   Switzerland   Thailand   Turkey   Ukraine   Vietnam

Copyright © 2008 by Ethan Rarick

Published by Oxford University Press, Inc.
198 Madison Avenue, New York, NY 10016

www.oup.com

First issued as an Oxford University Press paperback, 2009

Oxford is a registered trademark of Oxford University Press

Library of Congress Cataloging-in-Publication Data
Rarick, Ethan, 1964–
Desperate passage : the Donner Party's perilous journey west / Ethan Rarick.
p. cm.
Includes bibliographical references and index.
ISBN 978-0-19-538331-7 (pbk.)
1. Donner Party.   2. Overland journeys to the Pacific.   I. Title.
F868.N5R37 2008
979.4'37—dc22
2007023761

9 8 7 6 5 4 3 2 1

Printed in the United States of America
on acid-free paper

For Ellie

"We were full of hope and did not dream
of sorrow."
—Virginia Reed Murphy, a survivor
of the Donner Party, describing the
journey's beginning

"All of us have dark stirrings of doubt and fear
whenever the Donner Party is mentioned. In
such extremis what would we do? Snow-
trapped and starving in the Sierras with no
hope of relief, would we fall to devouring each
other? Our fathers? Our children? Our lovers?
How close to the animal are we? How far from
the desperate beast? In the purely physical
realm of survival, what justifies what?"
—James Dickey

Contents

DRAMATIS PERSONÆ

For members of the Donner Party, ages are given as of May, 1846, when the Donners and Reeds left Independence. Ages in the text may vary slightly, as they reflect the age at the appropriate moment of the story.

MEMBERS OF THE DONNER PARTY

GEORGE DONNER FAMILY

GEORGE DONNER, *husband*, 60-62
TAMZENE DONNER, *wife*, 44
ELITHA DONNER, *George's daughter from prior marriage*, 13
LEANNA DONNER, *George's daughter from prior marriage*, 11
FRANCES DONNER, *daughter*, 5
GEORGIA DONNER, *daughter*, 4
ELIZA DONNER, *daughter*, 3

JACOB DONNER FAMILY

JACOB DONNER, *husband, about* 56
BETSY DONNER, *wife, about* 38
SOLOMON HOOK, *Betsy's son from prior marriage*, 14
WILLIAM HOOK, *Betsy's son from prior marriage, about* 12
GEORGE DONNER, *son*, 9
MARY DONNER, *daughter*, 7
ISAAC DONNER, *son, about* 5
SAMUEL DONNER, *son, about* 4
LEWIS DONNER, *son, about* 3

REED FAMILY

JAMES REED, *husband*, 45 [*returned as a rescuer after reaching safety*]
MARGRET REED, *wife*, 32
VIRGINIA REED, *Margret's daughter from prior marriage*, 12
PATTY REED, *daughter*, 8
JAMES REED JR., *son*, 5
THOMAS REED, *son*, 3
SARAH KEYES, *mother of Margret Reed, about* 70

BREEN FAMILY

PATRICK BREEN, *husband, about* 51
PEGGY BREEN, *wife, about* 40
JOHN BREEN, *son*, 14
EDWARD BREEN, *son*, 12
PATRICK BREEN JR., *son*, 9
SIMON BREEN, *son, about* 8
JAMES BREEN, *son*, 5
PETER BREEN, *son*, 2
ISABELLA BREEN, *daughter, about* 1

THE MURPHY FAMILY

LEVINAH MURPHY, *widow*, 36
LANDRUM MURPHY, *son*, 16
MARY MURPHY, *daughter*, 14
LEMUEL MURPHY, *son*, 12
WILLIAM MURPHY, *son*, 10
SIMON MURPHY, *son*, 8

FOSTERS

WILLIAM FOSTER, *Levinah's son-in-law*, 30 [*returned as a rescuer after reaching safety*]
SARAH FOSTER, *Levinah's daughter*, 19
GEORGE FOSTER, *son*, 1

PIKES

WILLIAM PIKE, *Levinah's son-in-law, about* 32
HARRIET PIKE, *Levinah's daughter*, 18
NAOMI PIKE, *daughter*, 2
CATHERINE PIKE, *daughter, about* 1

THE GRAVES FAMILY

FRANKLIN GRAVES, *husband, about* 57
ELIZABETH GRAVES, *wife*, 45
MARY GRAVES, *daughter*, 19
WILLIAM GRAVES, *son*, 17
ELEANOR GRAVES, *daughter*, 13
LOVINA GRAVES, *daughter*, 11
NANCY GRAVES, *daughter*, 8
JONATHAN GRAVES, *son, about* 7
FRANKLIN GRAVES JR., *son, about* 5
ELIZABETH GRAVES, *son, about* 1

FOSDICKS

JAY FOSDICK, *Franklin's son-in-law, about* 23
SARAH FOSDICK, *Franklin's daughter*, 21

THE EDDY FAMILY

WILLIAM EDDY, *husband, about* 28 [*returned as a rescuer after reaching safety*]
ELEANOR EDDY, *wife, about* 25
JAMES EDDY, *son, about* 3
MARGARET EDDY, *daughter, about* 1

THE KESEBERG FAMILY

LEWIS KESEBERG, *husband*, 32
PHILIPPINE KESEBERG, *wife*, 23
ADA KESEBERG, *daughter*, 3
LEWIS KESEBERG JR., *son, less than* 1

MEMBERS OF THE DONNER PARTY, *Continued*

THE McCUTCHAN FAMILY

WILLIAM McCUTCHAN, *husband, about 30 [returned as a rescuer after reaching safety]*

AMANDA McCUTCHAN, *wife, about 23*

HARRIET McCUTCHAN, *daughter, about 1*

THE WOLFINGER FAMILY

———— WOLFINGER [*first name unknown*], *husband, age unknown*

DORIS WOLFINGER, *wife, about 20*

INDIVIDUALS

ANTONIO ————-, *role unknown, about 23*

CHARLES BURGER, *teamster for the Donners, about 30*

JOHN DENTON, *teamster for the Donners, about 28*

PATRICK DOLAN, *individual emigrant and friend of the Breens, about 35*

MILT ELLIOTT, *teamster for the Reeds, about 28*

LUKE HALLORAN, *taken in by the Donners, about 25*

———— HARDCOOP [*first name unknown*], *individual emigrant, about 60*

WALTER HERRON, *teamster for the Reeds, about 27*

NOAH JAMES, *teamster for the Donners, about 16*

HIRAM MILLER, *teamster for the Donners, about 29 [returned as a rescuer after reaching safety]*

JOSEPH REINHARDT, *individual emigrant, about 30*

SAMUEL SHOEMAKER, *teamster for the Donners, about 25*

JAMES SMITH, *teamster for the Reeds, about 25*

JOHN SNYDER, *teamster for the Graves, about 25*

AUGUSTUS SPITZER, *role unknown, about 30*

CHARLES STANTON, *individual emigrant, about 35 [returned as a rescuer after reaching safety]*

JEAN BAPTISTE TRUDEAU, *employee of the Donners, about 16*

BAYLIS WILLIAMS, *employee of the Reeds, about 25*

ELIZA WILLIAMS, *employee of the Reeds, about 31*

OTHERS*

EDWIN BRYANT, *a newspaperman who initially traveled with the Donners and Reeds, but later went ahead as part of a mule train*

CHARLES CADY, *rescuer, member of the second relief party, which was led by James Reed*

NICHOLAS CLARK, *rescuer, member of the second relief party, which was led by James Reed*

JAMES CLYMAN, *mountain man, skeptic about "Hastings' Cut-Off"*

WILLIAM FALLON, *rescuer*

JOHN C. FREMONT, *U.S. Army western explorer*

AQUILLA GLOVER, *rescuer, co-captain of the first relief party*

LANSFORD HASTINGS, *promoter of "shortcut" taken by the Donner Party*

HEINRICH LIENHARD, *emigrant traveling ahead of the Donner Party*

LUIS ————-, *Indian sent from Fort Sutter, age unknown*

WILLIAM RUSSELL, *captain of the party with which the Donners and Reeds initially traveled*

SALVADOR ————-, *Indian sent from Fort Sutter, age unknown*

JOHN SINCLAIR, *Sacramento alcalde, or top local official*

JOHN STARK, *rescuer*

CHARLES STONE, *rescuer, member of the second relief party, which was led by James Reed*

JOHN SUTTER, *owner of Sutter's Fort, at site of modern Sacramento*

REASON TUCKER, *rescuer, co-captain of the first relief party*

LOUIS VASQUEZ, *co-proprietor, with Jim Bridger, of Bridger's Fort*

SELIM WOODWORTH, *Naval officer and rescuer*

*This is not an exhaustive list of every rescuer or person connected to the story. These are figures mentioned prominently in the text.

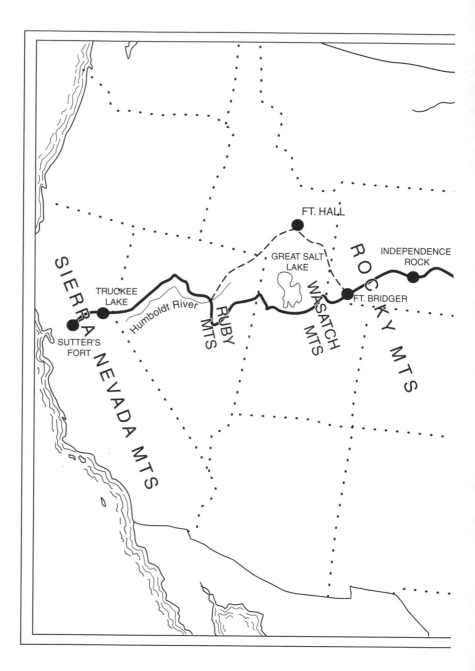

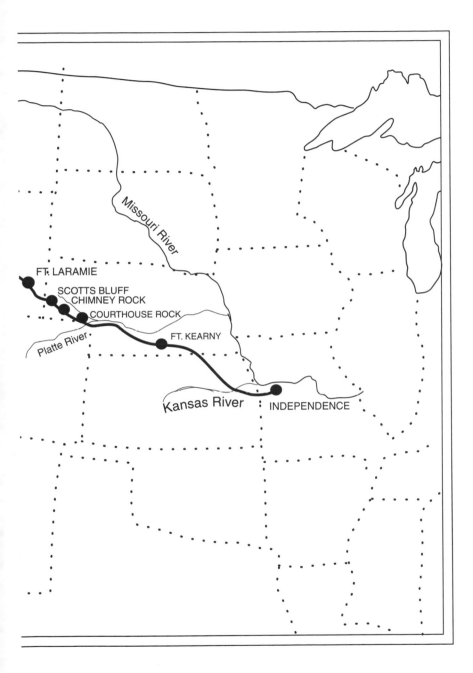

Desperate Passage

Prologue

Margret Reed spread out a buffalo robe for her children and then covered them with a shawl. It was snowing—"great feathery flakes," as one of the youngsters remembered—so every few moments Reed would rouse herself and shake the accumulation from their makeshift bedding, lest she and the children be buried alive in a muffling layer of white.

Huddled near a campfire, the forward section of the Donner Party had stopped for one last night of rest before the final assault on the mountains. Almost six months earlier, they had left Independence, Missouri, striking out for new lives in California. In the long ordeal of their journey, they had survived accidents, misjudgment, inexperience, disease. They had battled each other and helped each other. They had buried some comrades and abandoned another. They had hacked their way over trackless mountains and willed their way across murderous deserts. They had listened to the blandishments of a huckster promoting a shortcut that did not exist. Most important of all, they had fallen behind their fellow emigrants. That was the one unpardonable sin of the whole great venture, and now their penance was upon them.

The Donner Party is always remembered, of course, for the transcending horror that its members would be forced to endure. Unquestionably, the story says much about the mix of desperation and courage that allows human beings to survive seemingly impossible ordeals. But the tale also reflects a simpler and more practical truth about the journey to the American West—that it was a headlong dash for safety.

Pioneer families left Independence as soon as the warmth of spring gave them dry ground to travel over, crossed the broad middle of the continent at the height of summer, and—they hoped—reached the temperate climates of the Pacific before the first snows of winter closed the mountain passes. There was little room for error. Even at the slow gait of an ox or the creaking roll of a wagon, the journey was a race against time.

The Donner Party pushed that hurried schedule to the absolute limit and had spent much of the summer trailing in the dusty wheel ruts of the other wagons of 1846. For weeks now they had brought up the rear, the last, lonely party on the road from the comfortable familiarity of the Midwest to the alluring opportunities of the Pacific.

Yet they had endured, and pushed on, and were within reach of success. They faced one last barrier—the Sierra Nevada, the steep mountain range that separates California from North America's Great Basin. It was early November, snow was thick on the ground, and cold rains and dark clouds gave a hint of storms to come. A trailing band of the party—including the Donner families, for whom the group was named—was a few miles behind, but this forward group was approaching the pass that would take them over the mountains and down into the foothills, and then into the broad, verdant grasslands of California's Central Valley. Only another two miles, perhaps three, and they could start down toward their new lives. Two men had scouted ahead and predicted that if everyone kept moving, the entire group could crest the pass and make it through. But by the time the scouts returned, nothing could induce the weary party to move. The day's struggle had been monumental just to get this far, it was twilight already, and someone had managed to start a campfire, an irresistible bulwark of warmth and solace. The emigrants had settled around the fire and insisted they would camp there through the night and cross the pass in the morning.

Then the snow began falling, the "dreaded snow," as one survivor later wrote. It sizzled into the campfire, piled up on the backs of mules, covered tracks from earlier in the day. By morning, at least a foot of fresh powder had fallen. The drifts were far deeper still, the pass ahead a frozen barricade. The day before, escaping the mountains had seemed an arduous task that would require all that human beings could give. Now, it was simply impossible. They had no choice but to retreat down the mountainside, retracing their path so they could pitch camp at a lake far below, either to await a lucky break in the weather or, more likely, to winter over until the spring thaw. Even there the snow could pile to twenty feet and more. Drifts could cover cabins, even trees. Temperatures were sure to fall well below freezing. Game—their only potential source of fresh food—would be vanishingly scarce.

The Donner Party was trapped by a cruel combination of geography and time. Behind them lay nearly two thousand miles of wilderness; ahead, an impassable range of mountains. Behind them lay the days they had wasted; ahead, months of merciless winter. No longer could they afford fanciful thoughts of new homes and farms and lives. Now the men and women and children of the Donner Party were reduced to a single, elemental goal: to survive.

Part 1

Journey

Jumping Off

I

Sitting in her tent on the soft grass of a prairie spring, Tamzene Donner contemplated the vast expanse of wilderness she was about to enter and decided to bid her sister one last goodbye. She reached for a fresh sheet of stationery and carefully noted the date—May 11, 1846—and the location: Independence, Missouri. The next day she would begin a journey as exciting and dangerous as any that could be imagined.

Tamzene and her family were headed for "the bay of Francisco," two thousand miles away in California, a trip she guessed would take four months. The great migration of which they were a part literally engulfed them on the prairie. Tamzene guessed seven thousand wagons might be going west, and while the real number was less than a tenth so large, rigs stood everywhere. Owners tightened the wagon covers, laid out tack for the morning hitch, hammered home a final repair. Mounds of supplies vanished as crates and trunks and burlap bags disappeared into the wagon beds, stowed in precise array. Frying pans and tools and overalls succumbed to a final cleaning. Oxen and mules and horses grazed in the warmth of the sun, their tails flapping against ever-present flies. Children capered at play. The sounds—the edge of a tent flapping in the wind, the neighing of horses, the barking of dogs, greetings and farewells and talk of the trail ahead—mixed with the smell of sod and manure and campfires and freshly laundered calico. "I can give you no idea of the hurry of this place at this time," Tamzene wrote.

Tamzene and her husband, George, were going west with five children, their own three young daughters and George's two older daughters from a previous marriage. George's brother Jacob and his wife, Betsy, had come too, with their seven youngsters. So too had the Reeds, James and Margret and four children, another family from the Donners' hometown of Springfield, Illinois. Together, the three families had left Springfield a month earlier, but the trip thus far had been an easy prelude, an undemanding ramble through farmland and towns. The real voyage to California began here, at Independence, a boomtown at the edge of the frontier.

Tamzene had tried to write her sister once before, but the letter had been laid aside, perhaps because the preparations for the trip had left no time, perhaps because it was simply too hard to say goodbye. The old letter had been soiled—she rued the waste of a nice sheet of pink paper—and so now she was starting again. One of her children played with "an old indiarubber cap"; another pestered her with questions.

The children were the reason for the move, or at least part of the reason. A new life in the West would be "an advantage to our children and to us," Tamzene insisted, yet there was a hint in her letter of the anxiety anyone would have felt. "I am willing to go," she wrote. Willing, not eager.

As if to reassure herself as much as her sister, she outlined their ample gear and provisions: three wagons, each pulled by three yoke of oxen, food, clothing, even a few head of dairy cows for milk and butter along the trail. She added news of another family member, then closed with a promise to write that was really an acknowledgment of just how difficult, perhaps impossible, that might be. "Farewell, my sister, you shall hear from me as soon as I have an opportunity. . . . Farewell."

AMERICA IN THE 1840s hummed with energy and growth and ambition. The summer of the Donners' journey, the country turned seventy years old—an adolescent age for a nation—and its youthful vigor was unmatched. Since the turn of the century, the population had tripled. The geographic size of the nation had quadrupled. The gross national product had increased sevenfold. The United States was, in the words of historian James McPherson, "the *wunderkind* nation of the nineteenth century."

Technology seemed to be conquering everything. Since the opening of the Erie Canal in 1825, the country had been laced with man-made waterways. Steamboats, still a relatively new invention, plied the rivers carrying freight and passengers. Even the earliest railroads were belching along. Textile factories had supplanted individual weavers, rolling out affordable fabric by the ton. Inventors fashioned wonder after wonder: Samuel Colt the revolver, John Deere the steel plow, Charles Goodyear a vulcanized rubber that withstood heat and cold. The electric motor had been invented. America had the world's first dental school, and an American doctor had performed the first operation using general anesthetic. In 1844, Samuel Morse had sent the first telegraph message: "What hath God wrought?"

Yet beyond Independence, this cacophonous modern world faded to a hush. To pioneers, Independence was the "jumping-off point," a phrase that rightly suggested the dramatic abandonment of safety, and to the men and women about to undertake the journey, it was a dividing line between civilization and wilderness. To the west, boundless grasslands stretched toward the sunset, an ocean of grass streaked here and there with the trees of a river bottom. There were no great cities. There were no cities at all. The largest community of the west was Santa Fe, with perhaps a few thousand residents, and that was far to the south of the intended path. Where American settlers were headed, there were only a few small settlements—and those were two thousand miles away in California and Oregon. In between, there was nothing save Indians and a handful of trading posts. On many maps the vast expanse was labeled as the "Great American Desert." In the parlance of the day, those who made the trip were invariably "emigrants," people leaving their country for an unknown shore.

Some had personal reasons for going: a broken heart or a run of bad luck. Others were escaping hard times. An economic crash in 1837 had briefly halted the boom, touching off a painful depression. And yet the economy had started to grow again by the mid-1840s. Agricultural prices still had not rebounded fully, but the worst of the crisis was over.

The more common reason for starting the journey was simply the continual theme of America: going toward the sunset in search of a better life. Almost from the day the United States bought its way into the western half of the continent, with the Louisiana Purchase in 1803, Americans began to dream of using their newly acquired land as a highway to the Pacific. The hard and barren prairies seemed beyond the hope of cultivation, but they could still serve a purpose: access to the rich river valleys of Oregon and California. To go by sea was a grueling prospect—months of churning through the South Atlantic, then battering around Cape Horn, then sailing up through the whaling waters of the South Pacific and at last to California. Typically the trip took longer by sea, at least five months compared to perhaps four by going overland. And it was often more expensive, especially since the overland migrant's costs might be recouped at the journey's end if he sold his oxen or wagon. It is no surprise that Americans wondered if the overland alternative might not be better.

No one knew with certainty, because for the better part of four decades after the purchase, almost no Americans save a few hardy mountain men and a few inflamed missionaries dared venture into the Far West. The lack of experience did not, however, quiet a vigorous debate about the practicality of overland travel. The exploration party led by Meriwether Lewis and William Clark endured countless hardships in reaching the Pacific, dragging a boat up the Missouri River for much of the trip, but after their return it was not long before Americans were being told that repeating such a trip might actually become routine. Lewis and Clark arrived back in St. Louis in 1806, yet as early as 1813 the *Missouri Gazette* announced that wagons could reach Oregon with surprisingly little trouble. There was nothing along the way "that any person would dare to call a mountain," the paper claimed. Newspapers insisted that the trip to Oregon would soon be as simple as traveling among eastern cities, or even a carriage ride to a summer resort. The *American Biblical Repository* declared the path to the Pacific so inviting that it must have been "excavated by the finger of God." It was said in some quarters that crossing the Rocky Mountains was so easy that a man driving a wagon would hardly notice the rise.

Skeptics, on the other hand, decried the idea as madness. The trip was compared to a journey to the moon. Livestock would starve along the way. Indians would kill the pioneers. Women and children could not conceivably survive the rigors. Horace Greeley, the famous editor of the *New York Tribune,* insisted that trying to take a family west amounted to "palpable homicide."

But the westward urge could only be contained for so long. The middle of the continent, which not so long ago had itself been wilderness, was starting to fill up and settle down, losing the edge that attracted a certain kind of man. Missouri joined the Union in 1821, Arkansas in 1836, Michigan the year after that. The result, by the 1840s, was a decade of expansionist fever. In 1844, James K. Polk won the presidency by promising to annex Texas in the south and Oregon in the north, in the latter case vowing a war if the British didn't abandon their claim as far north as Alaska. The following year, a New York journalist named John O'Sullivan coined a term for America's grand ambitions: It was the country's "manifest destiny" to occupy the continent from sea to sea, no matter that the British still claimed Oregon and that California was part of Mexico.

By that time, western settlers had already started fashioning a continental country. They crafted new lives at the edge of the Pacific, assuming more or less that if Americans forged ahead, America would follow. The first wagon train went west in 1841, the brainchild of a twenty-one-year-old Missouri schoolteacher named John Bidwell. His Missouri land stolen by a claim-jumper and his imagination fired by tales of a California paradise, Bidwell organized the Western Emigration Society and drew pledges of commitment from more than five hundred would-be followers. When fewer than a hundred people showed up at the May rendezvous to start the trip, Bidwell plunged ahead anyway. Merely setting out on the journey was a remarkable display of courage. "We knew that California lay west," Bidwell wrote later, "and that was the extent of our knowledge." By luck, the emigrants encountered a party of Jesuit missionaries guided by Thomas Fitzpatrick, an Irishman who had already spent a quarter-century in the West and was a legendary mountain man. Fitzpatrick led them all to the vicinity of Fort Hall, in present-day Idaho, where they split into three groups.

The Jesuits headed north, into modern-day Montana, and the settlers cleaved off into separate companies bound for Oregon and California. To quicken the pace, the Oregon group abandoned its wagons immediately and rode and hiked to missionary Marcus Whitman's outpost at Walla Walla, then survived a harrowing raft trip down the Columbia River to reach the Willamette Valley. The Californians clung to their wagons far longer, finally abandoning them at the foot of the Pequop Mountains in what is today eastern Nevada. Even without the drag of the wagons, they were soon desperate and half-starved. They ate their horses and mules, then the oxen, finally crows and even a wildcat. Without maps or a specific sense of the route, they could easily have disappeared and been lost to history. But they managed to survive, cresting the Sierra Nevada and then working their way down through the canyons and ridges of the western slope, finally reaching the grasslands of the San Joaquin Valley. On November 4, in what are now the outlying suburbs of San Francisco, the remnants of the Bidwell Party stumbled into a ranch owned by John Marsh, an American expatriate and charlatan who fled the United States one step ahead of an arrest warrant but then grew rich in the California sunshine. Regular people—not mountain men, but a schoolteacher and farmers and young adventurers—had reached the Pacific by land.

They had done so by abandoning their wagons, however, and wagons were critical to settlers. When a later party managed to take a few wagons all the way to Oregon, the focus of emigration fever shifted north. Pioneers heading for Oregon soon outnumbered the trickle to

California, and for a time it seemed that Oregon would grow to be the colossus of the West.

Then, in 1844, a small group bucked the trend, declaring for California and holding to their destination against all warnings of doom. The Stephens-Townsend-Murphy Party included fifty people at the start and fifty-two at the end, the result of a safe journey for the beginners and the addition of two babies along the way. The captain was Elisha Stephens, a blacksmith and trapper with a full white beard and an eccentric streak. The other namesakes were Martin Murphy, an Irish immigrant eager for the official Catholicism of Mexican California, and John Townsend, a doctor destined to become the first licensed physician in California. Like the California wagon trains of previous years— the ones that had been forced to abandon their wagons and pack over the Sierra—the group led by Stephens followed the Oregon Trail to Fort Hall and then turned southwest down the Humboldt River through the deserts of what is now Nevada. They followed the Humboldt until it literally disappeared, for the Humboldt is an unusual river in that it does not feed to the sea but ends in a sink, a boggy lake from which there is no outlet. The water seeps down into the thirsty earth or evaporates into the blistering sky, and the Humboldt dies, a waterway conquered by a surrounding, merciless desert.

From the sink, previous California-bound trains had headed south, marching down the eastern flank of the Sierra, searching constantly on their right for a mountain pass, a doorway through an imposing granite wall. (One group managed to get wagons to the Owens Valley, along the eastern edge of the modern state of California, but that marginal success didn't count for much. To the pioneers, reaching California meant crossing the Sierra.) The Stephens Party, on the other hand, headed west from the sink rather than south. In an astonishing stroke of good fortune, they had encountered a Paiute Indian who led them to a river running out of the Sierra Nevada. The banks were wooded and grassy, crucial for supplying fuel for the campfires and feed for the oxen. They named it the Truckee, which they mistakenly thought was the name of the Indian who led them to it.

They followed the river, then a creek that branched away due west, and finally, amid November snow flurries, found a lake at the base of the mountains, the granite face above them rising almost as high as the Empire State Building. They abandoned six of their eleven wagons so they could double-team those that remained and then carried the supplies and freight to the summit so the wagons could be taken over empty. Part of the way up, a sheer vertical face about ten feet high stood in their way, seemingly impassable for any wheeled vehicle. They unhitched the wagons and drove the oxen up a narrow defile in the cliff. Then they reyoked the animals and lowered chains to the wagons, which were hauled straight up the ledge, the oxen pulling from above and the people pushing from below. They crossed the summit on November 25, 1844, the first party to take wagons over the top of the Sierra Nevada.

The feat was in some ways a hollow victory. More than half the wagons had been left behind, those that crossed the summit had been taken over without freight, and on the way down the western slope the wagons had to be abandoned altogether, not to be recovered until the following summer. For much of the time the very survival of the emigrants had been in doubt. They were lucky to encounter an Indian willing to guide them, perhaps just as lucky to make it up and over the Sierra without some serious injury or other calamity. Still, wagons had been taken all the way through to California, and if something could be done once, it could be done again.

More than a year passed before news reached the East, but by the spring of 1846 word of the new wagon route to California was spreading. Men returning from the West talked up the discovery, and the newspapers began to publish enthusiastic accounts, including one wildly optimistic assessment that the Stephens-led group had found a "very good road." Enthusiasm for California heightened. In Independence, where the wagon trains readied themselves to head out over the prairies, camps buzzed with excitement about California's climate, said to be good for people and crops alike. One joke had it that when a Californian reached heaven, the archangel Gabriel said the man should return home—"a heap better country than this." For the first time in the brief history of the wagon trains, California surpassed Oregon as the destination of choice. A newspaperman in Independence claimed to have seen just one wagon bound for Oregon. "The word," he wrote, "is California." When Tamzene Donner's family set their wagons and their futures toward "the bay of Francisco," they were joining a rushing tide of optimistic Americans headed west.

A T FORTY-FOUR, TAMZENE DONNER had already endured one tragedy in life, showing a resiliency that would sustain her in the ordeal yet to come. Born in Massachusetts, she went south as a young woman to work as a schoolteacher. While living in North Carolina, she married and had a baby, a son who looked just like his father. But then, in three horrific months toward the end of 1831, the bedrock of Tamzene's life crumbled beneath her feet. For reasons that are not clear—perhaps an epidemic of some sort—all those closest to her died in quick succession: her son in late September, a premature baby daughter in November, her husband on Christmas Eve. Shattered and alone, she began the long process of reconstructing her life, chronicling the stages of her emotional convalescence in an extraordinary series of heartfelt letters to her sister.

"Weep with me if you have tears to spare," she wrote in January 1832, just a month after her husband's death. Later that year she grew so ill she thought she might die, an idea that did not entirely frighten her. "Sister I could die very easily. One after one of the bonds that bound one to earth are loosened and now there remains but few." The following spring, she remained deeply depressed, with little to look forward to except the occasional letter from her sister. She was plagued with nightmares, dreaming that she was wandering aimlessly while looking for lost relatives, or that she saw her sister "wasting with sickness." By 1836, five years after the deaths, she was struggling to reclaim her optimism. She resolutely insisted that despite everything, she was a lucky woman—"Think not I am unhappy. Far from it. I realize that on me heaven has been lavish of its blessings" —and was obviously proud that her abilities as a schoolteacher had allowed her to survive on her own. Responding to her brother's offer to "take care" of her, she wrote her sister, "I am abundantly able at present to take care of myself and to supply every necessary and unnecessary want."

Eventually she fled the South and its personal ghosts, taking a job as a schoolteacher in Illinois. "Think you that my wandering feet will rest this side the grave?" she wrote. Her health was improving, and she had even regained a sense of humor: "You need not fear having a brother in law, for I know not a man old enough for me in the county." Not completely healed, she had at least found an equilibrium. "To say that I have any particular source of anxiety or cause of unhappiness I cannot. To say that I have any particular pleasure I cannot. Life moves on as smoothly and quietly as a summer stream." She loved the prairie. The broad vistas—the wildflowers, the grasslands, the sunsets that spread a swath of crimson across the skyline—gave a sense of possibility. "I stop, I gaze and am awestruck."

In time, she was ready again to consider courtship. In Springfield, Illinois, she met a local farmer, George Donner, a man in some ways her opposite. If she was the lettered Yankee, he was the garrulous southerner. Born in North Carolina in the years just after the Revolutionary War, Donner had traveled through Kentucky, Indiana, even Texas, settling finally in Illinois. He was the kind of man people liked, a big fellow known around Sangamon County as "Uncle George." The nickname fit. He was more avuncular than firm, a friendly presence who was neither a natural-born leader nor merely a face in the crowd. Almost two decades older than Tamzene, he had been widowed twice and had ten children from those first two marriages.

They courted, then married in 1839 and soon began a family of their own that would eventually grow to include three daughters. It was a comfortable life. They owned 240 acres in two parcels, including their home, sixty acres of planted fields, and an orchard of apple, peach, and pear trees. "Our neighbors call us rich," Tamzene admitted. As a wife and mother she gave up teaching but indulged her intellectual bent by starting a "reading society," an antebellum version of a book club.

By 1842, ten years after the death of her first family, Tamzene Donner had started anew. With her baby daughter asleep in a cradle beside her, she paused on a spring day, the window open to the scent of apple blossoms, to write yet again to the sister who had so often received letters of woe. "Things have turned around very much to my satisfaction," she wrote. Her husband was kind, her children a constant delight. A decade after a calamity that would have destroyed many people, Tamzene Donner was a woman at peace with the vagaries of life: "I am as happy as I can reasonably expect in this changing world."

T HE DONNER FAMILY'S RELATIVE AFFLUENCE was not atypical of those who made the great westward migration. Reaching the Pacific Coast was an expensive proposition. Months of travel that produced no income, then the cost of establishing a new home in a new place—these were not expenses to be borne by the destitute. The very rich were rare in the wagon trains, but often the families heading for Oregon and California were substantial people, with established and successful lives. The Donners' departure from Springfield had been announced in the local paper, and they had hired younger, stronger men to go along on the trip and do the hard work of driving the teams. George Donner had been able to afford a recruiting advertisement touting the fact that his jobs offered the chance at a trip to California for free. "Who wants to go to California without costing them anything? . . . Come, boys!" People even said later that the Donners were carrying ten thousand dollars, some of it sewn into a quilt for safekeeping.

But for all their money, the Donners and their traveling companions, the Reeds, were just unremarkable families from Illinois, ready to join the great migration to the west. The problem was that they were late. James Reed had been told repeatedly to reach Independence by the first of April, or the middle of the month at the latest. The advice was needlessly extreme; nobody "jumped off" that early. Emigrants had to wait for spring grasses to grow so the animals would have forage. But if the Donners and Reeds had reached the town by late April or May 1, they would have had a chance to rest both themselves and their animals, to "recruit" their strength, as they would have put it. For some reason, however, the two families did not leave Springfield until mid-April and reached Independence only on May 10. The bulk of the California-bound emigrants were already out on the trail. The Springfield families took but a day to rest their oxen and other livestock, then hustled out of town in hopes of catching up. It was less obvious at the time than it would be later, but the sad fact was that the journey had barely begun, and the core of what would become the Donner Party was already lagging behind.

2

Margret Reed fretted. It had been a week of hard travel since they left Independence, but at last they had caught the main body of California-bound emigrants, a sprawling company led by a slightly pompous Kentucky lawyer named William Henry Russell. The extent of Russell's domain—nearly fifty wagons and 150 adults—offered a safety-in-numbers bulk that appealed to the Reeds and the Donners. But camp gossips spread the word that past applicants to the party had sometimes been rejected, and Margret feared that she and her family would also be turned aside.

Once, Margret had been a high-spirited young woman, dashing around on horseback with reckless abandon and proving herself an independent soul. Engaged at eighteen to an older man, she fell for one of her fiancé's younger friends, a would-be groomsman named Lloyd Backenstoe. Margret broke off the engagement and transformed Backenstoe from a groomsman to a groom, marrying him and having a daughter, a girl they named Virginia. But in 1834, just four days before their second wedding anniversary, Backenstoe died in a cholera epidemic, leaving Margret alone with a young child just months after her twentieth birthday. Widowhood stole her youthful zest, and when she married James Reed a little more than a year later, she was still bed-ridden with grief and sickness. During the ceremony, he stood next to the bed holding her hand. The ensuing years did little to improve her health. She suffered from "nervous sick headaches," migraines that debilitated her for days on end, and sometimes from fever and chills as well. The move to California was, in part, an effort to find a gentler climate.

Risking the venture was typical of her husband, a man with a full head of hair and a bit of a smirk and iron convictions, others be damned. James Reed liked the people he liked, despised those he didn't, and struck some as haughty, perhaps the legacy of the Polish nobility from which he supposedly was descended. He had made a success of himself under difficult circumstances. Born in Northern Ireland, he was brought to Virginia as a child by his widowed mother, a fatherless boy in a new country. As a young man he moved to Illinois and later served with Abraham Lincoln in the Black Hawk War. At home in Springfield after the war, he hustled through a series of businesses: furniture manufac-turing, a sawmill, the railroads.

By the time he decided to go west he was a man of means, and he did not mind if others knew of his status. Reed would never sew his money into a quilt, as George Donner did. Reed put his wealth to use, perhaps even flaunted it. Before leaving Illinois, he corresponded with a friend in Independence, picking up tips on what to bring. Reed's friend warned against skimping—"Don't be puny, get a good outfit"—and Reed heeded the advice. He had a special wagon built with an entrance on the side, like a stagecoach, and high-backed seats with handy storage areas beneath the cushions. Extensions built out over the wheels added room. A small stove, vented by a pipe running through the canvas top, provided heat on cold mornings or at night.

There were those who found Reed hard to take, but he was a born leader, and when his wagons and those of the Donner brothers rolled into the camp of the Russell Party, it was Reed who took the initiative. Hoping to make a good impression, he scrubbed the trail grime off his face and then went to see the captain.

Russell's position was less authoritative than it sounded, for wagon trains were remarkably democratic organizations. Out on the open prairie, emigrants were beyond the reach of the law, so to provide some semblance of order they usually formed into companies, electing officers to organize daily progress and settle disputes. Someone had to assign guard duty and get things moving in the morning, after all. But anything created by a show of hands could be undone just as easily. Companies shifted constantly, adding or subtracting members. Smaller groups split off, latecomers joined, individual families decided for whatever reason to change traveling companions. So too could captains be deposed, and thus they were closer to being first-among-equals than commanders of a hierarchy. Still, competition for the honor was fierce, politics carrying into the wilderness even if the law did not. Russell, who had once served in the Kentucky legislature, was undoubtedly proud of his post.

To Reed he proved "kind and obliging." The captain immediately gathered the men of the party in the center of the camp and gave a speech recommending that Reed and the Donners be admitted. Russell said he knew Reed by reputation and would vouch that he was a gentleman. Somebody moved that the new families be allowed into the company, and every hand went up to signify assent. Russell walked over to Reed's wagons to meet his family, a pleasant little visit. "We are all in good spirits," Reed wrote.

Reed's buoyancy was a little overstated, for one member of the group was suffering. Sarah Keyes, Reed's mother-in-law, was ill, too ill for the journey, really. She was seventy and afflicted with "consumption," probably tuberculosis, but she had insisted on going. Margret Reed was her only daughter, and Keyes had no intention of living out her days with her daughter and grandchildren vanished over the horizon. She may also have hoped to meet one of her sons, who had already gone west. So James Reed outfitted a special wagon designed to provide a comfortable ride for his mother-in-law, and Keyes began a trip that often defeated those half her age. The early stages seemed to do her good, her health and spirits improving by the day, but the recovery did not last. By the time the Reeds joined the Russell Party, Keyes had stopped eating. One of her eyes throbbed with pain. Increasing blindness left her unable to see a coffee cup placed near at hand.

The next morning, Keyes confided in her son-in-law. The trip had sapped her remaining strength, she told James, and she did not expect to live long. He thought the same thing, for it was plain that the old woman was fading. Unless there was "a quick change," he wrote in a letter back home, "a few days will end her mortal carear."

SIX DAYS LATER, THE EMIGRANTS STOOD looking down into the churning waters of the Big Blue River, muddy and menacing and wide as a football field. Driftwood bobbed on the swift surface. Trains typically forded here, in what is now northern Kansas, but rains had raised the water level until it was nearly even with the banks, and the normally gentle ford was instead a wagon-wrecking torrent. They were only hours too late. Two companies ahead of them had reached the river the night before, crossed safely, and could now be seen in the distance, rolling west over the broken landscape.

That night a thunderstorm hit. "The whole arch of the heavens for a time was wrapped in a sheet of flame," one man remembered. In the morning the river was higher than the night before, and the emigrants had to accept that they were stuck, probably for days.

Fortunately, they found a delightful place to wait. A few hundred yards short of the river lay a bountiful spring in a cool and shaded gully, the water "of the most excellent kind." There was good wood for campfires and grass for the stock, and even a short, steep hill nearby that offered a splendid view of the countryside. Edwin Bryant, a newspaperman going west who was the wordsmith of the group, dubbed the site "Alcove Spring," presumably because he thought a small cliff in the gully formed a natural alcove. Another man carved the new name in one of the rocks. Characteristically, Reed engraved his name and the date in big, bold letters.

Such an agreeable campsite should have done them good, but as they waited for the river to fall, Sarah Keyes's health flagged. She grew speechless, weakened before their eyes, and then, still in the presence of the daughter she had vowed not to leave, drew a final labored breath. The men of the party had already started work on a raft so the wagons could be floated across, but the rites of the dead took precedence. The men felled a cottonwood tree, hewed it into planks, and hammered together a coffin. About sixty or seventy yards from the trail they dug a grave. John Denton, a young Englishman traveling with the Donners, found a gray stone and carved on its face the dead woman's name and age.

At 2:00 P.M. the emigrants formed into a funeral procession and marched solemnly to the grave. They sang a hymn—"with much pathos and expression," Bryant noted—and then, gathered beneath the oak boughs, listened to a sermon by a Presbyterian minister along on the journey. Like any good preacher, he tailored his message to his audience. "Trouble yourselves not about those that sleep," he urged, taking as his biblical text the Book of Thessalonians. It was important, he said, to seek a "better country," a place without sickness, like the place where Keyes now rested. George McKinstry, a sickly Mississippi merchant heading west for his health, wrote in his diary that it had been a "sensible sermon." That was true, and the reasons were more than theological. In a race against time amid a great wilderness, the pioneers standing bareheaded at the grave of Sarah Keyes would do well to hustle along toward the better country they were seeking, not tarry over the old woman they had just laid to rest.

THE NEXT MORNING THE RIVER was still running high, too high to ford, and the men returned to building a raft for the wagons. They chopped down two more cottonwoods and hollowed them out to make huge canoes, at least twenty-five feet long and close to four feet wide. Then they laid a cross-frame over the tops of the two craft, creating a platform on which the wagons could be taken over. When it was ready to be launched, they named the raft the "Blue River Rover" and shouldered it out into the swift current. When it stayed afloat, cheers erupted.

They crossed nine wagons that day and were up early the next morning to continue the job. In the afternoon a cold wind blew in from the northwest, and as the temperature dropped rain began to fall. Many of the men were standing in the river working the raft from bank to bank with ropes, holding their footing against a current strong enough to knock a man down, and the brutal conditions began to take their toll. Two normally affable men got into a fistfight, even drawing knives, although peacemakers stepped in before anyone was seriously hurt. The last wagon finally crossed about 9:00 P.M., and they made camp in a brake of trees on the western side of the river, but with the cold and the wet and the exhaustion, many men were shivering violently by the time they reached their tents. They were back on the trail the following morning, but between the funeral and the raft-building, more than five days had been lost, time in which a lucky train might make seventy-five miles.

Cold north winds began to blow relentlessly, forcing the men to bundle up in overcoats, the women in shawls. Some of those who had been riding in the wagons started walking, the better to stay warm. Then, almost overnight, a heat wave struck, and people started looking forward to the shade of their tents or a cooling breeze. On the open prairie, Bryant wrote, the heat could be "excessively oppressive."

But they were making good distances across the tabletop flatlands of southern Nebraska, or at least good distances for a journey that occurred at the pace of an ox—fifteen to twenty miles a day. In early June they reached the first milestone of their trip: the Platte River. Too shallow for navigation, the Platte had been useless to trappers and fur traders, who used heavy keelboats to carry their supplies upriver and their spoils down. But for emigrants, the Platte was perfect—a gentle, unmistakable byway that pointed directly at an important pass in the Rocky Mountains. In the era of the wagon trains, the Platte, which pours down out of the Rockies and traverses the length of modern Nebraska before emptying into the Missouri, was the great highway of the West. The Donners and the Reeds and their companions encountered it about at the site of modern-day Kearney, Nebraska, where they turned west and began working their way upstream along the south bank.

On June 12, Reed shot the first elk taken by the company. Hunters had seen some antelope, but the fleet-footed animals were too fast for most of the horses, and it was hard to get within range. As a result, the meat in the emigrants' diet had been mostly the salted supplies they had purchased in Independence, and the tender, fatty flesh of Reed's elk was welcome.

The next day, Reed lost a little of his glory when two other men rode back from a hunt with fresh buffalo steaks. Reaching the buffalo herds was always a notable occasion for the westward emigrants, many of whom had never seen the great animals before. "If we had found a gold mine," one man wrote during the Gold Rush, "there could not have been a greater commotion." Not surprisingly, Reed's fellow hunters were feted as heroes in camp, and in a letter back home Reed made plain his feelings about their success. The men were hailed as "the best buffalo hunters on the road—perfect '*stars*.'" Reed, on the other hand, was thought a greenhorn, a "Sucker." The other men set out again, and the camp was full of talk that they would bring back more of the prized buffalo meat. When Reed organized his own party, almost no one wanted to go along. The snub rankled, and Reed decided to prove both himself and his horse:

And now, as *perfectly green* as I was I had to compete with old experienced hunters, and remove the *stars* from their brows; which was my greatest ambition, and in order too, that they might see that a Sucker had the best horse in the company, and the best and most daring horseman in the caravan.

So Reed mounted Glaucus, took three companions, and rode out until he found a buffalo herd so large that it darkened the plains. Disregarding the danger, he outran his friends and then rode straight into the herd. Within minutes, he had shot three buffalo—two bulls and a calf—and was so far ahead of his companions that he rode to a small knoll and sat in the grass to wait. He claimed to have counted 597 buffalo, although it's hard to imagine that he could really have kept track. From his perch, he watched his friends, whose balky horses refused to get close enough to the buffalo to bring one down. Reed had a laugh at their expense, then rode over and joined the hunt, chasing down a bull and shooting him. He shot one more calf, and then they set about the butchering, taking what meat they could carry and leaving the rest for the wolves, unmoved by the waste.

The fresh meat must have boosted spirits, but it was the acclaim that Reed cherished most. When they made it back to camp, he reported proudly, he was hailed as "the acknowledged hero of the day." Other men huddled around Glaucus and pronounced her the finest horse in the train. When he wrote home, Reed made sure to mention the compliment.

Vexatiously Slow

3

The pace could drive a man mad. The column creaked along at two miles an hour. Men could walk faster. They might stop by the trail to write a letter or butcher a fresh kill, and then an hour or two later they would rise and pocket their pencils or their hunting knives and, with a bit of brisk walking, catch the ponderously rolling wagons. Progress, one man said, was "vexatiously slow."

"Covered wagons" became the symbol of the journey, but in fact the rigs used by the emigrants were typically small and simple, not the huge Conestoga freight wagons of the movies. The beds were four or five feet wide and perhaps twice as long, a size that allowed them to maneuver through the canyons and forests and mountain passes the emigrants would eventually face. The running gear was simple: wooden axles and wheels, although strips of iron were wrapped around the wheels to serve as tires. There were no brakes. Going downhill, a wheel or two would be locked with a chain to take off some speed, or a felled tree would be dragged behind, the deadweight serving as a kind of land anchor. Typically, there was no seat for the "driver." Instead, he walked along beside the draft animals, controlling them with nothing but a whip and voice commands.

As a cover, canvas was stretched over bows of wood that had been soaked and bent. In a particularly strong wind, emigrants were known to take down the canopies to reduce the pressure and avoid damage or even being toppled. But almost always the canvas crowns shone out over the trains, a gleam of white against a stark prairie backdrop. That too produced a maritime analogy. As the wagons snaked along ridges and dropped to river crossings, winding with the aimless terrain, the wagon covers looked from a distance like the sails of ships. In time, the mirage produced a fanciful nickname for vehicles that were a thousand miles from the sea: prairie schooners.

The problem with the wagons was the engine. To pull great loads across the better part of two thousand miles, most emigrants used oxen, which were recommended over horses or mules in the tattered guidebooks bouncing in the wagon beds, books that had been thumbed through countless times during the months of preparation back on the farm. Oxen were cheaper, more durable, and said to be less likely to wander from camp. But the ox is not a fleet animal. Two miles an hour for a journey of two thousand miles meant a thousand hours on the trail, 125 days at eight hours a day, more than four months in all. And that ignored the inevitable—the odd day of rest, one of sickness, a busted axle or a shattered wheel. There would be rivers to ford, hills to climb, mud and sand where moving the wagons at two miles an hour was a fantasy even with every ox on the team straining at the front and every man in the company pushing from the rear. There would be obstacles they could not yet imagine. On a journey into the unknown, perfect progress is perfectly impossible.

Edwin Bryant, the newspaperman, was one of those who rued the crawling tempo. In the moving frontier village that was the wagon train, Bryant stood out—he had studied medicine and later worked as an editor at the *Louisville Courier*—and like all intellectuals he thought too much. Walking along, a troubling realization began to vex him. Some emigrants lacked the necessary impatience, the gut-level recognition of the potential disaster that delay might invite. There was no such thing as getting to California too early, but being too late might mean never getting there at all. Saving time at the early stages was like putting money in a bank. Later, when the inevitable difficulties and delays cropped up, the train could draw down its account and still make it over the final mountains in time. And as with any savings plan, the sooner you began investing, the greater your nest egg at the end. Yet there were those who wanted to pitch camp early and break it late. "I am beginning to feel alarmed at the tardiness of our movements," Bryant wrote, "and fearful that winter will find us in the snowy mountains of California."

T AMZENE DONNER WAS MORE SANGUINE. After more than a month on the trail, things were going well, she thought. The Indians had proven surprisingly amiable. The chiefs of a local tribe had taken breakfast at the Donner tent that very morning. "All are so friendly that I cannot help feeling sympathy and friendship for them," she wrote to a friend back home. No cattle had been stolen—at least not "where proper care has been taken"—and the previous night two men who had exhausted their horses in a hard hunt had slept out in the open, a sign they feared no attack.

The open spaces of the prairie provided "a first rate road," and the countryside was "beautiful beyond description." Even crossing the creeks, though difficult, presented no real danger. The grass, sparse from lack of rain the year before, was plentiful for the cattle, and the cows produced ample supplies of milk and butter. Russell had proved an "amiable" captain, although she had to admit the wagon train was a mixed band. "We have [some] of the best of people in our company, and some, too, that are not so good."

Tamzene herself was making time for reading and botany. She had found tulips, primrose, lupine, "the ear-drop," larkspur, creeping hollyhock, and a "beautiful flower" she could not identify but that resembled the bloom of the beech tree. Most of her time, she admitted, was consumed with cooking, but even that was hardly an onerous chore. She was a little concerned that their flour might run low, but rice and beans and cornmeal were proving good staples, and the hunters were bringing in plenty of meat. As fuel, "Buffalo chips are excellent—they kindle quick and retain heat surprisingly." That night they had dined on buffalo steaks that were as tasty as if they had been cooked over hickory coals.

She estimated they had traveled 450 miles since leaving Independence and had only 200 more miles to go before reaching Fort Laramie. Unlike the cautious Edwin Bryant, she was buoyed by optimism. "Indeed," she wrote, "if I do not experience something far worse than I have yet done, I shall say the trouble is all in getting started."

Pleasure Trip

4

Virginia Reed swung into the saddle of her pony and galloped out onto the prairie. She loved getting away from the dull plod of the wagons, out into the high grasses where the wind whistled through a girl's hair as she rode. She stopped from time to time and gathered wildflowers, the bright sunshine glinting off a dazzling palette of colors in her growing bouquet.

The oldest of the four Reed children, Virginia had been born Virginia Backenstoe, the daughter of her mother's first husband. He died when Virginia was barely a year old, and when her mother remarried a year after that, James Reed adopted her. He treated his stepdaughter as his own, and Virginia grew into a spirited young woman, twelve now and looking forward to her thirteenth birthday in only a few days. In time, she would show a gift for describing the Donner Party's plight in pithy, moving letters.

She could scarcely remember the first time she had been set in a saddle. Outings with her adoptive father had always leavened her mood, the two of them sharing their love of horses and riding, and as she had contemplated the westward trip the previous winter, it was the prospect of daily jaunts on her prized pony, Billy, that made Virginia smile. The valley of the Platte River, up which the wagons were now rolling, was a smooth and welcoming road, perfect for riding, and Virginia took full advantage. Every morning, she stroked Billy's face and talked to him as though he were human. "I wonder what we will see today," she would say, feeling the softness of his mane between her fingers. "Take good care of me, Billy, and don't let me get hurt." He would bow his head as if to promise her safe return, and off they would ride into the freedom of the prairie. To her, it was a portion of the journey that was nothing less than "an ideal pleasure trip."

With hundreds of miles behind them, the wagon trains had by now settled into a daily rhythm. At dawn or before, a trumpeter sounded reveille to rouse the camp. The women made coffee and fried bacon for breakfast, the wafting scent tempting laggards from their bedrolls. If the oxen had been set loose to graze the night before, they were driven into the corral formed by the wagons, and men began to hitch the teams. George Donner, perhaps still playing his hometown role of "Uncle George," liked to encourage a little hustle by mounting a small gray pony and riding about camp, bellowing out, "Chain up, boys! Chain up!" If things went well, wagons rolled out of camp by 7:00 or 7:30. At 12:00, they stopped for lunch, perhaps pickled pork and baked beans, cold ham, bread and butter, pickles, cheese, and dried fruit, with coffee and tea, and milk for the children. "Nooning," as the emigrants invariably called it, might be a short break or might stretch out for an hour, giving both the people and the animals a chance to rest. Depending on where they found water and grass for the animals, they stopped for the night sometime between 4:00 and 6:00, forming the wagons into a corral once again. If they were passing through a region where they feared Indian attack, the horses and oxen were driven inside the ring of wagons; if not, they were turned loose to graze, although guards were still posted to protect against wolves or other predators. Occasionally, the mosquitoes were so thick that emigrants feared for the health of the livestock, so the animals would be penned or picketed and fires lit nearby in hopes that the smoke would drive away the insects. To save space for the livestock inside the ring of wagons, tents and campfires were placed outside. Men worked on repair jobs or cared for the animals, while women and children fetched water for cooking and gathered wood or buffalo dung—euphemistically known as "chips"—for fires. In the evening, if exhaustion could be held at bay, a fiddler might scratch out a tune. If spirits were high there might even be singing or a little dancing. At the end of the night, families took to their tents and guards took up their weapons, although frequently the sentries fell asleep.

In all, there were nearly five hundred wagons in this moving community, perhaps half headed to California, half to Oregon. Unfortunately for the Donners and the Reeds, they were near the rear of the long column. In letters home, others traveling with them claimed to be trailing by design, convinced that their slow pace helped preserve their livestock. The lead wagons, they believed, were working the animals too hard. Draft stock were priceless. Driving the poor animals until they collapsed was the ultimate example of short-term thinking, a way to make a few extra miles now and suffer more later. The race, in the end, would go to the tortoise, not the hare.

THE WAIL OF A NEWBORN SANG OUT from one of the wagons, a happy broadcast carried along by the stiff prairie wind. Philippine Keseberg, a young German immigrant going west with her husband and three-year-old daughter, lay back, exhaled, and cradled her new baby boy. They named him for his father. Farther back on the trail, the family wagon had tipped over, throwing Philippine from the bed and plunging her into a pool of water, but the accident seemed to have had no major ill effects, and Lewis Keseberg Jr. emerged into the world as the newest member of the migration.

Although he would be the only trailside baby born to the members of the Donner Party, little Lewis was hardly unique. It was not uncommon for women to give birth during the journey, nor, interestingly, less than nine months after its completion. Pregnancy rarely slowed the trains, at least for long. Maybe the Kesebergs spent a little extra time in camp the next day, or perhaps the other women lent a hand with the family's washing, but Philippine Keseberg and her son, like everybody else, kept moving west.

LIKE ALL TRAVELERS, WESTERING EMIGRANTS wanted a record of their great adventure, so many of them found time around the campfire or along the trailside to keep a journal. In all, there are hundreds of such recollections, an archival treasure trove that accounts for much of what we know about the pioneer experience. Of the original Donner Party group that set out from Springfield—the Donners and the Reeds— the only surviving diary of the early portions of the trip was kept by Hiram Miller, a friend of Reed's who had signed on to work as a teamster for the Donners. Remarkably, Miller's record did not emerge into the public eye for a century. For decades, it lay unnoticed in the basement of a family home, and only in 1946 did a Reed descendant donate it to a museum in Sacramento.

Miller was apparently a no-nonsense fellow, for most of his entries offer nothing more than the daily distance traveled and the location of the nightly campsite. There is nothing about his ideas or emotions, nothing about his comrades in the train, not even a note about the weather. His chronicle reveals more about nineteenth-century spelling and punctuation than about the scenery. The day after the wagons crossed from the south branch of the Platte to the north branch, a striking piece of territory and a milestone of the trip, Miller's entire entry reads, "and from their wee traveled up the plat a Bout 18 mills and Camped near the plat." The next day, he allowed himself a rare burst of comparative lyricism:

> And from their wee traveled up the plat a Bowt 12 miles and Camped near the plat By a fine Spring. No timber. Off to the left of the Spring on the Bluffs is a Beautiful pine ridge, the first that i have Seen on the Rout.

Still, for all its just-the-facts simplicity, Miller's diary allows us to trace the movements of the Donners and the Reeds with some precision, especially when it is pieced together with the letters and journals of other emigrants traveling nearby.

With each mile up the Platte, the party slowly departed the vast grasslands of the Great Plains and entered the kind of arid, high-desert country that dominates the American West. Along the river valleys, bluffs soared higher into the broad open skies, "rugged and sterile, exhibiting barren sands and perpendicular ledges of rock." Wagon wheels sank eight or ten inches into the dry, sandy soil, the oxen straining to keep the axles turning. Shallow and muddy, the water of the Platte tasted terrible, but there was nothing else to drink, so the emigrants forced it down.

The terrain threw up memorable landmarks everywhere, and the wagons began to pass them daily. On June 22 Courthouse Rock loomed up, though many people thought it looked nothing like a courthouse. On the 23rd it was Chimney Rock, a spire that could be seen for thirty-five or forty miles. They guessed its height at anywhere from 200 to 800 feet; it was probably 450 or 500 feet, although weather has now eroded it significantly. The next day the wagons rolled beneath Scott's Bluff, a sandstone face rising straight up out of the flatland. The landscape brought fanciful thoughts to mind for an emigrant named Charles Stanton, who wrote to a relative back east to describe the "knobs, or hills, or bluffs, or whatever else they may be called. . . . The wagons will often wind along under these bluffs, and, in their broken appearance, you can trace houses, castles, towns, and every thing which the imagination can conceive." One formation, he wrote playfully, looked like a citadel placed there to guard "the genii and spirits which dwell in the caverns and deep recesses of the ragged peaks."

THE DONNER CHILDREN STARED WIDE-EYED at the family's breakfast guests, two Sioux warriors in full regalia: beads, feathers, seashells acquired by trade all the way from California, pieces of colored tree bark, even the hair of scalps they had taken in battle. It was all "tastefully arranged," according to George Donner, who, true to his gregarious nature, had invited the visitors to join the family meal. "The Indians all speak very friendly to us," Donner wrote in a letter to a friend back home.

They had stopped at Fort Bernard, a grand name for what was in fact nothing more than a small log building built by a trapper at the very eastern edge of what is today the state of Wyoming. Just eight miles farther along the trail stood Fort Laramie, an adobe-walled quadrangle enclosing the space of half a football field, perhaps a little more, and containing watchtowers and a two-story administrative building. Like almost all the "forts" of the West in 1846, these were not military facilities, merely private trading posts, although eventually the federal government would buy Fort Laramie for four thousand dollars and station troops there until 1890. For now, though, the name "fort" seemed a little grandiloquent. Amused, Bryant put "Fort Bernard" in quotation marks in his book.

The neighborhood bustled. Between the two forts, there were fur trappers, traders, passing emigrants, and hundreds of Sioux preparing to make war against the Crow. It was by far the largest community of people the emigrants had seen since jumping off.

"Our journey has not been as solitary as we feared," Donner wrote to his friend. Like his wife in her earlier letter written along the Platte, Donner was optimistic. "I can say nothing except bear testimony to the correctness of those who have gone before us," he wrote. A month and a half after leaving Independence, they had avoided serious accident. "Our company are in good health. . . . Our supplies are in good order." With a touch of pride, he noted that their preparations had served them well. Even the wagons were in good shape. The covers shed the rain quite nicely.

5

At 9:00 A.M. on Saturday, July 4, the Donners and the Reeds and some other families gathered near their campsite along Beaver Creek, a stream lined with box elder and willows. Brightly colored wildflowers poked through the grasses, and high red bluffs lined the little valley. There was no hurry to wash the breakfast dishes and hitch the teams, for they intended to stay in camp all day to celebrate the Fourth of July.

Patriotic feelings ran high, for the country was at war. A few days after the wagon train left Independence, latecomers rode into camp bearing the latest St. Louis newspapers, which told of hostilities between American and Mexican troops on the Rio Grande. The news was no surprise. The year before, President Polk had acted on his campaign promise by annexing Texas, ostensibly an independent country but one that had been unrecognized by Mexico and coveted by the United States. Mexico and the United States still disputed the southern border of Texas, and it had been easy to see that the situation could lead to war, but that didn't lessen the importance of the issue for California-bound emigrants. California remained a part of Mexico, and now the United States and Mexico were at war. Emigrants had no idea how they might be treated when they arrived, even whether they might be arrested as hostile foreign nationals. They must have huddled around the campfires and pored over every word in the papers, but anyone willing to take the risk of a new life in California was not easily dissuaded. "How this important event is to affect us upon our arrival in California, it is impossible to foresee," Edwin Bryant, the journalist who began the journey with the emigrants, wrote at the time. "No one, however, is in the least disposed to turn back in consequence of it."

When Independence Day rolled around, there were those in camp who saw the melancholy side—celebrating the founding of a country they were abandoning—but nobody wanted to be a killjoy, and so the celebration started early. The men fired off a salute, and then a procession formed and marched solemnly around the corral of wagons, returning to the shade of the trees. Somebody read the Declaration of Independence. Colonel Russell gave a speech, although nobody bothered to write down what he said. They sang patriotic songs and made patriotic toasts, firing off more salutes when they felt like it. Just before noon, James Reed pulled out a bottle of liquor saved for the occasion. Friends back in Springfield had told him that at twelve sharp on the Fourth of July, they would face due west and raise a toast, while he did the same facing east. Enjoying his luxuries as always, Reed saluted his distant friends, then treated the whole company to a drink. The children gulped down lemonade. Perhaps because they were leaving their country behind, the little band of emigrants at Beaver Creek took the holiday to heart and made it their own. The celebration had "more spirit and zest," one participant wrote, than the grand and gaudy festivals back home.

The next day they remained in camp, their second straight day of making no distance. It was Sunday, and they told themselves they were keeping the Sabbath, but if so religion came upon them suddenly. Never before had they failed to travel on a Sunday. More likely they were nursing hangovers from the previous day's festivities and managed to convince themselves that another day of rest would do them good. No need to sprint during a marathon, after all. It was the height of summer, and it would be months and months before the long, warm days faded into cold winter nights. Plenty of other companies were camped nearby, making about the same pace. Everybody was part of a massive moving community, and nobody seemed panicked. If anyone asked George Donner, he might have noted, as he did in a letter back home, that the journey seemed far from solitary. There was safety in such numbers. True, they were toward the back of the line, but they could always make an extra push somewhere down the trail.

O N MONDAY MORNING THEY BROKE CAMP sharply and "mouved off in fine Style," as Reed jotted down in the diary he was now keeping. They made sixteen miles, maybe twenty, the wagons rolling along beneath the towering snow-capped spire of 10,272-foot Laramie Peak, the tallest mountain that many of the emigrants had ever seen and the plainest proof yet that they were slowly climbing into the Rockies. The Platte showed a change too: the shallow, muddy river of the plains was now a clear, tumbling mountain stream.

The buffalo hunting remained superb. On the 9th, Alphonso Boone, a grandson of Daniel Boone and an emigrant bound for Oregon, rode into camp to say he and some other hunters had killed eight of the animals and would be happy to share the meat. During a hunt the next day, Reed wounded a buffalo and then managed to drive it right up to the wagons, as though it were a dairy cow being herded to the barn.

At about the site of present-day Casper, Wyoming, they finally left the Platte, the river that had been their principal guide for a month, and aimed for the Sweetwater, which would take them on the last portion of their journey into the Rockies. Even as they gained elevation, the summer heat held its force. For six straight days the high temperature averaged 102—brutal conditions for twenty-mile marches.

The trail struck the Sweetwater near one of the most famous landmarks of the entire journey: Independence Rock. It is an unmistakable site, a huge hunk of sloping granite shaped roughly as though someone had taken a cereal bowl and turned it upside down. The rock rises up from a particularly flat stretch of valley floor, the Sweetwater River winding by on one side. The day after Reed herded his buffalo to the wagons, the Donner Party drove to within a few miles of the great sight, which they estimated, with fair accuracy, to be six hundred yards long and 140 feet high. The next day was Sunday, and for the second week in a row they paused for services, taking the chance to rest and write letters. Virginia Reed wrote to her cousin, among other things describing the death of her grandmother, Sarah Keyes, weeks earlier. "We miss her verry much. Every time we come into the Wagon we look at the bed for her." Still, like so many of the adults in their letters, she insisted on a resolute optimism. "We are all doing well," she wrote, "and in hye sperits."

The next day, Monday, they headed over to the rock for a closer look, but ironically were disappointed. Considering the fame of the place, they expected it to be so high that the top could barely be seen. But compared to the mountain peaks that lined both sides of the river valley, the rock itself appeared "tame and uninteresting." Still, if they climbed to the top—and surely some of them must have—they were treated to a striking panorama. Behind them, along the way they had just come, spread the open and treeless plain of the valley, stretching down to the horizon, spotted here and there with similar, smaller hummocks of rock. Before them, along the way they must go, the Sweetwater snaked ahead, beckoning them toward an astonishing sight— a 370-foot-high gorge known as Devil's Gate where the river sliced through some nearby mountains.

They stopped to noon at the Gate, and most of the company walked over from the trail, which ran a little to the south of the chasm, to take a look. Three days later, they got their first glimpse of the Wind River Mountains. Perhaps the sight spurred them on, for they made especially good progress, passing three other companies in a single day. The next morning, however, started with an argument. The younger men wanted to stay in camp for a day to hunt buffalo and rest the cattle; others said that a delay would only give away the advantage they had just gained, allowing the other companies to sweep past them and use whatever pastures lay ahead for their own stock. The latter faction won, and they rolled out of camp.

Their goal now was the culminating achievement of the first half of the journey: South Pass, a broad and relatively easy crossing of the Rocky Mountains and the Continental Divide. In the middle of North America's most dominant chain of mountains, South Pass was a natural blessing for expansionism. At 7,550 feet, it's low—many passes in Colorado top 10,000 feet—and the upward slope toward the pass is, at least by the standards of mountain passes, a forgivingly gentle grade. It's also at roughly the right line of latitude. Wagons rolling along the Platte River were aiming, more or less, directly toward South Pass. Lewis and Clark, by contrast, had crossed the Continental Divide far to the north, along what is now the border between Montana and Idaho, using a pass that one western historian described as "more barrier than portal."

South Pass had been known to Native Americans for centuries, but white explorers first crossed it in 1812, when it was traversed by a small party returning from the Oregon outpost established by fur trade magnate John Jacob Astor. The ease and utility of South Pass went largely unnoticed, however, for the next twelve years, until Crow Indians recommended it as the route for a group of fur trappers led by a young mountain man named Jedediah Smith. Trappers soon made the pass the preferred path to the Far West, and when in 1836 the missionary Marcus Whitman took the first wagon over, his wife, Narcissa, became the first white woman to cross the Continental Divide. By 1846, the year of the Donner Party, South Pass was the universally accepted avenue through the Rocky Mountains.

To this day, the landscape approaching the pass remains unchanged. Windswept and treeless, the trail crosses an arid desert more than a mile in the sky, an escarpment named Pacific Butte standing just to the left of the trail and offering an easy navigational aid. Ironically, for all the importance that the emigrants gave to the moment, the exact point at which the Continental Divide was crossed was often unclear. The trail rose steadily toward a ridgeline that seemed far too modest for the spine of North America, then fell away mildly on the other side. A little farther on, a set of springs fed a small, meandering creek whose waters ran west, and often it was only here that emigrants fully realized they had crossed from one watershed to another. Accordingly, it was named Pacific Spring and was a common point for celebrations.

On Friday, July 17—the day that began with an argument about moving on or hunting—the Reeds and the Donners and their companions mistook a subordinate rise for the summit and thought for a time that they had crossed the Divide. The balloon burst that night, when they camped on a river running east. If they had already conquered the Divide, the rivers would be running west, eventually to empty into the Pacific. Instead, they had once again found the meandering Sweetwater.

They reached the real Divide the next day, Saturday, July 18, stopping for lunch right at the ridgeline. The days had been hot, and the cold wind at the crest felt good. Coming down the other side they decided to bypass Pacific Spring, fearing that the cattle would get mired in the boggy ground. But they needed water, and so Reed rode ahead on Glaucus to scout. At dusk he charged back at a full gallop with disappointing news. There was no water ahead, and the wagons needed to turn back toward a small gully they had already passed. It had little water and no grass, but nothing better could be found. Another scout, probably one of the Donner brothers, had become lost, so once they pitched camp, they fired off their guns and lit signal fires on the surrounding hills, and the missing man finally rode in about midnight. The next day, the poor campsite proved more costly than they had realized. The water had been bad, and some of the livestock died. The Donners lost two oxen, and Reed lost "old Balley," probably a steer.

To say that crossing the Continental Divide was a milestone of the westward journey is an understatement. As they rolled across South Pass, emigrants had traveled more than a thousand miles, and were, roughly speaking, halfway to their goal. The Donners had been on the trail a little more than two months and were near the rear of the line, but by no means were they shockingly behind. From the adults to the children, they remained confident. If the second half of the trip took as long as the first, they would reach California in mid-September, weeks or even months before winter struck.

The moment was especially auspicious for one member of the party. Charles Stanton was going west in search of a second chance in life. The seventh of ten children, he grew up in New York, a skinny kid who matured into a dogged adult. As a young man he moved to Chicago to make his fortune, but business soured and he fell into a funk. One of his brothers remembered later that for two or three years Stanton seemed to do virtually nothing, the old energies that had made him a favorite sibling now sapped. In early March 1846 he turned thirty-five, half the biblical lifespan of three score and ten, and perhaps it jarred him. No real ties bound him to Chicago, so he headed to St. Louis, discovering along the way that traveling agreed with him. "I have found it as hard to stop myself from going as I did in the first place to set myself in motion," he wrote in a letter. He had read some of the popular books of the day describing Oregon and California, and he decided that the great journey west was the way to complete his personal rejuvenation. He was eager for the "active busy life" of the trail, a sure tonic to the "dull monotonous one I have so long led."

The trip worked as he had hoped, restoring the optimism and brio of a faded man. Once, on the plains, he let the wagons pull on ahead as he sat and finished a letter to his family. By the time he was done, his comrades had been gone an hour and he was alone on the prairie. As he hustled to catch up, a band of Indians approached on horses, and one or two even pulled their knives across their throats. They may just have been trying to scare him, but Stanton understandably took the gesture as a threat. Still, he held his composure, gave them some tobacco, and then marched on unfazed.

But if there was a single event that crystallized the change in Stanton, that burned it into his bones, it was crossing the Continental Divide. The next day, he stopped to write his brother and realized that the water at his feet would pour into the Green and then to the Colorado and then to the Gulf of California:

Thus the great day-dream of my youth and of my riper years is accomplished. I have seen the Rocky mountains—have crossed the Rubicon, and am now on the waters that flow to the Pacific! It seems as if I had left the old world behind, and that a new one is dawning upon me.

He couldn't have known it then, but in time he would have the chance to display his newfound vigor in ways he could not imagine. Even beyond the standards of the other members of the Donner Party, Stanton would prove his courage and risk his life.

The Crucial Decision

6

From the jumping-off point at Independence to the crossing of the Continental Divide, the path for all westward travelers was identical. Everyone needed to reach the easy transit through the Rockies, so everyone traveled up the Platte and the Sweetwater, like ships aiming for a strait before reaching the open ocean. But west of the mountains, no similar geographical narrows constricted the traffic. Depending on their intended destination and their personal preferences, emigrants were now free to follow different routes. It was the first time they made a real decision about their course, and for the Donner Party, no choice would ultimately prove more important nor rest on a shakier foundation.

J AMES REED MUST HAVE BEEN PONDERING the options for weeks. Marching along hour after hour, California-bound emigrants would have found it impossible not to weigh the impending alternatives, for in a certain sense the wagons were going in the wrong direction.

Central Missouri and Northern California—the beginning of the journey and the end—are roughly on the same line of latitude. A straight-line trip would have produced a far different path: across Kansas, then through Colorado south of what is today Denver, then across Utah and

Nevada before arriving at Sutter's Fort, the site of modern Sacramento. The wagons would never have rolled through an inch of Nebraska or Wyoming. But nineteenth-century emigrants lived in desperate need of the holy trinity of wagon travel—water, wood, and grass—and thus they were slaves to the meanderings of rivers and the haphazard location of mountain passes. For those headed to California, the trip traced a huge arc, northwest for the first thousand miles out of Independence, then at some point southwest toward the destination. This was partly because the trail had first been broken to Oregon, but it had far more to do with the path of the Platte River and the location of South Pass. Crossing the Rockies, emigrant wagon trains were almost two hundred miles north of both Independence and Sutter's Fort. Yet the traditional trail would take them farther north still, up to Fort Hall, in what is today Idaho, before starting a long southward swing toward California. Not surprisingly, emigrants were tempted by the idea of a more direct route, one that was both enticingly straight and dangerously unknown.

Travelers knew that an alternate course existed because it had been described, albeit briefly, in a book that some of the wagons carried, *The Emigrants' Guide to Oregon and California,* written by a young lawyer from Ohio named Lansford Warren Hastings. Hastings had first gone west four years earlier, in 1842, when he signed on with a wagon train organized and captained by Elijah White, who had been appointed Indian sub-agent for Oregon. Hastings quickly displayed both ambition and a talent for self-promotion. He was only in his mid-twenties and inexperienced in the ways of the West, but when White's term as captain expired, Hastings was elected as his replacement. The new captain was "an aspiring sort of man," one fellow emigrant remembered, "and he worked it so that he got the command."

Once in Oregon, Hastings grew dissatisfied and decamped south to California, where the unbounded possibilities suited his striving soul. Hoping to attract American settlers to this new homeland, he set to work on his book, which combined travelogue observations from his own western adventures—salmon abounded in the Oregon rivers, California priests thrilled to cockfights—with practical advice for would-be pioneers. The final two chapters were a how-to list for emigrants, a do-it-yourself guide to crossing the continent. Never shy, Hastings made plain his preference for California over Oregon, and even dangled the gleaming lure of a shortcut. In a brief passage, Hastings noted that once the wagons crossed South Pass, California-bound emigrants could leave the Oregon Trail and head southwest to the Great Salt Lake rather than continue northwest into Idaho. From the lake, they could turn due west, cross the desert beyond the lake, and then take aim for California. Hastings offered little detail about the new route, and for good reason: He had never set foot on an inch of it.

Still, cocksure of his own skills as a literary evangelist, Hastings began dreaming of the multitudes his book might seduce. By the winter of 1845–46—the same winter during which the Donners and the Reeds were laying plans and readying equipment and stockpiling supplies for the long trip west—Hastings was literally plotting a California boom, laying out a town near Sutter's Fort. A bold army of pilgrims would bring culture to a benighted land, he thought. "A new era in the affairs of California, is about to arise," he wrote to the American consul in Monterey in March 1846. "These now wild and desolate plains must soon abound with all the busy and intresting scenes of highly civilized life." He had even begun to chat up the outsized idea that perhaps California should break away from Mexico and declare its independence, as Texas had done less than a decade before, and there were those who got the impression that Hastings envisioned himself as the future president of this would-be California Republic.

The problem for Hastings was that the American emigration—the linchpin on which all his grand plans relied—might bypass California altogether, choosing Oregon instead. And so in the early months of 1846, he decided to ride out onto the trail and lobby for California as the emigrants' goal. If settlers could not be trusted to find California, then California—in the person of Lansford Warren Hastings—would go and find settlers.

Hastings left Sutter's Fort on April 11, a month before the Donners and the Reeds jumped off from Independence. He gathered a small party and started over the Sierra, intending to travel his proposed cut-off backwards, from west to east, and then to await the emigration on the main trail. As the wagons rolled up, he would recruit them for California.

Joining Hastings was James Clyman, who lent extraordinary experience to the group. Born in Virginia little more than a decade after the Revolutionary War, Clyman grew up on land owned by George Washington, from whom Clyman's father leased a parcel. As a young man he went west as a fur trapper, distinguishing himself with displays of ingenuity and determination. He completed, for example, the first known circumnavigation of the Great Salt Lake. In 1827 he returned east to take up business in Wisconsin and Illinois, but nearly two decades later, in 1844, he decided once again to go west. He was almost fifty, perhaps looking for a better climate or perhaps just seeking a little of the old adventurous spirit of his youth, a nineteenth-century version of a midlife crisis. He went first to Oregon, then the next year to California, and by the spring of 1846 was ready to return home. Wisely choosing not to make the trip alone, he joined up with Hastings.

From the beginning, the old explorer doubted the feasibility of Hastings's proposed cut-off—"my beleef is that it [is] verry little nearer and not so good a road as that by fort Hall," Clyman recorded in his journal—and the farther they went the more his apprehension deepened.

By the time he stood amid the desiccated bleakness of the Great Salt Lake Desert, Clyman was awestruck by the lifeless vista. "In fact this is the [most] desolate country perhaps on the whole globe," he wrote in his journal, "there not being one spear of vegitation and of course no kind of animal can subsist." At the lake itself, he looked about and recorded simply that he was surrounded by "wide spread Sterility."

When Hastings and Clyman and the others of their little party at last completed the cut-off and rejoined the traditional trail, Hastings stopped to wait for the approaching emigrants, but Clyman kept on going, encountering one wagon train after another coming from the other direction. By extraordinary chance, he found an old friend—James Reed. Fourteen years earlier, Clyman and Reed had served together in the Black Hawk War, when the Sauk and Fox Indians tried to reclaim their tribal lands from white settlers and were massacred by U.S. troops. Clyman and Reed mustered in as members of Capt. Jacob M. Early's Company of Mounted Volunteers on the same day, along with another unknown private, Abraham Lincoln. "We didn't think much then about his ever being President of the United States," Clyman wrote decades later, after Lincoln's assassination.

At Fort Laramie, the two old friends talked late into the night, Reed questioning Clyman about what lay ahead on the trail, Clyman trying to warn Reed about the desolation he had just seen in the Great Salt Lake Desert. Remembering the conversation years later, Clyman said he told Reed to "take the regular wagon track, and never leave it—it is barely possible to get through if you follow it, and it may be impossible if you don't."

"There is a nigher route," Reed replied, insistently, "and it is of no use to take so much of a roundabout course." Clyman acknowledged that the Hastings Cut-Off might be straighter, but again warned his old friend that it might also be impassable.

Clyman was a rare combination, half southern gentleman, half mountain man. "Deliberate in all his movements," as one contemporary remembered, he was kind and well read, and his voice still held the syrupy tincture of an antebellum upbringing. But he was also an old denizen of the West, a man with hair that reached his shoulders and a forest of whiskers and a sun-burnished face glazed to the hue of "smoked buckskin." He was the kind of man, in other words, who should have received his due from greenhorn settlers. Some of those at Fort Laramie did listen, changing their plans and following the traditional route, or even striking out for Oregon rather than California. By rights, Reed should have been among those who heeded Clyman's advice. The two men had fought a war together, after all, a shared experience that often creates an unbreakable bond.

But if Clyman's warning resonated at all—a nettling abrasion undermining Reed's former certainty—such doubts were probably washed away two weeks later by another eastbound rider, this one a stranger rather than an old friend. Wales Bonney was traveling by himself all the way from Oregon to Independence—a daring if not foolish venture—and carried with him an impressive token of expertise: a letter from Hastings himself. The two men had met along the eastbound trail, and Hastings had given Bonney the letter to show to emigrants. The missive declared that Hastings would wait for the wagons up ahead and guide them along the new route mentioned in his book.

That must have been exactly what Reed wanted to hear. He had not transformed himself from a fatherless boy into a wealthy and successful man by playing it safe. Nor had he started the journey west intending to avoid risks. Danger was inherent in what they were doing, no matter what route they took. Hastings was even putting himself in jeopardy to prove his new shortcut, guiding the wagons personally over the last and most treacherous portion of the journey. And if Reed considered the relative position of his wagons—near the tail end of the season's migration—he surely must have been encouraged to try anything that might save time. So he ignored the sound warnings of his old wartime friend Clyman and began talking to his fellow emigrants about the gamble of a lifetime: an untried shortcut through an unknown wilderness.

ON JULY 19, THE DAY AFTER CROSSING the Continental Divide, the wagons reached a nondescript fork in the road that would soon be given a rather romantic nickname: the Parting of the Ways. To the right lay the branch northwest to Fort Hall, to the left the southwest route toward the Hastings Cut-Off. The next morning, most teamsters steered their oxen to the right, choosing the safety of an established trail. But a few families—the Reeds, the Donner brothers, a few others who had been traveling along in the same general pack of wagons—decided to bank on Hastings's promises. In all, about seventy people waved goodbye to their former companions and took the gentle bend toward the left. Most were upbeat, their spirits buoyed by the prospect of a shortcut that might save precious time. The exception was Tamzene Donner, who was wary. They had never met Hastings, she noted, and yet now they were trusting his word on an issue that might literally decide their fate.

As a practical matter, the split at the Parting of the Ways was the true emergence of the Donner Party. Throughout the first half of the journey, as hundreds of wagons all rolled along the same route, traveling arrangements mutated ceaselessly, families or groups of families combining or withdrawing as the inevitable alliances and frictions developed and changed. Sometimes these changes were not even formally recognized. The Donners and Reeds, for example, had initially joined the Russell Party, which in turn became the Boggs Party when Russell resigned his post and was replaced by former Missouri governor Lilburn Boggs, but it appears likely that along the Sweetwater River, they and some companions broke away from Boggs's leadership and traveled independently, although without any known organization or structure.

But now the small group of wagons turning toward the Hastings shortcut would be on its own, traveling down a spur trail without close company, and so they decided to organize formally. With only a few small changes, the emigrants who veered to the left at the Little Sandy River would be the group that faced the coming ordeal in the mountains. The Donners and the Reeds still formed the core, but other large families would prove just as important in the long run.

The Breens were a big Irish family, and devoutly Catholic. Patrick Breen, who was in his fifties, had been born in Ireland and emigrated to Canada in 1828. He married an Irish girl, Margaret Bulger, who was called Peggy, and eventually they settled on a farm near Keokuk, Iowa. The restlessness that pushed Patrick Breen from Ireland to Canada to the United States did not fade, and by the 1840s he was talking about joining the great migration west. Religion may have been one factor. Catholics were rare in Keokuk, but they dominated Mexican California. By 1846 he was ready to take the great leap, so he sold the farm and set out for the Pacific. By that time the Breens had seven children, six boys and a baby girl named Isabella. Not as wealthy as the Donners or the Reeds, they had no hired hands, but neither were they poor.

A woman headed one big clan. Levinah Murphy was only thirty-six but was already a widow with seven children and three grandchildren. Born to a prosperous family in South Carolina, she married her distant cousin four days after her sixteenth birthday and quickly began a family. When her husband died in 1839, Murphy was left to care for seven children. Apparently a convert to Mormonism, she moved to Nauvoo, Illinois, the home of Joseph Smith's new church, and then to Tennessee. No one knows exactly why she decided to go west, although she may have hoped to reunite with her fellow Mormons, who were already planning to flee the Midwest but whose final destination was uncertain. Her oldest children, nineteen- and eighteen-year-old daughters, were married and had children of their own but decided to go along. Murphy's brood was thus huge: her seven children ranging in age from eight to nineteen, two sons-in-law, and three toddling grandchildren.

An Illinois couple, William Eddy and his wife, Eleanor, had two young children, a three-year-old son and a baby daughter. A carriage-maker by trade, William Eddy was talkative, ebullient, eager to help. Early in the trip, a wagon belonging to a group of single men broke an axletree, a common problem on the trail. A number of wagons rolled past, but Eddy and some other men stopped to help. Eddy set to work with the needed tools—a saw, augers, chisels, hammers, etc.—and fashioned a replacement for the broken axletree. By sundown, the owners thought, the wagon was as good as new, maybe better. But Eddy could also exaggerate his role in a story. There were those who thought him a liar, the kind of man who made himself the hero of every tale he told. He was capable, a fellow emigrant remembered, of "eulogizing himself."

A group of native German speakers stuck together, although they were not all actually Germans. The most important was Lewis Keseberg, a tall, blue-eyed, thirty-two-year-old Prussian émigré who spoke English, French, and German and would eventually learn Spanish. Before leaving Europe for the United States he had married Philippine, who was almost a decade younger than he and pretty and, some said, flirtatious. They endured a troubled union. A nasty temper plagued Keseberg, and he sometimes directed his vitriol at his wife, a habit that offended some of his fellow travelers on the journey west. More than one member of the Donner Party remembered Keseberg beating Philippine, a "humble and unassuming" woman who was "cowed down." "He treated her like a brute," recalled Virginia Reed. "She was afraid of him and yet made all sorts of excuses for him." James Breen remembered Keseberg, a tall and powerful man, as "quick tempered and irritable."

The Wolfingers were another German couple, young and childless although apparently wealthy. Doris Wolfinger spoke little English but impressed everyone with a regal bearing, not to mention elegant clothes and expensive jewelry. There were several young, single men among the "Germans," and one old man known only as Hardcoop, a cutler from Cincinnati who wanted to see the west before returning to his two children in Belgium.

Patrick Dolan was one of the few bachelors who was not working his way west as a teamster. A neighbor of the Breens back in Iowa, Dolan had vouched for Patrick Breen when the Irishman took the oath as a naturalized American citizen. Perhaps thirty-five or forty, Dolan was not as rich as some of the well-established family men, but he had made a success of himself. He sold his farm in Iowa and went west with a wagon and some cows. Optimistic and jovial by nature, he was popular with the children.

The first task for this emerging new group was to pick a leader. Surely the men had been eyeing each other for some time, drawing one another aside or wandering by someone else's campfire to discuss the likely candidates, glances thrown back over their shoulders to make sure no one was eavesdropping. Perhaps some men campaigned for the job while others refused it. As the wagons prepared to pull away on their new course, the men finally gathered around to settle the matter.

Reed, the only man keeping a regular diary at that point, failed even to mention the decision. We do not know with certainty that he wanted the job, but he was an obvious potential choice. Assuming he expressed an interest, it's easy to see why he was passed over. He was aristocratic and headstrong and rubbed people the wrong way. He was not the kind of man to win a popularity contest. But he was also not the kind of man to bring up someone else's victory in his own journal.

Charles Stanton, who had been so excited to cross the Continental Divide, had the courage and commitment of a leader, but he was a young man traveling alone, far less established than the older family men. The same was true of William Eddy, whose family was small and young. Patrick Breen headed a big clan, but he was an Irishman and a Catholic, and nobody volunteers to be led by an outsider.

And then there was the easiest choice of all: George Donner, the older of the two Donner brothers, a friendly fellow with enthusiasm and goodwill. He led one of the three families from Springfield that lay at the core of the group. Perhaps he wasn't the most commanding of men, but then all the captain needed to do was get the group moving in the morning and pick the campsite at night. In a pinch, somebody else could even take those duties. Maybe Donner was a little malleable, but better that than a self-important blowhard like Reed.

They counted the votes, and the new company assumed the name by which it would enter history.

B ILLY, THE PONY THAT HAD CARRIED Virginia Reed so joyfully across the plains, could go no farther. Worn down by the long days of endless walking, he simply stopped. James Reed could have shot him to save the beast a lingering death, but perhaps Virginia could not stand the idea, and so instead they simply abandoned the exhausted little animal by the trail.

Virginia agonized at the harsh ethos of the western trail: keep moving or die. "When I was forced to part with him, I cried until I was ill, and sat in the back of the wagon watching him become smaller and smaller as we drove on, until I could see him no more."

Gambling

7

Edwin Bryant decided to gamble. The newspaperman was now well ahead of the Donner Party on the trail, for his lingering doubts about the pace of the wagon trains had finally crystallized into action. At Fort Bernard, Bryant and his traveling companions traded their wagon for pack mules and rode ahead as fast as they could.

More than a week before the Donner Party, he reached Fort Bridger, a small trading post along the Black's Fork of the Green River in what is today the southwestern corner of Wyoming. Fort Bridger was the last chance to decide which route to pursue toward California, since in effect it offered a second chance at the decision the emigrants had faced at the Parting of the Ways. As at the Parting, the trail split at Fort Bridger: To the right lay a well-established route via Fort Hall; to the left was the untried Hastings Cut-Off.

When Bryant arrived, Lansford Hastings was there, touting his new course. But so too was the legendary Joseph Walker, a mountain man with decades of experience in the west. Walker "spoke discouragingly" of the Hastings route, Bryant wrote.

Nonetheless, Bryant and his friends resolved to risk the new path. The whole trip west was a risky venture, and the timid were still on the farm, a thousand miles back and probably regretting the missed opportunity.

But Bryant also worried about the families farther back on the trail, the ones with which he had begun the journey. With their ponderous ox-drawn wagons, they should try no new and untested routes. At their slower pace, they would spend longer in the desert. With their live-stock, they required more water and feed. And then there were the children. Family men should stick to the proven and rutted road. "Our situation was different than theirs," Bryant recalled. Single men on mules "could afford to hazard experiments, and make explorations. They could not."

Bryant could not wait around at Fort Bridger to voice his reser-vations in person. Even on the relatively fast mules, he still wanted to keep moving. Fortunately, an alternative was at hand. Louis Vasquez, who owned and operated the fort along with Jim Bridger, offered to see that letters were held for the oncoming wagons. Undoubtedly thankful for the kindness, Bryant scrawled out his doubts in messages to some of the key men, one addressed to James Reed. Then he rode off, trusting that the honorable men who ran Fort Bridger would see the missives safely delivered.

THE DONNER PARTY REACHED THE FORT nine days later, on July 27, a Monday, and pitched camp in a pleasing meadow half a mile down-river, hoping the rich valley grasses would rejuvenate their exhausted oxen. To let the animals rest, the emigrants planned to stay a few days.

As soon as the stock was turned loose and the bedrolls unpacked, the men went looking for Hastings. According to his own letter, he was supposed to be at the fort, waiting to guide them on his new and untested cut-off. It was crucial that they find him. Since Hastings's pro-posed route had hardly been traveled before, it bore none of the guide-posts that dotted heavily traveled trails—wagon tracks, well-worn fords, old campsites. Without Hastings, the Donner Party would be forced to feel their way along blindly, following a trail that did not really exist through terrain they did not know.

Yet Hastings was nowhere at the fort. He had gone ahead with other wagons. He had promised to wait for those who heeded his call, and now he had vanished. For Reed and the Donner brothers and the others of their company, it must have come as a brutal shock. They had banked their fate on an unreliable man.

Another option remained: the branch of trail leading northwest, toward Fort Hall. Take it, and soon enough they would be back in the ruts of the main route, perhaps even reunited with those to whom they had bid farewell at the Parting of the Ways. Clyman's knowledgeable warning about the Hastings Cut-Off argued for that option, and now so did Hastings's failure to wait for them.

One more stone might have tipped the scale, but the warning letters from Bryant lay as hidden as a miser's heart. Bridger and Vasquez had opened their fort just three years before, in 1843, as a trading post and way station for westward emigrants. The location seemed first-rate. Fort Laramie was well back to the east, on the other side of the Continental Divide; Fort Hall was still 150 miles away, at least a week's hard travel. Fort Bridger would do a booming business selling supplies and livestock to weary travelers. What's more, it was on the main road. The primary emigrant trail—the route that led to Fort Hall and then to Oregon and California—passed right by the new establishment.

But in a striking case of bad luck, Fort Bridger was bypassed the very next year. In 1844 a party of emigrants blazed what came to be known as the Greenwood Cut-Off, a shortcut that saved several days' travel but went nowhere near Fort Bridger. When emigrants steered to the right at the Parting of the Ways, it was actually the Greenwood Cut-Off they were taking. By 1846 the shortcut had become the main road, and almost nobody was going by way of Fort Bridger. Bridger and Vasquez found themselves stranded on a back road, like an old-fashioned motel too far from a new interstate.

Hastings's proposed route offered a solution. His cut-off required that emigrants use the old and now largely abandoned trail down to Fort Bridger before striking off through the Wasatch and along the southern edge of the Great Salt Lake. Unavoidably, families that took the Hastings Cut-Off would roll right past Bridger and Vasquez. So perfectly did the needs of Hastings and Bridger mesh that rumors of pay-offs circulated, although some of the gossip suggested that Hastings was paying Bridger and some that it was the other way around.

For Bridger and Vasquez, therefore, Bryant's discouraging letters were a potential disaster. If word got around that the cut-off was too dangerous for emigrants with wagons, families would continue to take the Greenwood route, never approaching Fort Bridger. Business would collapse.

The solution was as obvious as it was devious. When the Donner Party arrived, Bridger said not a word about the warning from Bryant, the emigrants' old traveling companion. Instead, he claimed the Hastings Cut-Off was a "fine level road," rich with grass for the livestock and well watered most of the way. The shortcut might save hundreds of miles over the old route via Fort Hall, he insisted. A benign explanation washed away Hastings's absence: The route he had initially explored contained a stretch without water, and now he had gone ahead to scout for an even easier trail.

Even without reading Bryant's letter, Reed and the other members of the Donner Party should have been suspicious of Bridger's enthusiasm. Anyone could see that the trading post was in danger of being marooned, an anachronism past which the modern trail detoured. Clyman had already offered cautionary words at Fort Laramie, and it's possible that at Fort Bridger the emigrants heard doubts yet again. Walker, the legendary mountain man who had warned Bryant about Hastings's route, may still have been there when the Donner Party arrived, telling people of his doubts. But if Reed heard of Walker's views, either directly or through local gossip, he seems to have disregarded them. Far from wondering about Bridger's possible motives in promoting the cut-off, Reed fell for the man. Bridger and Vasquez, he wrote, were "very excellent and accommodating gentlemen" who could be trusted to do business with emigrants "honorably and fairly."

So far as we know, no one else raised any strong objections, and so the wagons turned away from the tested trail to California. In less than two weeks, the Donner Party had faced essentially the same dilemma twice: Stay with the traditional route or take a chance on Hastings's promises. Both times they made the same decision. Sooner than they could imagine, they would have reason to wonder about the wisdom of their choice.

A New and Interesting Region

8

The young rider bounced off his mount and thudded sickeningly into the hard earth of Wyoming. The fall knocked Edward Breen out cold, and when he regained consciousness his left leg throbbed with pain. Adults arrived and examined the boy and found a bad break between the knee and ankle. There was no doctor in the company, but they were only a little ways beyond Fort Bridger. Perhaps someone there boasted medical training. A rider galloped off, and in time he returned with the nearest thing to a doctor the fort had to offer, "a rough looking man with long whiskers" who had probably acquired what medical knowledge he had through long experience on the frontier. He unrolled a small bundle he was carrying and produced a short saw and a long-bladed knife, obviously the tools of amputation.

Edward shrieked at the sight and began begging his parents to prohibit the operation. It was no easy decision. If the leg didn't set properly—and what were the odds of that in a jouncing wagon?—gangrene could fester. The boy could die. But Edward was adamant, and in time his parents agreed. They gave the would-be surgeon five dollars for his trouble and sent him on his way. Edward exhaled and tried to lie easy.

CHARLES STANTON BASKED IN THE SUMMER SUN, letting it warm both his body and his spirit. Snow-capped mountains glittered in the distance, yet another sign that the emigrants had long since left behind the flat-lands of their midwestern homes. Taking up a letter he had written to his brother two weeks earlier, Stanton added a short, optimistic postscript. "We take a new rout to California, never travelled before this season; consequently our route is over a new and interesting region." Perhaps too new and interesting. It was August 3, three days since the Donner Party had pulled away from Fort Bridger, and yet Lansford Hastings remained a ghost.

Then, on the sixth day out from the fort, they found some shadow of the phantom. Someone spotted a note protruding from the top of a sagebrush and called out to tell the others, and when they reached it they found it was from Hastings. In a way, it was a remarkable find— the paper could have blown away or been taken by an animal or simply overlooked—but in fact it was a common method of trailside com-munication. Paper being valuable, emigrants occasionally used what-ever lay at hand for their impromptu billboards—pieces of wood or even buffalo skulls.

The wagons had reached Weber Canyon at the base of the Wasatch Mountains, the steep and rugged range that lay between Fort Bridger and the Great Salt Lake. Up ahead, the forward group led by Hastings—the Harlan-Young Party—had already spent a grueling week struggling down the forbidding canyon, which grew narrower as it went. Wagons crossed and recrossed the river, sometimes driving straight down the rocky bed, with no guarantee they might not topple. One man watched some of his comrades trying to build a road through the canyon and proclaimed in his journal that it was "an exhibition of most consumate folly."

Hastings had never intended to travel down the canyon; a guide working for him had taken the wagons down that route while Hast-ings was briefly away. Now, in the note he left for the Donner Party, Hastings urged the trailing emigrants to stop where they were and send a messenger ahead so that he could return and take them along another route through the Wasatch. Finding the note, the men of the Donner Party huddled together and decided that three riders would search out Hastings while the rest of the party waited and rested. Ever at the center of events—and at least partly responsible for convincing the others to chance the shortcut—James Reed was chosen to go, along with Charles Stanton and William Pike, a son-in-law in the big Murphy clan. They mounted up, waved goodbye to their families and comrades, and rode off into the mountains to pursue the vanishing "guide" on whom they had staked so much.

THE THREE MEN RODE HARD, but by the time they caught Hastings they had crossed the Wasatch and descended to the beginning of the pancake-flat country that nuzzles up against the Great Salt Lake. None of the three had ever met Hastings, but somewhere in camp they were introduced. Reed must have noted acidly that his party relied on Hastings's promise to guide them from Fort Bridger, only to arrive and find that he had already left. Now they were here to collect on the promissory note. Hastings should return and show the way.

Hastings agreed, and he and Reed headed back toward the Wasatch, Reed on a fresh, borrowed mount. Stanton and Pike, their horses gasping for water and rest, stayed behind, promising to follow along when they could.

Reed and Hastings had not even reentered the Wasatch before Hastings yet again broke his word, announcing that he would not return to the stranded wagons and instead would simply point out the preferred route to Reed. There was no time to go all the way back, Hastings insisted. He needed to stay with the Harlan-Young Party and guide them across the salt desert west of the lake. Reed and Hastings camped together that night, and the next morning climbed a nearby peak from which Hastings vaguely indicated a course the Donner Party wagons might take through the mountains. "He gave me the direction," Reed wrote later.

Then, his duty grossly unfinished, Hastings turned away from Reed and rode off to the west. For the rest of their journey, the members of the Donner Party would never again speak with the man who had promised to lead them.

Consigned to his own ingenuity, Reed rode down off the mountaintop and found an Indian trail, which he began following back toward the wagons, blazing trees to mark the path more clearly. He rode back into the ring of the Donner Party corral on Monday evening, August 10, four days after he, Stanton, and Pike had gone ahead to find Hastings. Everyone must have crowded around eagerly to hear his report, in which he told of Hastings's refusal to come back and act as guide. The canyon route of the Harlan-Young Party was too risky, he insisted. Many of the wagons would be destroyed. On the other hand, the path he had just blazed through the Wasatch was "fair, but would take considerable labor in clearing and digging."

There is no record that Reed and the others discussed another option, one they should at least have considered: backtracking to Fort Bridger, returning to the traditional trail, and forsaking Hastings's chimerical cut-off altogether. Traveling from Fort Bridger to their current position had required six and a half days, but since they now knew the country the return trip would have been quicker. And they now had abundant evidence of Hastings's rash judgment, if not mendacity. Clyman had told them the shortcut was probably impassable. Hastings had promised to wait for them at Fort Bridger, then gone ahead without them. Then he had promised to return and guide them through the Wasatch, only to abandon them with little more than a wave of his hand toward a route he had never taken. Surely they did not want to be seen as fainthearts who lost courage in a crisis, staggering back into Fort Bridger ignominiously. But on the other hand, their circumstances had changed—they no longer had any promise of a guide to show them the way—and when fresh evidence emerges settled decisions must often be revisited. Judicious reappraisals were common on western trails. The same year as the Donner Party, one group of emigrants took the so-called Applegate Cut-Off toward Oregon, a new and reputedly easier route. But just fifteen miles past the fork, they found a handwritten note warning that it was two or three days to grass and water, a dangerous and difficult haul. Consultations were held, and the group resolved to change its destination and make for California.

For the Donner Party, backtracking would have cost precious time, but their only other options were equally grim: try to follow the Harlan-Young Party's disastrous route through Weber Canyon, or take their chances with Reed's newfound path, which had never been traversed by wagons of any kind, which in fact barely existed at all. Still, Reed "reported in favour" of the new route, as he put it in his diary, and no one was in a position to argue. Of those who were present, only he had seen the narrow end of Weber Canyon, and only he had crossed the Wasatch. If he thought the mountain route was the better way—and it may have been—it was simple logic to bow to his judgment. Reed seemed to acknowledge that he bore some special responsibility for the decision. In his journal, he noted that his account of the mountains "induced the Compay to proceed."

So, as they had before, the men of the Donner Party ignored the increasing evidence that Hastings was a charlatan and vowed to forge ahead along his untried bearing.

U NTIL NOW THE JOURNEY HAD BEEN ACROSS the open plains or up the relatively gentle slope of the Rockies, and always in the wake of those who had gone before. But in the Wasatch, the Donner Party began to bushwhack, clearing a road through a thicket of mountain forest as impenetrable as a jungle. Virginia Reed thought it was incomprehensible to those who were not there:

> Only those who have passed through this country on horseback
> can appreciate the situation. There was absolutely no road, not
> even a trail. The cañon wound around among the hills. Heavy
> underbrush had to be cut away and used for making a roadbed.

In one canyon the trail crossed the same creek thirteen times, the teamsters weaving from bank to bank in search of clearance. Frustrated, James Reed thought they were making even less distance than they were.

Then suddenly progress stopped entirely. They were approaching a pass across what is now known as Big Mountain, and the pace of road building grew so glacial that moving the camp seemed pointless. Instead the men simply walked out every morning, hacked away what little territory they could, and then returned to the exact same campsite at night. Reed's journal entries became terse concessions of stasis: "in Camp all hands Cutting and opning a road through the Gap" and "Still Clearing and making Road in Reeds Gap." Then at last he allowed himself a quiet and exhausted declaration of triumph: "Still in Camp and all hands working on the road which we finished."

They rolled across the pass using the road they had just hewn from the forest, and then down an incredibly steep and treacherous descent on the other side. A search party located Stanton and Pike, unseen since Reed had been forced to leave them behind with the Harlan-Young Party near the Great Salt Lake. The two men had spent days trying to rejoin the Donner Party, struggling through the mountains and, at least according to one account, nearly starving to death. But no sooner had the group regained its two lost members and crossed over Big Mountain than it faced another seemingly immutable natural enemy—a canyon so clogged with heavy timber that the wagons again remained in camp while the men went to work. They chopped and sawed for two days before moving the wagons up, but then found the very end of the canyon so barricaded with foliage that it seemed impervious to road-building. The only option was to take the wagons over a frighteningly steep hill at the side of the canyon, a climb so precipitous that there was a real danger of rolling backwards down the grade. Virginia Reed remembered that almost every ox in the train was required to pull each wagon up the slope, which would mean that thirty or forty animals were needed to drag a single vehicle. But in time they reached the summit and were rewarded with a view of the valley of the Great Salt Lake. "It gave us great courage," remembered fourteen-year-old John Breen. Reed's journal entry, by contrast, does not even mention the struggle over the final hill and seems strangely nonchalant: "this day we passed through the Mountains and encampd in the Utah Valley."

More than at any other point on its long and emotionally powerful journey, the Donner Party's passage through the Wasatch created a tangible historical legacy. Just a year later, in the summer of 1847, Mormon emigrants used the route while seeking a haven for their faith. At times, the Mormons had to scour the earth for the faint traces of the Donner Party's presence, wagon ruts still vaguely visible. In other places, the residue of the 1846 journey was more obvious—a cleft through the thick forests that was plain evidence of the tenacity with which the new road had been hewed. Only at the end did the Mormons depart from the Donner trail. The final, infuriating gorge that defeated the Donner Party—forcing them to haul up over the nearby hill—was cleared by the Mormons in less than a day and became Emigration Canyon, the main entryway to the Latter-Day Saints' lonely, pious kingdom of Deseret.

The Donner Party's Wasatch crossing had required more than two weeks, a debilitating loss of precious time. It was now August 22. Soon the debilitating heat of summer would give way to the crisp nights of fall. The delays that had beset the earlier portions of their journey—the high water of the Kansas River, the death of Sarah Keyes, the mysterious Sabbath lull that followed their Fourth of July celebration—were nothing compared to the slog through the mountains. Maybe it had been the best of a bad set of options. Maybe it would have taken longer to follow the Harlan-Young Party down Weber Canyon or to backtrack to Fort Bridger and the traditional trail. But the hard facts of the calendar could not be denied. At Fort Bridger, Reed had optimistically predicted that they might reach California in seven weeks. Crossing the Wasatch had required a third of that time, all for a paltry thirty-five miles. Virginia Reed remembered that by the time the Donner Party cleared the mountains and reached the exotic shores of the Great Salt Lake, they were "worn with travel and greatly discouraged." They had six hundred more miles to go.

Unearthly

9

If the Donner Party received any brief encouragement as it struggled against the Wasatch Mountains, it must have come from the startling realization that other emigrants were even farther behind. At some point during the Wasatch ordeal, newcomers unexpectedly rolled up from the east.

The three wagons belonged to Franklin Graves, a big, amiable man whose life had been a fitting prelude to the deprivations of the California Trail. In Illinois, where Graves and his wife had carved out a hardscrabble life in a one-room cabin along the banks of the Illinois River, Graves had gone shoeless in summer and hatless in winter. The family kept chickens and bees, and every morning Graves crossed the river in a handmade canoe to trade game, furs and buckets of honey with settlers in town. In the afternoon, the equally resourceful Elizabeth Graves showed up in the same boat with butter, eggs and soap. When the river froze, she kept up her errands by walking across the ice. They were cheerful, happy people, and it isn't entirely clear why they decided to make the journey west, especially since Franklin was in his late fifties. They may have been trying to escape the fevers of the Midwest—a common complaint of the day—or perhaps the country was just growing too tame for a man like Graves. The farm sold for $1,500, at least some of it paid in coin that Graves hid in the box of one of the wagons for the trip west. Presumably, the money also helped pay for the traveling costs of their nine children, one son-in-law, and a teamster named John Snyder.

Later even than the Donners, the Graveses jumped off from St. Joseph, Missouri, in late May with the last group of the season. Most members of the party kept to the traditional trail, but the Graveses showed characteristic pluck and turned for Hastings's unknown cut-off even though they numbered only thirteen people. When they caught the Donner Party, they must have felt a sense of relief at their newfound fellowship, even as the Donners and the others must have endured mixed emotions—gratitude for the extra hands, unease that they were now unquestionably the hindmost runners in the race to California.

Whatever the emotions—and strangely James Reed made no mention of the company's expansion in his diary—the arrival of the Graves family was the last time anyone would join the group of wagons destined for tragedy. The Donner Party was now complete.

THE EMIGRANTS DIDN'T KNOW IT, but as they left the Wasatch the wagons were rolling onto the bed of ancient Lake Bonneville, a sprawling inland sea that was once 325 miles long, 135 miles wide, and more than 1,000 feet deep, roughly the equivalent of Lake Michigan. Lying in the Great Basin, a vast depression hemmed in by the Rockies on one side and the Sierra Nevada on the other, Bonneville was what geologists call a "terminal lake," meaning that it had no outlet to the sea. Fed by rivers tumbling down out of the mountains, it eventually grew into an aqueous behemoth that created its own release valve by pushing across Red Rock Pass in what is today southern Idaho. In one riotous spasm, Lake Bonneville emptied much of itself into the Snake River drainage, the torrent pouring through the pass at a rate well above that at which the Amazon River discharges into the ocean. Then, almost as quickly as it began, the flood abated. The lake level dropped below the height of the pass, and Bonneville returned to its traditional boundaries.

In time, the lake bequeathed two legacies, both essentially lifeless. As the last Ice Age ended and temperatures rose, evaporation rates increased until the atmosphere began sucking away more water from the lake than the rivers could pour in. Unable to sustain itself, the lake began to die of thirst, the waters receding until evaporation and input came into rough annual equilibrium, creating the body of water we know today as the Great Salt Lake, the runt child of Lake Bonneville. Like its parent, the Great Salt Lake has no outlet, and thus the minerals carried in by feeder rivers cannot be swept away by drainage streams. The result, of course, is increasing salinity; today the lake is brinier than the ocean, and home to virtually no marine life.

To the west, Bonneville's receding waters deposited billions of tons of salt, spread across the playa as though troweled on by a giant mason. Seepage from the lake itself soaks the underlying surface, creating vast bogs of soft alkaline loam. The liquid rarely breaks through, and even if it did it would not be drinkable, so the salt flats present a strange paradox: a moist and muddy desert devoid of potable water. Almost nothing grows there, and almost no animals can be seen. The only break in the relentless, blinding whiteness of the salt is a few tiny mountain chains, the tops of which were once islands poking up through the frothy waters of Lake Bonneville. Yet the Great Salt Lake Desert lay directly in the wagons' path as they came down from the Wasatch. The Hastings Cut-Off, in other words, led straight through one of the most inhospitable places on earth.

European or American parties had rarely penetrated the heart of the desert. A train of emigrants had crossed the northern section in 1841, nearly dying in the process. The southern portion—the route now proposed by Hastings—had been traversed only twice, and both times without wagons. The explorer John C. Frémont had led a paramilitary party through in 1845, and Hastings himself had crossed from west to east earlier in 1846, the trip that convinced Jim Clyman that Hastings's plan was madness. With superior local knowledge, Indians may have crossed the desert from time to time, though we have no written record of such ventures. Or they may have known enough to give the region a wide berth; emigrant records make no mention of Indian trails, as they often do in other portions of the West.

Marching along toward this great plain, the Donner Party found the trail of the Harlan-Young Party, the group up ahead that Hastings was leading, and fell in behind. If Hastings refused to return and guide their wagons as he had promised, at least they could follow his tracks.

LUKE HALLORAN HOPED THE WEST would cure him, not kill him. A young, entrepreneurial Irishman who owned a small store in St. Louis, Halloran was a success—he owned six lots in town—but decided to give up his comforts to search for better health. He hoped that the western climate might cure his tuberculosis, what emigrants called "consumption." Little is known about the early part of his journey, but at the Parting of the Ways he was abandoned by the family with which he was traveling. Alone and in poor health, he sought refuge with George and Tamzene Donner, who displayed a characteristic kindness and took him in. Too weak to walk, Halloran rode in a wagon, though even such luxury could not stop the ravages of his disease. He traveled with the Donners for more than a month, but died just after they came down out of the Wasatch and was buried in the salty soil of Utah. Having rescued him from abandonment once, perhaps the Donners did not want to leave Halloran alone in the wilderness again. They dug his grave next to that of an earlier emigrant who had also succumbed to the rigors of the great journey west.

TAMZENE DONNER, THE WOMAN WHO had doubted the wisdom of the Hastings Cut-Off from the beginning, gathered the fragments of paper scattered before her on the Utah desert. The note, apparently written by Hastings, had been torn apart by birds or animals or simply the elements. Donner assembled them like a jigsaw puzzle and produced a reconstructed missive that was both cryptic and fearsome: "2 days— 2 nights—hard driving—cross—desert—reach water."

At Fort Bridger, the emigrants had heard warnings about the salt desert, rumors that it required a "dry drive" of forty miles without grass or water. Arid stretches of trail posed a particular hardship for the pioneers, since their overburdened wagons could carry little added weight, and water is an extraordinarily heavy commodity. A fifty-five-gallon barrel, for example, weighs close to five hundred pounds when filled. Even a fifteen-gallon barrel—a container only about two feet high—weighs well over a hundred pounds, the equivalent of asking the oxen to drag another full-grown woman across the desert. Hastings's note, found at a spring, presumably signaled the last oasis before the wastelands. The wagons stayed in camp the next day, "wooding watering and laying in a Supply of grass for our oxen and horses," as Reed put it in his diary. They expected to spend one night out on the desert, he noted, but doubted they would find "grass wood or water of sufficentt quallity or quantity to be procured."

The desolation they were about to enter has challenged even modern expeditions armed with the benefits of technology. In 1929, when a small group set out to track the route in a Model A, the vehicle became mired in "soapy slime" and could be freed only when the men dismantled the bed of an abandoned pioneer wagon and forced the boards under the car's wheels for added traction. Fearing a similar fate, a later expedition resorted to a converted Caterpillar tractor. As recently as 1986, archaeologists working in early September, exactly the season of the Donner Party's crossing, found it impossible to cross the "semisolid mud flats" in modern, four-wheel-drive trucks and were forced to use all-terrain vehicles instead.

For nineteenth-century emigrants like the Donner Party, the bogs clung tenaciously to hooves and wagon wheels. Mules sank to their knees, sometimes to their bellies, floundering forward and kicking up vast clouds of suffocating dust as thick as fog. Riders often had to dismount, lessening the burden on the horses but slowing the pace. Heat waves baked the days; frigid winds chilled the nights. With wood scarce, some parties swore off a cooked breakfast, starting the day's march on cold tack or even an empty stomach. Water was more valuable still, so only tiny rations were allowed. Often, thirst gave way to hallucination, and families imagined themselves marching toward cooling lakes or lush, verdant meadows or even magnificent cities dotted with grand homes and shaded, regal avenues. If there was any other living thing for miles, the emigrants could not see it. "The hiatus in the animal and vegetable kingdoms was perfect," wrote Edwin Bryant, the journalist who had once traveled with the Donners. The desert, he said, was "unearthly."

By midday on Wednesday, September 2, the members of the Donner Party had been marching through this lifeless vacuum for more than two days with little sleep or rest. It had been three days since they passed the last spring with drinkable water, and the oxen began to give out. The line of march elongated—families pulling ahead if they could and lagging behind if they could not—but even the forward-most group could not make it with all their wagons. So teamsters unhitched their animals and drove them onward, hoping merely to keep the beasts alive and return later for the abandoned cargo. Teamsters kept their eyes on Pilot Peak, an aptly named and plainly visible mountain at the desert's western edge with a well-known freshwater spring at its base.

The Reeds struggled near the rear of the line. James Reed decided to ride ahead to fetch water and then return, telling his hired teamsters before he left that if necessary they should unyoke the oxen and drive them forward, along with the cattle he was taking west as livestock. Reed reached the encampment beneath Pilot Peak about dark, just a few hours after the other families had made it. He stayed for an hour, drinking from the spring and resting, and then started back toward his family. Sometime before midnight, he encountered his own teamsters, driving his oxen and cattle toward the spring, and told them to water the animals and then follow him back out onto the desert.

He found his family in the morning, and together they kept a day-long vigil, peering vainly to the west in hopes of seeing the returning teamsters and animals. By nightfall, with their water running low, it was clear that another day on the desert might prove fatal, so they decided to abandon the wagons and set out on foot for the spring, carrying some bread and what little water they had left. James Reed carried the youngest child, three-year-old Thomas; the other three children walked.

The youngsters eventually grew exhausted and lay down to sleep, covered as much as possible by shawls. A wind kicked up—James Reed remembered it as "a cold hurricane"—so he and Margret sat upwind of their children, their backs forming a makeshift break, and encouraged the family's five dogs—Tyler, Barney, Trailor, Tracker, and Cash—to crowd around for more warmth. "It was the couldes night you ever saw," thirteen-year-old Virginia wrote later in a letter. "The wind blew and if it haden bin for the dogs we would have Frosen."

If they needed an incentive to get moving again, it came by accident before dawn, when one of the dogs suddenly jumped up and began barking. The others did the same, and as the Reeds roused themselves, one of the family steers suddenly bolted out of the night and ran straight for them. Luckily it changed course, although, as Reed noted dryly, "There was no more complaining of being tired or sleepy the balance of the night."

Resuming their march, they reached the wagons of Jacob Donner, whose oxen had also grown so weak that they had been unhitched and driven ahead to water. From the Donner family, Reed learned why his teamsters had never returned with the livestock: As they approached the spring at Pilot Peak, the unyoked animals sensed water and bolted into the desert, and now were missing. (The animal that ran at the Reed camp in the night had obviously wandered around and eventually stumbled across the family, almost literally.) Once again, Reed temporarily abandoned his family, leaving them with the Donners, and walked ahead to the spring, where the other families were camped and waiting. That night, Reed and Jacob Donner returned to the desert and brought out the Donner wagons, which now carried the Reed family as well. Five and a half days after they walked away from the last freshwater spring on the eastern edge of the desert, all the members of the Donner Party had made it across.

They spent nearly a week camped at Pilot Peak, alternately resting, searching for missing cattle, and going back into the desert to bring up wagons that had been left behind. Perceptions varied as to the cause of the delay, doubtlessly deepening existing tensions within the group.

Reed remembered later that most everyone had lost some stock, universalizing the cause of the delay; others thought they were hunting specifically for Reed's animals, as though he alone were the cause of the extra effort. Two days after the Reeds and the Donners reached the spring, some of the men set out for the Reeds' abandoned wagons, the farthest out on the salt flats. Judging by Reed's own journal and modern archaeological evidence, the wagons were probably about twenty-five miles from Pilot Peak, a hard day's travel. In one case, Reed and the others may have freed a wagon by digging a small pit, perhaps a yard wide and a foot deep, at the same time discarding a broken wheel and replacing it with a spare. Since most of their cattle had been lost, the Reeds were forced to permanently abandon two of their three wagons, leaving behind most of their household goods.

The cost of the desert crossing had been incalculable. In all, they had lost thirty-six cattle, either because the animals bolted and ran off or because they simply could go no farther and collapsed. George Donner and Lewis Keseberg each abandoned a wagon, but it was clearly the Reeds whose fortunes had been the most deeply damaged. Left with only one ox and one cow, they were forced to borrow an extra team merely to pull their one remaining wagon, the richest family in the train reduced to accepting frontier charity. Even among the families who made it through with their animals and wagons intact, the livestock had suffered, weaker now as draft animals and scrawnier as a potential supply of meat. Perhaps most significant, the company was increasingly divided and dispirited, families eyeing each other as sources of hindrance rather than help. When the Reed family divided its provisions, which could not fit into the one wagon that remained, the result was a near-universal sense of martyrdom and grievance, the Reeds convinced they had generously victualed their comrades, the other families certain of their beneficence in helping the newly impoverished. Like most wagon trains, the Donner Party had never been a truly unified force, but now it was more fragmented than ever, wilting in both spirit and body. John Breen, who was fourteen at the time of the journey, thought back to the desert passage years later and recalled simply, "Here our real hardships commenced."

T HEY STARTED FORWARD AGAIN on a morning when a snowstorm dusted the nearby hills, a reminder of the advancing calendar that, as John Breen remembered it, "made the mothers tremble." In fact, desperation was beginning to suffuse more than just the maternal contingent of the Donner Party. Fearful that their provisions might not carry through to California, the company agreed that each family would inventory its foodstuffs, then provide a written status report to Reed, another sign of his de facto status as leader. The result was apparently pessimistic, for Reed suggested that two riders hurry on to Sutter's Fort, fetch fresh supplies, and then backtrack to meet the rest of the party somewhere on the trail. His recent setback on the desert had hardly diminished Reed's enthusiasm for the expansive gesture: He wrote a letter to Sutter personally guaranteeing payment for the supplies, assuming he eventually reached California.

The resupply effort would be an astonishingly dangerous mission— two men alone would be easy prey for hostile Indians or unscrupulous emigrants in other trains, or even simple mishap—and so it would have to be strictly a matter for volunteers. None of the men with large families—Reed himself, the Donner brothers, Graves—stepped forward, perhaps because they dared not abandon their wives and children, perhaps because they were too old, perhaps both. Either the hired hands were unwilling or their employers balked at losing the help, so it was left to men with smaller, younger families or to those traveling alone. The first to step forward was William McCutchan, a giant of a man with a bushy mane of hair who was going west with his wife, Amanda, and their toddler daughter, Harriet. Left behind by some previous train for unknown reasons, they had joined the Donner Party at Fort Bridger, apparently traveling without a wagon and carrying what supplies they could on a horse and a mule. His offer was conditional: The rest of the party must vow to help his wife and daughter, a reasonable demand that was granted quick acquiescence. The other volunteer was Charles Stanton, the former Chicago merchant hoping to rekindle some inner flame after a bout with depression, who said he would go if someone provided a mount. His family now assured of aid, McCutchan agreed that Stanton could take his mule.

Physically, the men were opposites—Stanton diminutive, McCutchan said to be six-feet-six—but there were plenty of other reasons to find them a strange selection. McCutchan had not even been a member of the Donner Party for most of the trip, and Stanton was a bachelor with no relatives or loved ones in the train, and thus a man who might balk at returning if he reached safety in California. But absent other volunteers there wasn't much choice, so the unlikely pair of couriers packed food and blankets onto their saddles and set off toward the west.

FOR THE FIRST TIME IN WEEKS Edward Breen swung into a saddle. Through the Wasatch, when the young man's labor had been desperately needed to help clear the way, he had been lying in a wagon, his broken left leg gripped by handmade wooden splints. Now he moved gingerly at first, not wanting to risk some further trouble with the limb. His parents watched nervously, then breathed a sigh of relief as the boy touched his heels to the animal's flank and moved off.

SOME PLACES ON THE TRAIL SEEMED CURSED. The air or the water or the soil brought out the snippy side of people, all the collected antagonisms of a long journey simmering like a low-grade fever. Somebody remembered the time that Smith held up the train for no good reason. Or the way Jones always commandeered the best campsite. Or the fact that Johnson was lazy about guard duty. Or the way somebody talked too much or talked too little or just plain annoyed folks. Weeks and weeks and weeks of hard travel built up the pressure until something sparked an eruption, and sometimes it seemed to be nothing more than a spot along the path, even a good spot.

Up ahead of the Donner Party, Edwin Bryant and his friends in the mule train found one such spot when they camped in a grassy dale where springs bubbled up a water supply and the foliage offered rich feed for the animals. The next morning, two men argued over some minor slight, "a very trivial matter," Bryant wrote. The dispute grew heated until both men leveled rifles. Bryant thought the whole affair was crazy. Here they were in the middle of nowhere and people were threatening to kill the very comrades on whom they depended. He rushed into the middle of it and started giving both men a lecture, telling them that killing each other was as bad as an attack by some outsider. Tempers cooled and the barrels were lowered.

The Donner Party reached the same exact place five weeks later and weathered a broader if less acute quarrel—a war of the sexes. "All the women in Camp were mad with anger," Reed wrote in his diary. He gave no more details, other than suggesting that the site should be known as Mad Woman Camp.

Maybe it was just boredom that tweaked the nerves. After crossing the salt desert of Utah, the wagons entered what is today eastern Nevada and endured a repetitive geology where the earth has furrowed itself into a succession of small mountain ranges, like the lines of a wrinkled forehead. Heinrich Lienhard, traveling the same route but well ahead of the Donner Party, could not avoid echoing the region's monotony in his journal entries. "We came into a valley which was very much like the one we had left," he wrote. Then the next day: "We went through another gap and came into a dry valley." And the following day, after yet another mountain crossing: "The valley lying before us was again broad, and resembled in every respect the one we had just crossed."

And then they squared up against the Ruby Mountains, the last obstacle on Hastings's ill-advised cut-off. On the other side of the mountains lay the Humboldt River, where they would rejoin the traditional trail. On his eastbound journey earlier in the year, Hastings had crossed the Rubies via a small, steep defile that later came to be known as Secret Pass, a route that required little detour. But Secret Pass was too rugged for wagons; another way had to be found. The point at which the trail collided with the mountains lay toward the northern tip of the range, and so the easiest and quickest choice would have been to turn north and circle around that end. But no one had ever taken that route, so nobody knew how close the wagons were to an easy passage. Guiding the Harlan-Young Party, days in front of the Donner Party, Hastings instead turned to the south—yet another mistake, this one born mostly of ignorance. He began paralleling the mountains, looking constantly to his right to find a workable pass.

When the Donner Party wagons came along, they were following the plainly visible tracks of the earlier group, and so they too headed south. They trudged along beneath the precipitous rise of the mountains for three days, interrupted by one baffling and inexcusable Friday on which they remained in camp, going nowhere and achieving nothing. Finally, they came to a shallow pass—Reed described it as "a flatt in the mounton"—and followed it up and over the crest. Streams led them down the other side, and on September 26, a little west of what is today Elko, Nevada, they at last reached the Humboldt, where they found the main California trail that ran down from Idaho. The Hastings Cut-Off was finished at last.

It had been more than two months since they separated from the other California-bound trains along the Little Sandy. At Fort Bridger, the last place where they could change their minds and stick with the main trail, Reed had optimistically written that he hoped to reach Sutter's Fort in seven weeks by taking the cut-off. When they arrived at the Humboldt, more time than that had already passed, and they were still far from their goal. Edwin Bryant, their onetime traveling companion who had joined the Fourth of July celebration before trading in his wagon for mules, was now more than a month ahead.

Ironically, it was the presumed advantage of Hastings's route that was in fact its central flaw. Like a modern engineer building a freeway, Hastings laid his course with a straight-edge, heedless of the constraints of mountain or desert. In this, he was in some respects the first modern westerner, struggling to impose human preference on an unforgiving geography, but he was foolishly ahead of his time. Mountain men or military units might conquer whatever barrier lay before them, but family wagons and livestock needed to treat the most difficult topography with grudging respect, circumventing obstructions rather than assaulting them. Travel by compass bearing alone was an arrogant fantasy. The traditional trail curved and buckled and detoured for a reason: Western terrain demanded a circumspect and sinuous approach. Crossing the Wasatch and the Great Salt Lake Desert—tasks more onerous than anything emigrants faced on the traditional trail—not only slowed progress horrendously but also weakened people and animals alike, both physically and mentally. Lienhard, the fellow emigrant who was ahead of the Donner Party on the trail, pondered the realities of the Hastings Cut-Off and declared in his diary that it would more appropriately be called "Hastings Longtripp."

In rough terms, the delay could be measured. Using information from Indians or other emigrants or even trailside notes, parties that used the Hastings Cut-Off could gauge themselves against those who had gone the traditional way. One group estimated they had lost seventy miles, at least four days of hard travel, probably more. Another party pegged their delay at nearly two weeks. For the Donner Party, the last of the groups along the cut-off, it was even worse. The gamble probably cost them a full month in lost time, as though they had simply stopped traveling and lollygagged about camp for thirty precious days.

Yet there was no time for recriminations or pouting, nothing to do but to keep moving. They could neither go back nor remain in place. Like their wagons, they had no brakes, no way of stopping the high-stakes journey on which they had wagered their lives and fortunes. The only alternative was to push forward, exhausted marathoners hoping for a second wind. They could not know that, as at every stage of their long ordeal, their situation would soon grow more precarious still. And this time, the fault would lie not with a hostile geography or an unreliable promise, but with the bitter divisions of their own comrades.

One Bad Hill

10

Most of the wagons had already climbed the long, sandy hummock. John Snyder, the teamster for the Graves family, was toward the back of the line when he began urging his charges up the slope. It was rough terrain—emigrants recalled it as a "very bad ridge" or "one bad hill"—and most men stopped to double-hitch, combining five or six pairs of oxen to haul just one wagon, like a truck driver dropping into a lower gear.

Snyder spurned such caution. Perhaps it was pride in his animals, or in his own skill as a teamster. Maybe he was just tired and exhausted and sick of the wearying delays. Maybe it was simple exuberance, for Snyder was a young man. Whatever the reason, he insisted his charges could conquer the hill unaided, and he started up the climb.

Suddenly there was trouble with the teams: confusion, a tangle of reins, animals shouldering their great bulks into one another, wagons crunching together. Angry words flew. Snyder and one of the Reed family teamsters shouted insults. James Reed himself stepped into the fray, and he and Snyder flared. After all those months of walking across a continent, the fatigue and the delays and the aggravations finally combined into one irresistible moment of wrath. Adrenaline shot through the veins. Fury rose in the chest. Fists clutched weapons and raised them in the air. Rage conquered all.

IT WAS BARELY A WEEK since the Donner Party had completed the disastrous Hastings Cut-Off and regained the main trail along the Humboldt River, the waterway that would guide them across what is now the state of Nevada. Rejoining the traditional road had been a milestone: For the only time in his long diary, Reed noted the party's location even before mentioning the date.

But the Humboldt itself proved a disappointment. Drought plagued the West in 1846, and the river had withered until it was "more a succession or chain of stagnant pools than a stream of running water." At places the soil was so dry that it resembled ash. Kicked up by the draft animals into vast white clouds, the dust caked the emigrants' hair and skin until they were "as cadaverous as so many corpses." The Humboldt was better than Hastings's nonexistent shortcut, but it was hardly easy. The hard work and long days and constant exertion still sapped the body and frayed the nerves. And then on Monday, October 5, the wagons reached the hill where Snyder refused to double-hitch.

As Snyder and Reed argued, Reed barked that they should get the teams to the top of the hill and then settle the matter man-to-man. Snyder insisted on a more immediate brand of satisfaction. He raised the butt end of his ox whip and struck Reed in the head. At almost the same moment, Reed pulled a hunting knife and lunged at Snyder, stabbing him deeply in the chest. As soon as the fight began, it was over, Snyder collapsed to the ground with a mortal wound, Reed gashed across the head, both men soaked in blood. Snyder's friends carried him up the hill and laid him on the ground, but there was nothing anyone could do for him, and within minutes he was dead.

The company cleaved in two, both figuratively and literally. The Graveses and their friends pitched camp near the top of the hill, Snyder's body lying nearby and surely fueling anger at Reed. The Reeds stopped near the bottom of the hill, perhaps with the Eddys, who seem to have taken Reed's side almost immediately. Opinion was as divided as the tents, split between those who thought Reed had merely defended himself and those who denounced him as a murderer. Later, Reed's friends and family members recalled a man deeply saddened and working to make amends: casting the knife away in disgust, rushing to Snyder's side to hear his dying words, offering boards from his own lone remaining wagon for a coffin, standing at the gravesite till every clod of dirt had been patted down over the body.

Nobody knew quite what to do. They had quit the United States when they crossed the Continental Divide—the western boundary of the Louisiana Purchase—and so technically they were no longer subject to American law. Nevertheless, the developing credo of the western migration was one of remarkable commitment to legal procedure. When crime struck, emigrants typically formed courts to try the defendant, often with a rather elaborate legal structure that included a judge, jury, and lawyers for both the prosecution and defense. In at least one case, a "sheriff" was appointed to watch over the jury, which returned its verdict in writing. Nor were these show courts. Emigrants took great pains to ensure some element of fairness, often recruiting people from other companies to act as judge or jury so as to gain greater impartiality. In some cases, even though the wagons were racing against time, parties halted their progress to find suitable jurors in other companies or spent precious hours tracking down suspects or investigating a crime scene.

Yet for a variety of reasons, it was hardly clear that the Donner Party would observe the niceties. For one thing, there were no other companies nearby to provide a ready pool of disinterested jurors. For another, there was no agreed-upon set of rules. The Russell Party—the company in which the Donners and the Reeds first traveled—had established a set of bylaws, but these were mostly concerned with procedural matters like organizing the day's march and assigning guard duty, not punishing capital crimes. In any event, the rules had been adopted before the Donners and the Reeds joined the company, and when they and the other families split off from the main emigration to follow the Hastings Cut-Off, there was, as far as we know, no discussion of the legal procedures that might apply to the newly formed party. In later years, most emigrant parties abandoned the practice of formal bylaws for precisely this reason. Companies divided and re-formed with such frequency that the original signers were often long gone by the time the rules were actually needed.

Worse still for the Donner Party, their nominal leader was not at hand. As happened periodically throughout the journey, the train had, for whatever reason, split in two a few days before the fight, and the Donner families were traveling separately, two days ahead on the trail. Revealing the tenuous nature of hierarchy in emigrant trains, nobody thought to ride ahead and fetch the elected leader of their band, and so the half dozen or so family groups now camped at opposite ends of the fatal hill were left to their own devices to settle a matter of life and death.

As is often the case with explosive moments of trauma, even the eyewitnesses could not agree on precisely what happened. The cause of the original dispute was never exactly clear. Perhaps it centered on Snyder's refusal to double-team. Perhaps it was about the order or pace of the climb. The teams may have become tangled. Snyder may have started to beat his animals or use foul language. There was no un-animity on which man struck first, or whether Margret Reed, who had stepped in as peacemaker, was hit as well. Reed's backers always maintained that Snyder took the blame for the whole thing with his dying words, but that too was disputed.

Favoritisms and resentments bubbled to the surface. Snyder had been a popular fellow, an upbeat and jovial type who liked to take the hind gate off the wagon at night and use it as a dance floor, enter-taining the camp with a jig. In contrast to the ostentatious wealth with which Reed began the journey, Snyder was a young man trying to make it on his own, having struck a deal with Franklin Graves to work his way west in return for his board. He was handsome in a rugged, outdoorsy sort of way, and he may even have been romancing Mary Ann Graves, the nineteen-year-old daughter of his employer and the belle of the train.

By contrast, Reed was disliked. His haughtiness rankled from the start, and he had been the biggest advocate of the Hastings Cut-Off, now plain to all as a disaster. Lewis Keseberg may well have harbored some private grudge against Reed—there were those who said that early in the journey Reed upbraided Keseberg harshly for beating his wife or using foul language in the presence of Reed's wife—and now the German apparently tried to exact his revenge by propping up his wagon tongue, the silent call for a hanging.

Most of the emigrants opposed anything so drastic. "Perhaps the intimate friends of Snyder favored extreme measures, but this sentiment was not generally approved," remembered James Breen, who was only five at the time but talked about the event later with his older brother.

Instead, in what must have been a compromise of sorts, the emigrants turned to the most common form of serious punishment meted out on the overland migration: banishment. Executions certainly occurred—almost always by hanging or firing squad—but it was much more common that wrongdoers were simply forced out on their own, perhaps because the emigrants recognized that most trailside killings were not premeditated murders but, as in the case of Reed and Snyder, sudden explosions of temper, what one historian aptly called "unleashed antagonisms, small personal matters greatly magnified." By avoiding a killing, banishment also helped to keep the peace among those who remained in the company, a consideration that may well have influenced Reed's case. It's easy to imagine that Reed and his supporters would have tried to fight off an execution.

In later years, when the Gold Rush crowded the trail with thousands of wagons, some emigrants began to complain that banishment lacked the needed severity, so easy was it for the expelled man to latch on with some nearby company. But that was hardly the case for Reed. The emigration of 1846 was far smaller, and in any event the Donner Party was lagging far behind all the other companies. Told that he would have to ride alone to California, he faced the real possibility of death.

At first he refused, and while we have no evidence, it seems reasonable that he must have contemplated another option: abandoning the train with his entire family and pushing ahead on their own. The idea had a certain minimal plausibility. The Graves clan had been alone on the trail until it caught the Donner Party west of Fort Bridger, and the Reeds, with five employees, made a comparably sized group. But there were also sound reasons suggesting that it was impractical for the family to forge onward unaided. Their losses in the salt desert had reduced them to borrowed oxen, and the owners might have demanded their animals back. What was more, the Reeds had precious few supplies left, and without the help of fellow emigrants, they would have been reduced solely to hunting for food.

Talking over the family's options, Margret Reed emphasized their scarce provisions and told her husband that if he refused the banishment and somehow avoided a hanging by the other emigrants, he might simply watch his children starve. If he rode ahead, he might return with food and save them all. Indeed, some people remembered Reed's departure as motivated less by the killing and more by a desire to push forward quickly. He left, Mary Ann Graves insisted, "because he would rather travail with one man than the company." Whatever the exact mix of reasons, Reed mounted up and struck out alone, his head wounds swathed in bandages.

When he caught the Donner families farther along on the trail, he offered a sanitized version of his departure: He was simply going ahead for provisions, in effect reprising the effort of Stanton and McCutchan, the volunteers sent out a few weeks before. One of Reed's teamsters, Walter Herron, was traveling with the Donners, but now he joined Reed, providing help and companionship that could easily prove crucial to survival.

In less than a month, Reed had been transformed from the richest man in the train to one of the poorest, and now he had been rejected altogether, forced to abandon his family and the few material possessions he retained. He was leaving his wife and children with a group of people who had just banished him, some of whom had wanted to kill him. And yet the loss may have been greater for the others than for Reed. For all his airs, he possessed admirable qualities. William Graves, who disliked Reed, acknowledged that he was "as true as steel." Reed often made the day-to-day decisions about where to camp or noon or water the stock, and the others had relied on his intelligence and tenacity. When three men were sent ahead to find Hastings and ask about the route, Reed was the only one who returned quickly. Through the Wasatch—and perhaps beyond—it appears that he was effectively the captain of the party, titles notwithstanding. Others recognized such traits. At Fort Bridger, Louis Vasquez turned to Reed when he wanted to recover three missing horses. The animals had strayed or been stolen, and Vasquez wrote out a short note in effect making Reed his agent. "We do hereby authorise Mr. Jas. Read," Vasquez wrote in a full, rounded hand, "to take where ever he should find three horses stolen or strayed from us." He could have turned to any man in the train, but Vasquez picked Reed. Now, short on both provisions and time and still hundreds of miles from its destination, the Donner Party would have to push ahead without its one true leader.

Abandoned

11

The old man struggled to keep up. The sterile terrain and the long journey had weakened the draft animals until they could no longer bear the extra weight of passengers in the wagons, so everybody was walking, even children and the elderly. Hardcoop, a Belgian whose first name is lost to history, was struggling along as best he could, but the muscles and bones and joints that had carried him through sixty hard years were finally giving way.

The same thing had happened the day before, after he had been booted from his normal seat in Lewis Keseberg's wagon. He had fallen so far behind that when the others pitched camp at night, they realized the old man was missing and dispatched a rider on a rescue mission. Hardcoop was found five miles back on the trail.

Now, the following morning, they were again on the march. It had been less than half an hour since they broke camp, and Keseberg had renewed his refusal to carry Hardcoop. Searching for a ride, Hardcoop asked William Eddy for a seat in his wagon. Eddy balked too. They were struggling through a sandy patch, where the loose ground sucked at the wheels, and Eddy thought his oxen could handle no extra weight. If Hardcoop could keep going on his own for a time, Eddy said, perhaps he could ride in the wagon when the trail improved. The old man vowed to forge ahead.

But when the emigrants stopped that night, they again found Hardcoop was missing, just as he had been the night before. Boys who had been driving cattle recalled him sitting by the side of the trail, physically played out and unable to go on. Another rescue ride so late at night was impossible, so they built a signal fire and hoped he might stumble in to camp. The night guards stoked the flames through the wee hours, but Hardcoop never appeared.

Eddy set about organizing a rescue effort, but he had no horse, so he asked Patrick Breen and Franklin Graves, the two men with saddle animals that could be used.

Breen said it was impossible to save the old man. Graves flashed with anger and said he would not risk losing a good horse to search for a man who was probably already dead. He declared he wanted to hear no more of the idea. Desperate, Eddy and two other men offered to walk back and search. The others said they would not wait. The night had been cold, perhaps too cold for a weakened old man to survive. Even if he was still alive, he could be miles in the rear, a half day's walk just to reach him. And what then? How would they get him back to the main party? And what about the next day, or the next, or the next? This wasn't a military unit, men bound to one another with unshakable allegiance. Nobody had promised Hardcoop anything. Out this far, you could look to your family members, but not much beyond that. If Hardcoop couldn't keep up, or so the argument must have gone, then sooner or later he was destined to die. They broke camp, hitched up the wagons, took a final look backward, and rolled out to the west. Parents must have told their children to stay extra close that day.

Keseberg has often been described as the villain of Hardcoop's abandonment, and there is little doubt he was a hard man, if not an overtly mean one. Yet Keseberg should not shoulder the blame alone. Eddy was the main source for the story, especially the details about his efforts at a morning rescue, yet even he admitted that the previous day he refused to let Hardcoop ride in his wagon when the old man asked for help, and Eddy apparently made no effort to learn what happened to him the rest of the day.

Nor did anyone else. On the day Hardcoop was left behind, most members of the party must have had some inkling of the old man's struggle, must have noticed that he was faltering or was sitting by the trail or was nowhere to be found at the noon break. Only the day before, after all, he had been unable to keep up; it would have required no great act of collective mercy or prescience to mind his progress with a protective eye. Anyone could have helped, but no one did.

Hardcoop would have labored on until he was past exhaustion. He had a son and daughter in Antwerp, and after the trip west he intended to return to Belgium and spend his declining years with them. If only he could somehow make it to camp, perhaps he would see them again, bounce grandchildren on his knee and spend a peaceful old age amid the pleasures of home. He had risked everything for one last adventure—a glimpse of this far-off place called California—and now the dream was darkening into nightmare. He could be halfway to Belgium now, not out here stumbling through the wilderness and fighting for his life.

If he made it through the night, he must have gazed at the morning horizon hoping for some approaching figure of rescue. Perhaps someone was coming back. Perhaps they had not forgotten him. Perhaps they would take pity on a weak old man. But at some point he faced the facts. He could go no farther forward, and they were not coming back. He may have just walked to the end and collapsed onto the trail when he was fully spent. Or perhaps he found some piece of shade where he could sit down and await the inevitable.

AHEAD ON THE TRAIL, THE BANISHED James Reed and his teamster Walter Herron had only one horse between them, so they took turns riding and walking, half the day in the saddle and half on foot. Freed from the wagon train's crawling pace, they made good time—close to forty miles one day and often twenty-five or more, by Reed's reckoning. His unfinished diary remained with his family, but now he continued the effort as best he could, using a scrap of spare paper to scrawl out a crude map, mileage notations, and a few taciturn comments. "Hard pass. You must double teams," he wrote at the start, presumably referring to the hill where he had killed Snyder.

Despite "all the economy I could use," as Reed wrote later, their provisions ran out in a few days, forcing them to hunt for food. Still, he and Herron survived the Nevada desert, even stopping long enough at a hot springs to use the scalding water to make a cup of tea. Near the lake where the rest of the party would eventually be trapped, Reed noted that they endured eight miles of "the worst road in creaton," and then began climbing into the Sierra Nevada. Game grew scarcer, and in any event they had little time for hunting if they wished to reach the California settlements and return with supplies before winter. The result was that starvation became a very real possibility. They managed to gather a few wild onions, but eventually they grew so famished that Herron wanted to kill the horse for meat, although Reed held him off, insisting that destroying their best means of transportation should be a last resort. At one point, while Herron was riding and Reed walking, Reed found a single bean, apparently dropped by previous emigrants, and they began scanning the ground. "Never was a road examined more closely for several miles," Reed wrote later. In all, they found five beans; Herron, who had briefly become delirious from hunger, ate three of them, Reed two.

Stumbling on some abandoned wagons, they ransacked the contents but found no food. Desperate, Reed checked a bucket slung under the bed of one of the wagons and used to store axle grease. He scraped away the tar normally used as grease and at the bottom found "a streak of rancid tallow"—animal fat that was sometimes also used as a lubricant. As an animal product, it was theoretically edible, and so Reed used the bucket's tar paddle to scrape up a ball of tallow about the size of a walnut. As repulsive as it sounds—old, congealed animal fat that had been sitting beneath a coating of tar—they each ate a piece, and then Herron had another. They walked on, but Reed went only fifty yards before his stomach rebelled and he became "deadly sick and blind." He had to stop and rest against a rock, leaning his head on the muzzle of his gun. He looked so ashen that Herron asked if he was dying.

In time, they spotted wagons belonging to a group of emigrants who had stopped to rest their cattle at a place called Bear Valley. Amazingly, they also found Charles Stanton, one of the two men who had left the Donner Party six weeks earlier to ride to California and fetch supplies. Stanton had safely reached Sutter's Fort and now was returning to the company with mules loaded with flour and dried meat. William McCutchan, the other volunteer and a man whose wife and baby daughter were among the emigrants, had also reached Sutter's Fort but had been too sick to return, so it was Stanton, the diminutive bachelor with no relatives at risk, who started back eastward over the Sierra.

Reed and Stanton exchanged news and then, as soon as possible rode off in opposite directions: Reed westward, toward Sutter's Fort and more supplies, Stanton eastward, toward the struggling party he had vowed to rescue.

B ACK ON THE HUMBOLDT RIVER, the main contingent of the Donner Party was enduring a fresh adversity: conflict with Indians. Hollywood depictions notwithstanding, violence between wagon trains and tribes was actually quite rare. Over the long span of history, of course, the European conquest of the Americas was devastating to native peoples, seizing their homelands and effecting a genocide on the population. In North America, British, French, and Spanish settlement reduced the pre-Columbian population by at least half, perhaps far more than that. Estimates vary hugely, but it's clear that the European triumph cost hundreds of thousands, if not millions, of lives. But in the shorter term, the overland migration to the West actually produced far less bloodshed than has commonly been portrayed in the popular culture, either in vintage movies that depicted all Indians as bloodthirsty savages preying on innocent families or in more recent fare that reversed the roles. John D. Unruh Jr., the best historian of the overland migration, tried to count the deaths of emigrants at the hands of Indians, and vice versa, using reasonably reliable contemporary sources. His admittedly imprecise tally for the two decades between 1840 and 1860 found only 362 emigrants killed by Indians and—even more surprising—only 426 Indians directly killed by emigrants. Even among the few hundred deaths Unruh could identify, most occurred in 1849 or later, when the Gold Rush increased traffic on the trail drastically, unavoidably exacerbating discord with Indians. In some early years, Unruh found no deaths directly attributable to emigrant-Indian skirmishes. In 1846, the year of the Donner Party, he recorded only four emigrant deaths and twenty Indian fatalities.

Typically, emigrants started the journey with great fear of the Indians but soon found their concerns unwarranted. At Fort Kearny in Nebraska—two hundred miles or more into the journey—a correspondent reported in 1850 that most of that year's trains had yet to even see an Indian. When the two groups did encounter one another, relations were usually friendly. Indians gave directions to those who were lost, helped extract wagons that were stuck, provided water or firewood to families short on provisions, and in at least one case rescued a drowning man. Mutually beneficial business deals were common, with Indians hired to serve as guides, guards, interpreters, and packers. So peaceful was the trip that some emigrants concluded almost all dangers were mythological and discarded their weapons. Lansford Hastings, who had written the guidebook read by many emigrants of 1846, noted that earlier parties had disarmed in what is today Idaho. In 1850 one party was no farther than western Nebraska when they lightened their load by throwing out their guns.

Almost all emigrants viewed the Indians with what we would regard as gross racism and sometimes acted on an attendant belief that they could behave toward natives in any way they liked. There are stories not only of kidnapping but of wanton murder. But there were also many cases of emigrant-Indian interaction that were charmingly human and universal. Heinrich Lienhard, ahead of the Donner Party on the trail in 1846, once struck up a sign-language friendship with a Shoshone by asking him to dig some edible roots. Lienhard ate one of the roots—it reminded him of a parsnip—and enjoyed it. But that night he suffered horribly from stomach cramps and diarrhea, so when the Indian brought him more roots in the morning Lienhard was aghast. "Since I could explain why only by signs, I bent over forward, held my stomach with both hands, and groaned as if I had severe stomach pains. Then I imitated a certain sound with my lips that could come only from another part of the anatomy, and at the same time I made a quick gesture to my behind. The Indians understood completely, and they all burst out in a storm of laughter. My friend laughed loudest of all, and threw his roots at my back. We naturally joined in the laughter and parted as good friends in spite of all."

When trouble did arise, emigrants sometimes found that Indians were wrongly blamed. In 1844 a minister named Edward Parrish noted in his journal a developing crisis that was by turns a story of suspicion and exculpation, all in a single morning: "Preparing to make an early start, But the cattle are not all lined up. Indians accused of driving them off. Indians not guilty—cattle found." White criminals sometimes disguised themselves as Indians, although in at least one case the ruse failed. In 1859 a woman was raped by five apparent Indians, although she was able to identify her attackers as white men because, in the words of a government report on the incident, "They had not taken the precaution to paint the whole body."

We have fewer written records revealing the Native American perspective about the migration, although we know that some chiefs initially urged cooperation and amicable relations. The West was a polyglot place, after all. Aside from hundreds of distinct Indian tribes, there had long been French, British, and American trappers and traders, occasionally even Spanish explorers roaming up from the south. It would not have been immediately obvious that the new groups of white people in covered wagons represented a stark departure from the past. When the emigrants did begin to appear, one record of Indian perception suggests a progression of emotions not unlike that of the emigrants: initial fear followed by a growing acceptance and realization of common humanity. Sarah Winnemucca Hopkins, the daughter of a chief, remembered that when she was a girl, her people first heard stories of slaughter and even cannibalism by emigrant trains. Caught too near a band of approaching whites, the little girl's mother became so fearful that she briefly buried her two children alive as a way to hide them, propping sage bushes over their exposed faces to provide more cover.

If a single rough grain of contention abraded the relationship between emigrants and Indians—at least from the perspective of the emigrants—it was the theft of horses and other stock. For California-bound trains, theft was worst of all along the Humboldt, a hardscrabble region inhabited by Indians whom the emigrants denounced as "diggers." The name came from the native practice of using a stick to dig for edible roots and grub, but it was also meant to suggest that the local Indians were primitive, filthy people. Mark Twain denounced them as "the wretchedest type of mankind I have ever seen," and the perception continued into the twentieth century. The Pulitzer Prize–winning historian Bernard DeVoto, who in another context chastised Americans for insufficient comprehension of Indian life and folkways, described the "diggers" as people without a culture, even insisting that many were "physically decadent." In fact, the Indians of the Great Basin—mostly Paiute, Shoshone, and Ute—had shrewdly adapted to their difficult surroundings. The digging that earned the white men's epithet was a reasonable way to reach foodstuffs, but it was hardly their only method of acquiring nourishment. They snared game, irrigated small plots of land, and collected large quantities of pine nuts, some of which were buried in order to preserve them for the winter months. DeVoto was wrong about a lack of culture: They were renowned for their artistic basketry, painted hides to depict important events, and specified rites to mark mileposts of life such as the birth of a couple's first child. Though hardly the richest native people of North America, neither were the Indians of the Humboldt River the filthy savages reported by the emigrants.

At every step of the journey, the Donner Party fit the pattern of emigrant-Indian interaction: initial fear, then friendly relations, then trouble along the Humboldt. The fear began before the trip did. On the long winter nights in the months before they left, Virginia Reed's grandmother entertained the girl with yarns about a relative supposedly kidnapped and held captive by Indians for five years, tales that so frightened Virginia she would back up against the nearest wall, lest a marauder attack her with a tomahawk from behind. When the Donner Party wagons encountered Indians operating a ferry service across the Kansas River, Virginia wondered if the strange entrepreneurs would sink the vessel halfway across so as to drown their white passengers. No such confrontation occurred, of course, and by the time they reached Fort Laramie, the members of the Donner Party were comfortable enough with Indians to invite them for meals. But conflict began almost as soon as they hit the Humboldt. A yoke of Graves's oxen was stolen by two Indians who wandered into camp and stayed the night, at one point helping to put out a grass fire. Two days later, Graves lost a horse, again apparently to thieves. Farther down the river, all of Graves's remaining horses trotted away under the reins of new and unknown owners. Then the serious depredations began. In a single night nineteen head of cattle went missing. A few days later the overnight guards, apparently thinking the danger had passed with the darkness, came into camp for breakfast. When they gulped down their last swig of coffee and rose to prepare for the morning march, they discovered that twenty-one more animals had disappeared in the time it took a man to eat a rasher or two of bacon. The losses imperiled transportation—cattle pulled the wagons—but the real cost was far greater, and one the emigrants could not yet fully appreciate. A good portion of the Donner Party's potential food supply had vanished.

The Mouth of Hell, the River of Life

12

Down the dwindling waters of the Humboldt, they set their course by taking aim toward Lone Mountain, a desert butte that reminded some emigrants of pictures they had seen of ancient Mayan pyramids. A broad, open meadow provided good fodder for the stock—the coarse grass "as thick as hair on a Dogs back"—and then they were at the Sink, the strange and somber spot where the river died. In wet years it formed a broad, shallow lake; in a drought it simply vanished into the desert. Most years it was something in between, a boggy marsh that one slightly poetic Gold Rusher described as "a veritable sea of slime, a slough of despond, an ocean of ooze, a bottomless bed of alkaline poison," all of which created "the appearance of utter desolation." Given the conditions of 1846, the Donner Party almost surely found little or no water in what was sometimes called, too optimistically, Humboldt Lake. James Clyman, the mountain man who had tried to warn Reed about the Hastings Cut-Off, had passed by the area earlier in the year and spied "the most thirsty appearance of any place I ever witnessed The whole of several large vallies is covered in a verry fin clay or mud which has vimited from the bowels of the earth."

At the end of the sink stood a strange earthen berm, perhaps twenty feet high, extending across the riverbed. Probably created by the wave action of an ancient lake, this natural dike guarded a small slough where emigrants were known to fill every available vessel, sometimes even using their boots for water storage. They were eager to collect all the water they could because they were about to enter a stretch of the journey almost as brutal as the desert just beyond the Great Salt Lake. With the Humboldt now gone, they needed to cross to the Truckee River, which would lead them toward the pass over the Sierra Nevada and into California. But between the Humboldt and the Truckee lay a desolate forty-mile desert.

Like most trains, the Donner Party tried to cross at night, hoping the cooler temperatures would ease the agony of the long, waterless push. At 4:00 A.M., halfway across, they found a hot springs, where steam spewed up from the ground "like the mouth of hell," as a later emigrant wrote. Brackish and foul-tasting, the water was still good enough to drink once it was cooled, and in the meantime offered the chance to make coffee or tea. Eddy got some coffee from the Donners and made some for his wife and children, who seemed to get a boost of energy. They rested for a time, then started again a few hours later and drove all through the day, then into the wee hours for the second straight night. For the last ten miles, deep sand covered the road, and the animals slipped and slid as they heaved the wagons through. When the Gold Rush hit a few years later and the trail turned into a crowded highway, the rotting corpses of collapsed animals lined the route. One man reported in 1849 that he and his companions had to stop "every few yards" to rest their teams, despite the overpowering stench of decay. "All our traveling experience," he wrote, "furnishes no parallel to this." The Donner Party was no exception: Three yoke of cattle died of fatigue.

But at the end of the desert, a verdant reward awaited. After hundreds of miles of the arid, rocky sterility of the intermountain West, the Truckee River was a thing of beauty, a cool and inviting oasis lined with trees. No member of the Donner Party left a direct record of the moment they saw the river, but if their experience was like that of other trains, the arrival at the Truckee was an occasion for glee. For weeks they had seen virtually no trees; now they rushed toward a river lined with a shady bower of cottonwoods and willows. They paused a moment or two to scan the trees for hidden Indians, then turned loose the animals and ran toward the clear, clean water. They waded out into the knee-deep stream and, side by side with the stock, drank long and delicious draughts. Elisha Brooks, who made the trip in 1852, remembered her first sighting of the Truckee as though it were a mirage or a miracle. "We beheld the green banks and crystal clear waters of the Truckee River by the morning sun; and it was to us the River of Life."

Still, the Donner Party that arrived at those resuscitating riverbanks was a slowly disintegrating unit, both materially and spiritually. The Eddys were nearly destitute now, their wagon and possessions abandoned back on the Humboldt when Indians stole their last yoke of oxen. With no other choice, they had resolved to finish the journey on foot, Eleanor carrying their baby daughter and William shouldering their three-year-old son, three pounds of sugar, some bullets, and a powder horn. (His rifle no longer fired, but apparently he assumed he could borrow one later.) Margret Reed, her children, and her employees were hardly better off. They had been forced to abandon their wagon shortly after James Reed's departure, and although for a time they borrowed a lighter vehicle from the Graveses, soon they too, like the Eddys, abandoned most of their property. "We had to cash all of our close except a change or 2," Virginia Reed wrote. The Breens agreed to haul the family's last few garments, and three-year-old Thomas Reed and five-year-old James Reed were put aboard their two remaining horses. The fact that a three-year-old boy was not joined by another rider offered plain testimony to the pathetic condition of the animals. The other Reeds walked, although across the desert the Donners let them ride in a wagon. Worst of all was the fate of a German named Wolfinger, reputedly a rich man. When he stayed behind to dig a cache for his wagon before the desert crossing from the Humboldt to the Truckee, he mysteriously disappeared, and the various recollections of survivors could never quite clarify the circumstances.

So with the party still struggling, it's not surprising that talk soon turned toward another effort to secure more provisions from California. Stanton and McCutchan, the two volunteers, had been gone for more than a month, and no one knew if they had even survived to reach Sutter's Fort, let alone return. As for Reed and Herron, occasional trailside notes had offered evidence of their initial survival, but no one knew their ultimate fate. It was conceivable that none of the four men had reached safe haven across the mountains.

The two men who emerged as the would-be saviors this time were the sons-in-law of Levinah Murphy, the Mormon widow leading a three-generation clan. William Foster was married to Murphy's oldest daughter, William Pike to the second oldest. They had joined the family somewhat by chance. In the winter of 1842, when the Murphy family was leaving Nauvoo, Illinois, for Tennessee, ice floes captured their ship and held it fast in the Mississippi River. Foster and Pike were both crew members, and as the vessel lay motionless, romances flowered with the two oldest Murphy daughters, sixteen-year-old Sarah and fourteen-year-old Harriet. Both couples were wed four days after Christmas, and by the time they went west four years later, the Fosters had one young child, the Pikes two.

For an engineer on a riverboat, William Pike was a man of glorious pedigree. His grandfather had been an officer in the Revolutionary War; his uncle was the explorer Zebulon Pike, the discoverer of Pike's Peak. At the time of the Donner Party expedition, William was in his early thirties, an impressive and intelligent figure with a mechanical bent, a man almost as old and experienced as his mother-in-law. It says something about his standing in the company that near the start of the Hastings Cut-Off, when three men were needed to ride ahead and find the company's absent guide, Pike was one of those chosen. Now, he was ready to begin a risky new venture with a man he surely must have trusted, his former shipmate and current brother-in-law. But as the two men readied supplies and equipment, a small pistol that was being loaded somehow fired, striking Pike in the back. One of his wife's sisters remembered that he lived for half an hour, suffering "more than tongue can tell."

Accidents with firearms on the trail were more common than might be expected, especially given our modern conception that everyone in the nineteenth century was a backwoodsman or a hunter. In fact, many emigrants were new to life in the wild, as nothing so vividly attests as their experiences with weapons. More than once, someone pulled a gun from a wagon muzzle-first—and paid for the mistake with his life. Gold Rusher Andrew Orvis shot himself in the hip and noted that "there has been several kiled and wounded on the road in the same way by just being carless with their fire arms." Occasionally, the circumstances were simply bizarre. In one case a gun went off accidentally because the hammer caught on a woman's skirt.

But Pike's death offered a broader lesson too. In less than a month, the Donner Party had lost four of its members: Snyder stabbed, Hardcoop abandoned, Wolfinger the victim of an unknown fate, Pike shot accidentally. Even before the mountain entrapment that would mark their tale for generations, the Donner Party was proving the hazards of the way west. Life was risky everywhere—cholera was cholera, no matter where it struck—but the weight of the historical evidence suggests that death was more common for emigrants who braved the trip than for their more timid brethren back home. A budding new industry recognized the risks. Only three years before the Donner Party headed west, the first commercial life insurance company in the United States was founded, sparking a quick proliferation of competitors. But almost all the policies forbade travel beyond the Mississippi River, so likely was it that the companies would have to pay beneficiaries. Not until the Gold Rush sent thousands of policyholders scurrying toward the Pacific did the insurers allow western travel, and even then there was typically a surcharge on premiums, an added tariff for adventure in America's great natural wonderland.

A LONG THE TRUCKEE, THE WAGONS SNAKED through the river canyon, fording the current again and again, the water pushing up against the wheel rims. At times the canyon pinched to a sheer-walled gorge that barely offered room for a trail.

Then on one of the endless days marching westward they finally saw a cheering site ahead of them. Stanton bumped along at the head of a little mule train, returning with supplies, just as he had promised. After bidding farewell to Reed on the west slope of the Sierra, the intrepid Stanton had crossed the mountains with two Indians sent along by John Sutter, and now, somewhere on the eastern side, he reappeared before his old companions. Provisions were extraordinarily low, but Stanton brought flour and fresh meat, and the Dutch ovens soon produced biscuits. Patty Reed loaded her apron and distributed the welcome victuals to the children—one biscuit apiece. "I don't know when we had had bread before," remembered Frances Donner. "It was a great treat to us then." For the Reeds, Stanton brought another godsend as well: news that James Reed had made it safely over the mountains. Stanton recounted his meeting with Reed, "not fur from Suters Fort," as Virginia Reed described it, and said that although Reed had eaten only three times in a week, he was at least healthy enough to ride onward.

To the bedraggled, half-starved members of the Donner Party, it must have seemed that the worst of their problems had passed. They had already endured more than many emigrants ever did. Leaving the main road, they had been forced to hack a new path through the Wasatch and then to cross the Great Salt Lake Desert, a more desiccated and debilitating environment than most trains ever encountered. Comrades had been deserted callously and killed violently, and a man had been banished to the wilderness. At various points, water and provisions had run so low as to threaten the very survival of the party. Yet now they had a replenished larder and, perhaps more important, a guide who could lead them over the lone obstacle still to be conquered. Stanton had crossed the Sierra twice, once westward to fetch supplies, once eastward to bring them back. What was more, he was a man they could trust, not merely one of their own but a selfless volunteer who had proven his fealty merely by reappearing. Surely he could lead them all over the mountains to safety. Surely the ordeal was done.

Part 2

Tribulation

A Great Snowy Range

13

By the time westward emigrants reached the Sierra Nevada, they had completed all but a hundred miles of a two-thousand-mile journey. Yet that final, brief stretch constituted a singular and frightening obstacle as testing as any they had yet endured.

Lying almost entirely within the modern state of California, the Sierra Nevada is the largest single mountain range in the contiguous United States. (The Rockies and Appalachians, although covering a greater area, are collections of geologically distinct chains.) Slathered across an area almost as large as the Alps are more than five hundred peaks that exceed 12,000 feet in elevation, including Mt. Whitney, at 14,494 feet the highest point in the country, save Alaska. Such pinnacles are the topmost portion of a vast and mostly subsurface mass of granite, actually consisting of hundreds of individual pieces but known collectively to geologists as the Sierra Nevada batholith. Millions of years ago, this underground behemoth thrust upward through the earth's surface, eventually transforming what had been a range of low hills into the majestic spires visible today. The boost was greater in the east than in the west, so that the mountains tilted as they grew, and the Sierra Nevada came to be a range with two starkly different slopes:

precipitous on the east side of the summit ridge, gradual on the west. This geology mattered to the overland migration because it meant that as the wagons creaked slowly toward the final obstacle of the journey, they faced not a staircase of gently rising foothills but a dizzying cliff face of nearly vertical escarpments, some of which dropped thousands of feet from the alpine heights to the desert floor beneath.

As if to double the curse, the geological challenges of the Sierra are matched by climatic ones, for the mountains offer some of the snowiest conditions on the continent. On April 2, 1772, a Spanish missionary named Pedro Font spied the peaks from 120 miles away and described them in his journal as *"una gran sierra nevada"*—a great snowy mountain range. The name stuck, perhaps because no cartographer could have devised a more apt moniker. Arrayed down California's spine from north to south, the mountains sit at a right angle to the prevailing westerly winds and, relative to other mountain ranges, are close to the ocean. Storms sponge up moist air over the Pacific and then are blown directly at the peaks. The clouds are pushed upward as they scrape against the western slope of the Sierra, an effect meteorologists call "orographic uplift." Air masses cool as they rise, and this cooling condenses the moisture back into water, which then plummets from the sky as rain or snow. As a result, the Sierra can experience extraordinary deluges, single storms dropping foot upon foot of heavy, wet snow.

The earliest meteorological records for the Sierra owe their existence not to a desire to measure the range's ferocity but to conquer it. When the transcontinental railroad subdued the Sierra with ties and track, Southern Pacific maintenance crews began to record weather conditions on a daily basis. Fortunately for the study of the Donner Party, the line goes right over the point at which the emigrants aimed to cross the ridge of the Sierra. Thus we have weather records for the spot dating back to 1870, the longest stream of meteorological data for any location in the Sierra.

The resulting picture is one of almost mythical snowfall. In 1938, apparently using a particularly conservative method of measurement, the railroad crews recorded a winter-long total of sixty-eight feet. Because snow compacts—the heavier new snow on top pressing down the old layers beneath—the amount on the ground at any one time is less than the seasonal accumulation, but Donner Pass can still feature extraordinary totals. It is not uncommon to have fifteen feet of snow on the level, and that is far from the maximum. In 1880, just a decade after the railroad opened, the diligent observers of the Southern Pacific recorded a depth at Donner Pass of thirty-one feet, enough to cover a three-story building.

TWO THOUSAND MILES FROM THE SLOWLY MOVING WAGONS of the Donner Party, a storm rose from the unruly waters of the Gulf of Alaska. Evaporation sent countless tons of water vapor pirouetting up into the sky, loading up the clouds like soaked sponges. Winds gathered strength until they howled across the whitecaps like a flood down a gully. The jet stream began to push the front southward, shoving it along at the speed of a hardworking freight train.

The storm smashed into the redwood forests at the mouth of the Klamath River, almost up by Oregon, dropping sheets of rain that soaked deep down into the roots, ensuring another lush green winter at the ocean's edge. The heart of the maelstrom rushed farther south, cascading over the coast ranges, whipping through the Golden Gate, casting long and threatening shadows across Sutter's Fort. At last the clouds began their long climb up into the Sierra, aiming directly for the pass the emigrants intended to use. As the clouds rose, they cooled. Gaseous molecules condensed into liquid droplets; droplets froze into ice crystals; crystals coalesced into snowflakes. The flakes grew too heavy to resist the call of gravity. It began to snow.

THE NIGHTS WERE GETTING COLDER. Early risers found the buffalo skin blankets rimed with hoarfrost and the water buckets glazed over with ice as thick as a windowpane. The peaks before them were sheathed in clouds, a sign of storms that spurred the prudent to push on as fast as possible.

Some families drove themselves harder than others, and the company again broke into pieces, the Breens and some other families in front, the two Donner clans lagging behind at the rear, an uncertain array of small groups in between. On October 31 the forward group reached Truckee Lake, a pristine swatch of blue that sits at the base of a massive, nearly vertical slope reaching more than a thousand feet straight up into the high Sierra. At the top lies the pass for which the emigrants were aiming, a notch between the peaks. If you are headed west from the lake, there is nowhere to go but up.

Snow covered the ground at the lake, the depth increasing with every added foot of altitude, but the lead families made a quick try for the summit anyway. It proved a hopeless attempt, for they had no guide. Charles Stanton and the two Indians from Sutter's Fort, Luis and Salvador, were the only members of the company who had been over the pass, but they were with some of the trailing families. Unable to follow the route through the snow, the lead group retreated to the lake and waited until the following day, when Stanton and some others caught up. They decided that the following morning they would make a try.

Some hung back, preferring the relative safety of the lake to the exposed heights above. William Foster dictated a note authorizing Milt Elliott, one of the teamsters, to buy mules and cattle in California on Foster's behalf and promising to pay for the animals once he arrived. The Breens, who had led the previous day's attempt, probably abandoned the second day's effort sooner than most. John Breen remembered them advancing no more than two miles before the heavy snows brought them to a downhearted halt. "We were compelled to retrace our steps in despair," he wrote.

Others forged on: the Reeds, the Eddys, the Graves family, Stanton and the two Indians. Lewis Keseberg went along, though he was too lame to walk. Weeks earlier, when he was out hunting geese, Keseberg had stepped on a willow stub that had punctured his moccasin and pierced the ball of his foot. As the party reached the Sierra, he still could not put weight on it, and so he made the great push up the mountains in a saddle.

Writing to her cousin a few months later, Virginia Reed remembered the start of that day's climb in almost plucky terms. "Well we thought we would try it so we started," she wrote. Rain had been falling at the lake, and some of the flatlander emigrants naively hoped that it had rained higher up the mountains as well, beating down the powdery snow and creating a firmer walking surface. Instead, they learned a hard lesson of life in the Sierra: Rain in the valleys is almost always snow at higher elevations. "The farther we went up the deeper the snow got," Virginia remembered. As on the day before, the wagons were soon abandoned in favor of pack animals, but the process was slow and troublesome, the oxen trying to dislodge the unfamiliar loads, the people grumbling and debating about what would be taken, what left behind. "One wanted a box of tobacco carried along; another, a bale of calico, and some one thing and some another," as Keseberg recalled.

One of the mules handled the drifts better than the others, so the animal was put at the head of the line to stamp down a trail, but in time it too began to pitch headfirst into the swallowing snow. Stanton and one of the Indians scouted ahead and reached the summit, but when they returned to urge a final push, they found a party collapsed in exhaustion. A campfire had been kindled on the snow, and the desperate and dispirited emigrants clung to it like a raft amid the sea. Stanton insisted that if no more snow fell the pass could be crested, but it was useless counsel. Whether from fatigue or despair, no one would move. They bedded down, intending to forge ahead in the morning.

But in the night, the storm that would prove the ultimate undoing of the Donner Party reached them at last. Snow pummeled down so heavily that it almost buried the unsheltered emigrants. Margret Reed tried to stay awake, brushing the snow from her children. Keseberg remembered waking at one point to feel a heavy weight pushing down on his chest, impeding his ability to breathe:

Springing up to a sitting posture, I found myself covered with freshly fallen snow. The camp, the cattle, my companions, had all disappeared. All I could see was snow everywhere. I shouted at the top of my voice. Suddenly, here and there, all about me, heads popped up through the snow. The scene was not unlike what one might imagine at the resurrection, when people rise up out of the earth.

Daylight brought a grim realization: The snow was far too deep to go on. Plainly, there was no chance of reaching the pass and descending the other side. Not that reaching the crest would have guaranteed their safety. A long slog down the western slope of the Sierra would have awaited, something that might have proved beyond their weakened bodies. Or they might have been trapped near the top of the pass, at high altitude and exposed to the weather's full brunt. They might have all died there, mere bones to be found the following spring.

But at least there had been some hope. At least they had still been moving forward, going in the direction of their goal. Now they could face nothing but the bleak truth. "The rest you probably know," Keseberg wrote years later, reflecting the resignation that must have suffused the group. They turned around, retraced their labored steps from the day before, and headed down toward the lake they had just left.

The bold and desperate vanguard of the Donner Party had failed the final, terrible test of the great gamble of their lives. Leaving as soon as spring allowed, marching an extra mile or two in the gathering gloom of dusk, seizing a promised shortcut in the hope of saving time and distance—all these had been aimed at a single goal, to cross the mountains and reach safety before the changing of the seasons wreaked a vengeful havoc. Now it had all come to naught. "We had to go back...," Virginia Reed remembered, "and stay thare all Winter."

This Prison

14

James Reed reached Sutter's Fort just as his family and the others were approaching the Sierra. The first storm of autumn greeted Reed's arrival, sending a torrent of rain down upon John Sutter's keep.

At the fort, Reed found William McCutchan, the tall, bushy-haired man who had left his wife and daughter with the main party six weeks earlier to ride ahead for supplies with Charles Stanton. McCutchan had been too sick to go along when Stanton returned, but now, his health restored, he was ready to go back for his family. He talked with Reed, and the two men—both fathers with children in the mountains—decided to set out on a desperate mission of rescue. Sutter offered a discouraging assessment. Looking up at the peaks coated in white, the master of the fort declared ominously that the snow "was low down and heavy for the first fall of the season."

Sutter had fled his native Switzerland when a failed business overwhelmed him with debts. He made his way to St. Louis and then on to the West—New Mexico and Oregon and even Hawaii before finally settling in California, where in time he took Mexican citizenship. Blessed with a generous land grant from the territory's governor, Sutter built an adobe fort on a little rise near the Sacramento River, with

Indian laborers to do most of the work and cannon in the guard towers to discourage marauders. He dealt in furs and cattle and brandy, and by 1846 Sutter's Fort was well established as both the end point of the overland migration and the hub of the burgeoning American community in California.

Sutter looked generously upon overland pioneers, either because he was also an immigrant or because they might buy supplies at his fort. When Reed and McCutchan resolved to launch their rescue effort, Sutter provided Indian helpers and some supplies—flour and a hindquarter of beef. Reed and McCutchan lashed the provisions to a train of packhorses and set out as quickly as possible.

Optimistic and confident as always, Reed hoped they might not have to cross the peaks. Perhaps the wagons had slipped through the vise just in time and were already rolling down the western slope. If only he and McCutchan could get up there with some fresh provisions, the whole bruising trial might be over. Everyone would make it after all, safe and sound, to new lives in California. Perhaps they would even forget—or at least forgive—the foolishness of the Hastings Cut-Off and the ugly trouble with Snyder.

But as they climbed the western slope, Reed and McCutchan found no trace of their families, instead encountering a stranded and starving emigrant couple from another company. Desperate for food, the couple had butchered their dog, the last piece of which was now cooking in a Dutch oven. A storm had prevented Reed and McCutchan from lighting a cookfire, so they were famished, and Reed wrote later that they quickly accepted the couple's offer of a canine meal:

> Raising the lid of the oven, we found the dog well baked, and having a fine savory smell. I cut out a rib, smelling and tasting, found it to be good, and handed the rib over to Mr. McCutchan, who, after smelling it some time, tasted it and pronounced it *very good dog.*

They provisioned the stranded couple, then moved on through snow that grew deeper with each added increment of altitude—knee-high, then up to their waists, finally so deep that the horses would rear up on their hind legs and crash down with their front feet, sinking until only their noses and the top portions of their heads were visible. Sensing the hopelessness of the task, the Indian helpers sent by Sutter deserted in the night, and the next day Reed and McCutchan abandoned the horses and forged ahead on foot. At last, still well short of the crest of the mountains, they could go no farther, "the snow being soft and deep," and they stopped to face the unavoidable.

Both men had every motivation to fight onward; their families were stranded up there somewhere. But then again, they would hardly be much help as dead men. And for all they knew, the trapped emigrants might not be truly desperate. When McCutchan and Reed left the main party—McCutchan in mid-September, Reed in early October—the Donner Party still possessed a small but decent herd of cattle. Only later, along the Humboldt River, did the emigrants encounter hostile Indians who killed dozens of the animals. Nor did Reed and McCutchan know where the emigrants had stopped. The location could have been worse than it was—atop the pass, for example—but it might also have been better. For all they knew, their families were trying to winter over at a substantially lower elevation, and doing so with an ample larder of meat on the hoof.

At last, prudence and reality won out over the urge toward a foolish if courageous heroism. The two men took a last longing look, and turned their backs on the mountains that held their families captive. "I state," McCutchan wrote a quarter century later, "that it was utterly impossible for any two men to have done more than we did in striving to get in to the people."

The crestfallen pair retreated to Sutter's Fort, where the proprietor validated their decision. Reed described how many cattle the company possessed when he was banished, and Sutter, unaware of the later losses on the Humboldt, did some rough calculations. If the emigrants butchered the animals immediately and froze the meat in the snow, he said, they should have enough to eat until the spring thaw made it feasible to bring them out.

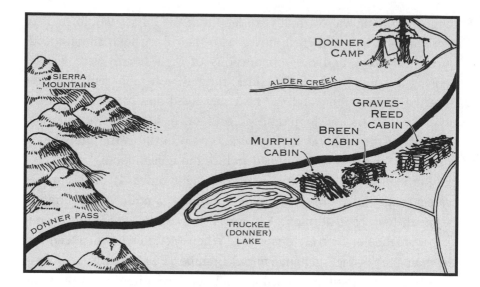

The families trapped in the mountains did not know it, but their last slim chance of immediate help had vanished. They were on their own.

THE FIRST NECESSITY WAS SHELTER, and so the men rummaged in their wagons for axes and saws. In the wake of their final attempt at the summit, the leading group had carefully picked its way back down the mountain face, retracing the way toward Truckee Lake. As they descended, they could peer straight down into the basin that would be their home for months to come.

It was not a hospitable place to spend the winter. Sitting at almost exactly six thousand feet in elevation, the lake averages more than fifteen feet of snow each year. And although large—roughly three miles long and a half mile wide—the lake can easily freeze over during a cold winter, as it did in 1846, when the emigrants found it impossible to successfully ice-fish.

So why did the Donner Party stop there? Truckee Meadows, the welcoming valley where Reno sits today, is thirty-five miles east and fifteen hundred feet lower, a substantial difference in the dead of winter. The wagons had come right through the Meadows before starting their climb up the Truckee River, so the emigrants knew the valley was there.

It was an option that must have crossed their minds. George Tucker, whose family was in a company just ahead of the Donner Party on the trail—a company that had itself barely slipped over the mountains in time—wondered about a tactical retreat. Tucker's family had stopped to winter at Johnson's Ranch, the first settlement west of the Sierra, but they knew the Donner Party was behind them on the trail. Looking up at the snow, just as Reed and Sutter had done, Tucker hoped that the Donners and their comrades had retraced their steps back down the river to find a location "where they could winter their stock and find some way of sustaining life til Spring."

If the Donner Party considered that alternative, no one ever mentioned it in a diary or journal or letter, at the time or in the years to come. Partly it was the triumph of hope over realism. They kept thinking that perhaps they could sneak over the mountains—maybe there would be a break in the weather or a little rest would revive their strength—and so wintering at the base of the range kept them closer to their goal. So too would they be closer to the prospect of rescue. They knew Reed, McCutchan, and Herron were on the west side of the mountains, and any or all of them might return, just as Stanton had.

Then there was simple exhaustion. After nearly two thousand miles on the trail, giving back ground must have seemed a dispiriting idea. Who wanted to keep walking—in the wrong direction—just to drop a few hundred feet? How much better to stay put, to finally take a breather from the endless marching. "We arrived here betraveled, weary, already half-starved, and almost desperate," remembered William Murphy, who was then ten. "My friends, what would you have done, indeed? . . . Behind you is a desert two thousand miles uninhabited to the Missouri River; before you is—what? There is no San Francisco, no Sacramento . . . no nothing."

But the most significant reason for staying at Truckee Lake may have been their ignorance of the territory into which they had wandered. Back at home, Midwest winters froze noses and turned fingers numb, but a storm was fierce if it dropped three feet of snow. For the most part, the men and women of the Donner Party had no experience with the kind of mountain climate they were about to experience, no idea that snowstorms could bury livestock or buildings or a decent-sized tree. In the end the extraordinarily deep snows of the Sierra Nevada would have much to do with their suffering, but in the beginning their expectations were a blank. The families must have stayed at the lake, in other words, in part because they knew so little about it. Had they understood more about their surroundings, they might have left.

Fortunately, one cabin already existed, which may have been another reason for staying. Two years before, another party of emigrants had been forced to abandon its wagons and livestock and cross the pass on foot. One man stayed behind to guard the prized possessions, and the cabin where he passed the winter still stood. It was in bad shape; the rain poured through a roof that was nothing but boughs spread across the top of the walls. But it was better than nothing, and the Breens moved in immediately, perhaps because they were the first to come back down from the final assault on the pass, perhaps simply because they were one of the bigger families.

The other clans pulled out tools and set about building shelters from scratch. They felled trees, dragged the logs to the building sites, hewed out notches at both ends, hoisted them up as the walls rose—exhausting labor under any circumstances, let alone for people who had just walked nearly two thousand miles. The Murphys saved themselves some sweat by erecting their cabin against a huge rock, the face of the boulder serving as one wall. The Graves and the Reeds—or really the Reeds' teamsters, since the family itself now consisted only of Margret and her children—pitched in together, building a "double cabin," a large structure with a fireplace at each end and a dividing wall running down the middle, "leaving a few chinks in the partition through which we might talk to plan a way out of this prison," as Patty Reed remembered.

The smaller families found homes where they could. Amanda McCutchan found room for herself and her infant daughter with the

Graveses. The Murphys took in William Eddy and his wife and two children. Stanton and the two Indians from Sutter's Fort managed to bunk with the Reeds. Keseberg apparently wanted a roof of his own, or perhaps no one would house him, but he was still lame from his wounded heel and could manage only a rough hovel, a lean-to really, banking tree boughs against the side of the old cabin that now housed the Breens.

As neighbors, they hardly huddled up with one another. The Graves/ Reed cabin was said by some to be half a mile from the others, a ready reflection of the tensions coursing through the group. "Father built his cabin where it was most sheltered from wind and storm and wood near by regardless of company interest, I supposed," recalled Mary Graves. Patty Reed seemed to think that Franklin Graves led a slightly bull-headed bunch: "he, & all of his family, had minds & wills of their own."

THE TWO DONNER FAMILIES, INCLUDING George Donner, the ostensible leader of the enterprise, were involved in none of this, for they were miles to the rear.

Coming down a steep hill well before they reached Truckee Lake, the front axle broke on one of George Donner's wagons. The vehicle tipped, and the contents scattered into a heap. The two youngest children, three-year-old Eliza and four-year-old Georgia, were riding in the wagon, and their father and their Uncle Jacob rushed to pull them free. They found Georgia quickly and pulled her out, but Eliza lay hidden in the messy jumble, not answering her father's frantic calls. The two men tossed aside items until at last Jacob found his niece. "You would not have stood it much longer," remembered her older half-sister, Elitha. The men set to work fashioning a new axle, but the delay meant that the other wagons moved even farther ahead.

When the snow came the Donners were seven miles behind the rest of the company. Tamzene wanted to push onward and make a try at the pass, but her husband and brother-in-law ruled that an impossibility, and so they camped where they were, near a small stream called Alder Creek. They made a brief attempt at building a cabin, but the walls were only four logs high when a blizzard hit, rendering work impossible. The small wagons packed with possessions offered little room or comfort, so the families pitched what they described as "tents," although these may only have been quilts, coats, and other covers spread over boughs propped against a tree. An even cruder brush structure was also erected, variously described by survivors as a lean-to, a "shed," and a "wigwam." The conditions made the lake cabins seem luxurious.

In all, eighty-one people were trapped, about three-quarters of them scattered among the three cabins at Truckee Lake, the others at Alder Creek. The wails of babies competed with the giggles of toddlers, for the camps teemed with children, a reflection of the fact that the entire overland migration was a family affair. More than half of those trapped were under eighteen, and a quarter were five or younger. There were half a dozen babies.

WILLIAM EDDY KNEW HE WAS BEING GOUGED, but what choice did he have? Franklin Graves wanted twenty-five dollars for an ox carcass, and not even a good carcass at that. Alive, the animal had been mostly hide and bones. The remains were more baleful still. Back in Independence twenty-five dollars would have bought a full yoke, two healthy oxen ready to pull a wagon across the continent. Now it bought only a pathetic, emaciated carcass. From Graves's perspective, it was just good business sense, of course. For Eddy, it was an outrage.

The high price was perhaps the most striking example of the degree to which food supplies immediately became a paramount issue for the trapped emigrants. Larders varied from family to family. The Breens sat atop a hoard, for a good many of their cattle had come through unscathed. The Eddys, by contrast, had little. William Eddy started hunting and took a coyote the first day and an owl the next. But the meat soon ran short for a family of four, so Eddy set his jaw and agreed to Graves's exorbitant price.

Margret Reed stood in similar straits, dickering to save her children's lives. She promised that if others provided the Reeds with one cow now they would be repaid with two later, when everyone reached

California. Given that her once-wealthy family had lost almost all its possessions and that her husband had ridden away to an uncertain fate, it was impossible for her to know if she could repay the debt, but the strategy worked anyway. She got two animals each from Franklin Graves and Patrick Breen. Sadly, the half-starved beasts provided little food. After walking nearly two thousand miles, they were so thin and weak that when they lay down on the snow they could hardly get back up again.

WHEN THE FIRST STORM HIT, snow fell for eight straight days with almost no break. To flatlanders from the Midwest and the East, it was a blunt introduction to mountain winter. Most families felt trapped until spring—building cabins was a sure sign of that—but visions of escape persisted. On November 12, almost as soon as the storm broke, about fifteen of the fittest set out to walk over the pass. They were almost all young and childless, although Franklin Graves, the independent-minded, fifty-something patriarch of his clan, went along, as did a couple of other parents. Stanton joined up, and so did the two Indians from Sutter's Fort, Luis and Salvador, which meant that the group had the incalculable benefit of guides who had seen the route before. Still, for all their advantages, they made almost no progress before the snow—soft and ten feet deep—forced them to turn around.

Eddy shot two ducks on the first day back in camp, but it was the next day that he hit the hunter's mother lode. He crossed the tracks of a grizzly bear, a notoriously ferocious animal that lone hunters typically avoided. A single shot rarely fells a grizzly, and in the age of muzzle-loading rifles, the significant time required for reloading could be a fatal interval. But two ducks will not feed a family for long, so Eddy pursued his giant prey. He saw the bear about ninety yards away, nose down and digging for roots. Hiding behind a fir tree, Eddy put his one spare rifle ball into his mouth to speed reloading, then took steady aim and fired. The animal reared up on its hind legs and charged, Eddy trying to reload as fast as possible. By the time he finished, the bear was virtually upon him. He dodged around the tree to buy himself another split second, then raised the rifle and fired his last shot. The bullet hit the animal in the shoulder, disabling but not killing it. Out of ammunition, Eddy picked up a club of some sort, presumably a tree branch, and hit the bear in the head with all his might, a blow that finally ended the battle. When he examined the corpse, he found that the first shot had hit the bear in the heart, a wound that would have slowed and weakened the animal. Had the first shot been less true, Eddy would almost surely have been killed. The animal weighed eight hundred pounds, but Eddy convinced Franklin Graves to bring out oxen and drag it back to camp. They got in after dark, dividing the meat among Eddy, Graves, and William Foster, who had loaned his gun to the rifle-less hunter. Eddy claimed he also gave some to the impoverished Reed family.

Lone and weakened hunters do not normally take grizzlies with just two shots and a club, and since Eddy was the only survivor who ever recounted the tale, there were those in the ensuing decades who suspected the whole thing was a fabrication, a grab for glory by a man renowned for bragging, or at least that the animal was misidentified, and that Eddy's trophy was not a grizzly but the far smaller and less ferocious black bear. But in the 1980s, excavations at the site of the Murphy cabin, where Eddy lived, revealed bear bones among the remains of cattle. Judging by the size of a bear tooth that was found, scientists concluded that the emigrants may indeed have eaten a grizzly.

THEY LUCKED INTO A RUN OF GOOD WEATHER—the nights cold but the days clear and warmer, the snow almost melting away completely at the lake—and a week after the first escape attempt, twenty-two people marched out of camp to try again.

They reached the top of the pass, even crossed it and started down the western side according to some accounts. But finally the mules could go no farther, the snow being too soft and the animals too exhausted. The only choice now was to kill them and pack out what meat could be quickly butchered or even just abandon the beasts to their fate. Then suddenly Stanton balked. He had promised to return the mules to Sutter's Fort, where he had borrowed them from Sutter himself, and Stanton intended to keep his word. He had returned to the entire company based on nothing more than a promise, and he would abide by his vow now just as he had then. Stanton insisted that he, Luis, and Salvador would take the mules back to the lake.

Arguments erupted. Turning around now was insane. They had vanquished the mountains and were heading downhill. Food was in perilously short supply back at the cabins. It was imperative that somebody get through to California, and here was the best opportunity. They had come so far, worked so hard, and now an unbending little man was ready to throw it all away just for a promise over a few mules. Sutter wouldn't want people to die for mules; nobody would. Sutter would understand that dire circumstances demand hard decisions. If necessary, somebody else in the company would pay for the damn mules. By returning with provisions, Stanton himself had already risked his life to give them a reasonable chance at survival. Now he was heightening the odds of their demise.

Through it all, Stanton stood as immutable as the granite mountains beneath his feet. Dedication to principle had calcified into obstinacy. He and the Indians were going back, mules in tow.

The rest of the little group considered its options. They could go ahead on their own, but Stanton and the Indians were the only ones who knew the way. An unguided journey through snow-covered mountains without a known trail was a near guarantee of death. Angry and stupefied, they turned back toward the lake with Stanton.

At nightfall, they were still high in the mountains, and the wee hours turned bitterly cold. The following morning broke clear and sunny, and they reached the cabins at midnight, grateful for the shelter, frustrated at the failure, and right back where they had started.

The First Death

15

Patrick Breen took out a few sheets of paper that had somehow survived the cross-continental journey and folded them so as to fashion a small booklet. Inevitably, human beings record the circumstances of their existence—we paint our stories in caves or write them in books or record them on film—and Breen had decided to make himself the chronicler of the Donner Party's entrapment.

What prompted this decision remains a mystery, but he proved diligent at the task, writing daily entries for more than three months, never missing a day, not even because of Christmas or illness or hellish travails that would have sapped the resolution of most men. His entries are typically short, almost always practical, occasionally revealing a deeply held religious faith or a keen observation about his fellow emigrants. Taken together, they constitute the only surviving daily record kept by a member of the Donner Party during its captivity.

The first entry was made November 20, three weeks after the initial entrapment and the day before the escape attempt that would end with Stanton's stubbornness. Breen noted that the forward party had arrived at the lake at the end of October, had tried to cross the mountains twice before settling in for the winter, and had already killed most of their cattle, "having to stay here untill next Spring & live on poor beef without bread or salt." The next day Breen noted the departure of the twenty-two hikers, and then two days after that their sad reappearance: "the Expedition across the mountains returned after an unsucesful attempt."

Remarkably, the marchers—Breen called them "our mountaineers"—were ready to try again just three days later, intending to leave on Thursday, the 26th, so long as the weather allowed. But the evening before, a low and cloudy sky let loose a blizzard, huge snowflakes falling so thickly that visibility faded to a few feet. The storm raged for days, eliminating any hope of immediate escape and reducing Breen's diary to serial images of wintry repetition. On the 27th: "Continues to snow. . . . Dull prospect for crossing the Mountains." On the 28th: "Snowing fast. . . . Snow 8 or 10 inches deep. Soft wet snow." On the 29th: "Still snowing. Now about 3 feet deep." On the 30th: "Snowing fast . . . about 4 or 5 feet deep, no drifts. Looks as likely to continue as when it commenced." On December 1: "Still Snowing. . . . Snow about 5½ feet or 6 deep. . . . No going from the house. Completely housed up." It was vivid testimony to the mind-numbing stasis of a Sierra blizzard, and in time it led the emigrants to a blunt realization that mountain weather could hold them as securely as any prison. In the midst of it, Breen was reduced to summing up their immobility in a single, gripping phrase: "no liveing thing without wings can get about."

Snow finally stopped falling on December 3. The night was clear, and although the sky was cloudy in the morning, the emigrants were hopeful. "Snow lying deep all round," Breen noted in his diary. "Expecing it to thaw a little today." The optimism proved premature, and a few hours later he was forced to add an addendum of resignation. "The forgoing written in the morning. It immediately turned in to snow & continued to snow all day & likely to do so all night." The real break came the next day, when clouds raced by in the sky but neither snow nor rain pelted down. "It is a relief to have one fine day," Breen wrote.

But the blizzard had effectively cut their food supply when they could least afford it. The remaining cattle and horses had been left unstaked—another example of the emigrants' inexperience with mountain winter—and now the massive snowfall simply buried the beasts, with no way for the emigrants to find the frozen corpses. At the Alder Creek camp, one of the Donner teamsters used a long stick with a nail on the end to poke down into the drifts, hoping to strike a carcass, but he had no luck. Even Stanton's precious mules were lost beneath the muffling layer of white, a tragic irony that made the circumstances of the previous escape attempt all the more heartbreaking. His determination to keep the animals alive now seemed utterly pointless. The cabins grew buried too. As the snow depth increased to the height of a man and more, the little huts increasingly sat in holes, depressions dug out by the occupants.

The physical marks of starvation follow a set pattern, and now they must have afflicted the emigrants. Cheekbones and ribs and shoulder blades protruded. Muscle-bound arms shriveled to sticks. Joints ached. Buttocks grew so bony that sitting became painful. Skin dried and scaled to the rough texture of parchment. Around the fire or across the cabin, emigrants stared at the kind of gaunt, skeletal figure that would eventually be associated with death camps. Irritability spiked, even among those who were normally even-tempered. The cold dug deep into the bones, more painful than in past winters. Blood pressure sagged so low that someone who leapt to his feet too quickly could faint.

Often, the emigrants remained "housed up" even after the weather cleared. "The people not stirring round much," Breen wrote on the 8th, although it was a fine day. Weakened by their diminishing rations, they were finding it "hard work to [get] wood sufficient to keep us warm & cook our beef."

By the next day, at least one emigrant had grown so weak he could no longer care for himself. Augustus Spitzer, a mysterious figure about whom little is known, had been living in Keseberg's lean-to, but now he staggered down the snow-steps leading to the Breen cabin and fell into the doorway. He was too weak to get up without help, and it was obvious that the harsh conditions of the lean-to were more than he could bear. The Breens took him in, though he was so enfeebled that he required nursing just to survive.

Stanton too was short on food, although his pleas for help landed on deaf ears, perhaps because of his role in the failure of the previous escape attempt. In his diary, Breen noted that some of the families had very little beef left. "Stanton trying to make a raise of some for his Indians & Self," he wrote. "Not likely to get much."

TWO WEEKS HAD PASSED since the children's clothes or blankets had been dry, and Tamzene Donner was worried. When the family couldn't get a fire started, she kept the girls tucked into bed even at midday in hopes of keeping them warm, but the idea hardly worked if their bed-clothes were soaking.

In the tents at Alder Creek, it was getting harder and harder to maintain decent conditions. For one thing, labor was in short supply. When the axle broke on one of the Donner wagons—the accident that left poor little Eliza temporarily buried beneath a jumbled crush of household goods—George and Jacob went to work shaping a replacement. But as George Donner held the wood and his brother swung the axe, the tool slipped and came across the back of George's right hand, opening a long diagonal gash from the wrist almost to the little finger. An infection rose, and soon the arm lay useless at his side. Jacob Donner took up no slack, for he had always been sickly, and now a good many of the younger men began to fade as well. The result was that most of the work devolved to a teenager, Jean Baptiste Trudeau, a sixteen-year-old with a frontier background who had joined the company at Fort Bridger as a hired hand. It was Trudeau who searched for the animal carcasses buried under the snow, plunging downward with a long pole with a nail at one end, hoping that his improvised fishing hook might come up with a tuft of hair or hide to signify success. Memories varied as to Trudeau's work ethic—he viewed himself as a workhorse, some thought him a layabout—but whatever the details of his efforts, the relative lack of able-bodied men meant that circumstances at the Alder Creek camp suffered even more.

Dry wood was a treasure. Fetching it was a fatiguing and sometimes impossible task, and so there were the heatless days that imprisoned

the Donner daughters in their beds. On nights when a fire had been kindled, a large kettle was placed atop the coals, and the children gathered
round and pressed their hands against the warm comfort of the pot.

Tamzene struggled for a semblance of domesticity. Every morning,
she took her daughters in her lap and brushed out their hair. Schoolteacher to the core, she entertained them with Bible stories as she loosened the tangles. Often she chose Joseph's faithful persistence through
years of slavery or Daniel's deliverance from the fearsome horrors of the
lions' den—tales of tribulation and perseverance and eventual triumph.

FRANKLIN GRAVES MADE THE CASE PLAINLY: There was no alternative
but to try again. By early December, a month into the Donner Party's
mountain captivity, escape parties had been forced to turn back repeatedly, and it would have been easy to lose heart and passively await rescue.

Graves would have none of it. He was sure they should try again
to hike out, this time with better planning and equipment. Putting his
Vermont heritage to use, he began to make snowshoes, sawing lengthwise through the oxbows, the U-shaped pieces of wood that fit under the
necks of the oxen and attached to the yoke. The shape was suitable for
the frame of a snowshoe, and by weaving strips of rawhide crosswise
and lengthwise, Graves was able to fashion a reasonably effective sole.

Going from cabin to cabin, he recruited members for the proposed
new party, mounting a logical and largely indisputable case. The more
people in camp, the quicker the food supply dwindled. If a contingent
of healthy adults took minimal rations and made a headlong push for
Sutter's Fort, the remaining supplies might be stretched—just barely—
until the hikers could summon help and return. It was a risky calculus,
but unavoidable. "It is our only choice," Graves insisted. In his diary,
Breen recorded the preparations: "Stanton & Graves manufacturing
snow shoes for another mountain scrabble."

Two of the young teamsters, Milt Elliott and Noah James, set off on
foot for the Alder Creek camp to tell the Donner families of the new
plan. Stanton, industrious as always, found a small piece of paper and
neatly wrote out a note to George Donner asking for a pound of to-

bacco and the loan of a pocket compass, "as the snow is so very deep & in the event of a storm it would be invaluable." He added that the troublesome mules were "all strayed off," and asked that if any of the animals wandered through the Alder Creek camp the Donners get news to the lake cabins as soon as possible.

But the same day Elliott and James left, the weather turned foul, and as a diarist Breen was once again reduced to redundant invocations of helplessness. "Commenced snowing about 11 Oclock. . . . Snows fast," he wrote on December 9, a Wednesday. Then on Thursday: "Snowed fast last night with heavy squalls of wind. Continues still to snow." And Friday: "Snowing a little." And Saturday: "Continues to Snow." And Sunday: "Snows faster than any previous day." Finally, after four and a half days, the storm cleared, and Monday morning broke sunny and fine. "Don't thaw much," Breen noted, "but fair for a continuance of fair weather."

Elliott, who had intended to join the snowshoe party, had yet to return from Alder Creek with the much-needed compass, but the clear weather was too good an opportunity to pass up. The hikers needed to leave immediately, and so it was decided that they would not wait for Elliott's return. He and James had walked away from the lake cabins on the same day the blizzard began, after all, and it was likely they had frozen to death before they even reached the Donner family tents. The snowshoe party would simply have to forge ahead by dead reckoning, one more handicap to an already hazardous undertaking.

INEVITABLY, PEOPLE BEGAN TO WONDER about the chances of their own demise. Franklin Graves had spoken of a morose expectation that he would die in the mountains, the victim of divine retribution for driving Reed from the party and abandoning Hardcoop in the deserts of Nevada. Still, it was a remarkable fact that after more than a month of captivity, no one had actually died.

That changed the night of December 15. Baylis Williams was a young man working for the Reed family, a mysterious figure whose sister Eliza was also a Reed family employee. Years later, Patty Reed wrote that Baylis was an albino who worked by night and slept by day, a peculiar description but almost the only one we have. We know nothing of his exact condition when the party arrived at the lake, and little of his deterioration thereafter, although given that the Reed family had almost no food it is easy to imagine that he slowly faded into weakness and starvation. Billy Graves, who was then seventeen, remembered that Williams lost his mind and eventually "was insane." In any event, on the evening of the 15th, as the snowshoe party was busy preparing to depart the next morning, Williams died.

There was little time for grieving, but the death must have played on everyone's mind. When the hikers tied on their snowshoes and walked away from the cabins the following morning, they knew with more certainty than ever that the families they were leaving behind could not last much longer, that help must be fetched or everyone would die.

The Forlorn Hope

For all that it is usually considered an unspeakable atrocity, cannibalism has a long and rich history. People have eaten people for thousands of years and for countless reasons: to appease gods, to honor ancestors or shame enemies, to cure disease, perhaps even to set a hospitable table for guests. Some stories may be exaggerated or even false; many of the more grisly versions were reported by European explorers eager to paint the natives as bloodthirsty savages in need of Christian salvation. But modern evidence suggests that at least some accounts are indisputably true. Archaeologists have found human remains showing the apparent signs of butchery or cooking, and a few years ago scientists studying a Colorado site used by the ancient Anasazi reported that they had found fossilized human fecal matter containing digested human tissue. Somebody, for some reason, was eaten.

Far better documented are more recent cases in which people who were isolated and starving resorted to eating human flesh because they had little choice, what experts sometimes call "survival cannibalism." Seafaring disasters produced the most numerous examples. Prior to the invention of radios or electronic safety beacons or airplanes from which a search might be conducted, a shipwreck or sinking often stranded people for weeks or months. Whether they were marooned on an island or drifting in a lifeboat, their only hope of rescue was that another ship, by purest chance, might come within sight. Often, other ships failed to materialize and eating the dead became the only hope for survival. The practice became so common that one authority on the subject described it as "normal." If a stranded crew managed to survive by some other means, they sometimes felt compelled to proclaim the fact to their rescuers, lest the typical assumption of cannibalism go un-challenged. Because there were so many cases, the chronicles of sea-going cannibalism are long and varied, and they illuminate the topic's dark history in striking ways.

One of the most closely documented examples occurred in 1710, after the *Nottingham Galley* set sail from London, bound for Boston. The journey was almost complete when a December gale blew up off the coast of Maine and ran the ship aground on a small rock island, barely a hundred yards long and perhaps half as wide. The mainland was visible in the distance. The crew abandoned ship, and by the fol-lowing morning all that was left of their vessel was debris: wood and canvas and a little of the cheese they had been carrying as cargo. Using the ship's timbers, they built a boat in hopes of escape, but the surf smashed it to bits as they attempted to launch. Later they built a small raft and successfully put it to sea with two men aboard, but they both drowned. For nearly three weeks they survived by harvesting what little edible material they could find: a few weeds and two or three mussels per day per man. They drank rainwater or melted snow. Then the ship's carpenter died, and the awful possibility of cannibalism pre-sented itself. With no other choice, they cut up the corpse and began to eat. Three crew members refused to join in at first, but by the next morning they all did. The captain rationed the meat, and within a few days they were rescued by a passing ship.

Other cases were more gruesome. Occasionally survivors on a derelict would take a half-eaten body and hang it in the rigging, as if in a slaughterhouse. On one ship a woman was said to have cut the throat of her recently deceased husband, insisting that if his blood was to be drunk she had the greatest right to the ghastly beverage. There are records of sailors refusing to eat human flesh, but there are also cases where cannibalism began relatively quickly, as if sailors felt no great need to delay the practice until the last conceivable moment. In 1835 the *Elizabeth Rashleigh,* sailing from Quebec to England, grew waterlogged and had to be abandoned by her crew, which took to the longboat. They had a store of potatoes and were rescued in nine days— an interval survived by many modern hunger strikers—but the crew had already begun eating their dead shipmates. The following year, the *Hannah* suffered a similar fate while sailing from Quebec to London. The survivors began eating a dead comrade on the fourth day.

If nature failed to provide a carcass, sailors sometimes killed someone specifically for food, the result of a far more complex moral calculus involving a single sacrifice for the good of all. In 1759 the *Dolphin* was dismasted by a storm while sailing from the Canary Islands to New York. There were only eight people aboard, and they drifted aimlessly for more than five months. They ate their supplies, then their dog, the ship's cat, even their shoes. Finally, they decided that one member of the group should be killed and eaten, so that the others might live. They cast lots to pick both the victim and the executioner. A Spanish passenger lost the draw and was shot through the head. The others ate his bowels first and then consumed the rest of the body.

One of the most famous maritime catastrophes of the nineteenth century resulted in a similar decision by survivors of the Nantucket whaleship *Essex,* which had been attacked and sunk by a whale, the prey turned hunter. The crew was forced into the whaleboats and bobbed on the sea for weeks. As men starved to death, the others resorted to cannibalizing the remains. When that food source ran out, the four men in one of the boats decided to cast lots to decide who would be killed and eaten, believing that otherwise they would all die. The loser was a sailor named Owen Coffin, eighteen years old and the cousin of the captain, who was also in the boat. Coffin accepted his fate and gave the others a message to be delivered to his mother. Sixteen-year-old Charles Ramsdell, who was Coffin's close friend, drew the lot as the executioner. He refused his duty for a time, but finally relented. Coffin laid his head upon the gunwale, and Ramsdell shot his friend.

As a rule, such events rarely produced feelings of shame among the participants or scorn among the public. Survivors often made no attempt to conceal the evidence of their desperation. Rescuers found partially butchered bodies in lifeboats even when the remains might easily have been thrown overboard. In one extraordinary case, survivors trapped on a derelict signaled to a passing ship by waving the hands and feet of a man they had butchered and eaten. Whether the deaths were natural or the result of a lottery, cannibalism was simply, in the decorous phrase of the day, "the custom of the sea"—a horror defensible under the circumstances, much as men's behavior might be different in wartime than in peace. Surviving cannibals could go on to distinguished careers. The captain of the *Nottingham Galley*—the man who oversaw the consumption of his ship's carpenter—was later made the British consul in Flanders. The captain of the *Essex* was given command of another whaleship and later in life became the night watchman on Nantucket Island, charged with ensuring the safety of the community's young people by enforcing the nightly curfew.

Even when survivors admitted that no lottery was conducted before a killing, little punishment was meted out. In 1884 the British ship *Mignonette* sank in the Atlantic amid heavy seas, forcing the captain and three crew members into a dinghy. When the youngest member of the crew became violently ill and appeared to be dying, the captain took a penknife and cut the boy's throat. The survivors drank his blood and, over the next few days, ate his flesh. When they were rescued, the captain freely said that one man had been killed and eaten, and later he even demonstrated the technique to the authorities back in England. In a breach with tradition, the captain and one crew member were charged with murder, perhaps because they had conducted no lottery, perhaps because cannibalism by sailors was viewed by some as a relic from a bygone age. Still, most public sentiment hailed the men as heroes for having done what was necessary. The dead man's father forgave them, and they were granted bail, which was unusual for a capital case. After they were convicted, Queen Victoria commuted their sentences to just six months in prison. Shortly after their release, the British government restored their maritime credentials, and at least one of the men returned to a career at sea.

The case of the *Mignonette* came almost forty years after the travails of the Donner Party, but the emigrants heading west in 1846 may have known about earlier examples of cannibalism's long seafaring history. Then as now, shocking tales were a staple of journalism, and some examples had become famous around the world. Many cases had been recounted in books and poems and even songs. The Donner Party included literate, curious people, and it's entirely conceivable they were aware of the macabre imperative that had long been the sailor's last resort.

A S THE SNOWSHOE PARTY WALKED AWAY from the Truckee Lake cabins, the Breens—and perhaps a few of the others remaining behind—gathered outside to watch them go. If they braved the cold and stayed there long enough, they saw their comrades shrink until they were nothing more than a line of trudging dark spots, miniaturized against the daunting mountain escarpment up which they began to climb. Although the emigrants didn't use the term at the time, the group eventually came to be known by a poetic nickname that captured the moment's utter desperation, the idea that either this small band would succeed or everyone would die. The snowshoers, it was said, were "the Forlorn Hope."

Mostly they were the younger people, men and women in their late teens and twenties. Among the women, the oldest was about twenty-three. Several were parents forced into a cruel dilemma: stay with the children and watch them die, or abandon them for now so that they might be saved later. William Eddy left his wife and both his children, and could never forget the look on his wife's face as he departed. William and Sarah Foster left their toddler son. Two women—Amanda McCutchan and Harriet Pike—left children behind even though the fathers were no longer present, William McCutchan having gone ahead to California and William Pike having been accidentally shot and killed.

Others at the lake camp promised to care for the children. The oldest snowshoer—the only one who might be counted as old—was fifty-seven-year-old Franklin Graves, who divided his family, taking along his two grown daughters and a son-in-law but leaving behind his wife and seven other children.

In all, the Forlorn Hope included seventeen people: ten men, five women, and two of the Murphy boys, thirteen-year-old Lemuel and ten-year-old William. They had only fourteen pairs of snowshoes, so one of the men and the two Murphy brothers planned to tag along at the rear of the column, hoping those in front would mash down the snow and create a firm walking surface. Limited to what their weakened bodies could carry, they each took a blanket or quilt but no extra clothing or tents. Among them, they had one rifle, a few pistols, and a hatchet. For food, they took a little dried beef and some coffee and sugar. By strict rationing, they hoped to make the supplies last six days.

THE SNOW WAS EIGHT FEET DEEP at the lake, deeper as they climbed the mountain pass, deeper still in the drifts, and it soon became apparent that the lack of snowshoes ensured a hopeless lagging. The one adult with regular shoes, Charles Burger, who was always known as "Dutch Charley," turned back the first day along with William Murphy. They picked their way back down to the lake and eventually reached the cabins, cold and exhausted but safe.

The others climbed onward. The lake dropped away, a cobalt mirror plummeting to the floor of a great basin circled by a jagged crown of white spires. Hands rose against the glare as eyes peered down toward the water, five hundred feet below, then eight hundred, then finally a thousand, as though they had been magically whisked to the observation deck of a modern skyscraper. Smoke floated from the cabins in lazy curls, a visible reminder of the comrades whose hopes they carried.

They had entered a mountain realm about which they knew little. Snow covered everything. It deepened invisibly beneath their feet, like water under the ice of a frozen lake, until they were walking in the sky, reaching out to touch tree branches that would have soared above their heads in summertime. Drifts rose up like cliffs, tall enough to cover the church steeples back home. Walking near the back of the file, Mary Ann Graves gazed at her companions up ahead and was reminded of "some Norwegian fur company among the icebergs." By night, they built fires on platforms of green logs, so the flames would not melt the surrounding snow and sink them all slowly into a pit.

The reached the pass on the second day—Graves remembered it as "a very slavish day's travel"—and were met with a vista so stunning that it pierced their exhaustion. "The scenery was too grand for me to pass without notice," Graves wrote. "Well do I remember a remark one of the company made here, that we were about as near heaven as we could get."

The next day they encountered a heavy snowstorm, "wind blowing cold and furiously," according to Eddy, who was apparently keeping a journal, a document that has not survived but that two men claimed later to have seen. One of them was James Reed, who eventually published what he said was a "synopsis" of Eddy's journal, which may be close to a verbatim reproduction. The pithy entries certainly read as though they were jotted down in the midst of the journey, when there was little time for writing. On the 19th, for example, three days out from the cabins, Eddy noted merely, "Storm continued; feet commenced freezing."

They were completely unprotected from the elements, struggling along day after day in clothes of wool and cotton that were either soaked with sweat and snow or frozen stiff as boards. They were in difficult, steep terrain and did not know where they were going. As rations dwindled, they could afford nothing but the smallest meals, if that. At night, lacking shelter, they simply stopped where they were, building their small fire and then huddling around it as temperatures plummeted and winds howled. In the morning, they simply rose and started walking.

At one point, Mary Graves thought she glimpsed smoke in a deep gorge off to the right. Believing it might come from a cabin or at least a campfire, she convinced the men to fire the gun as a signal, but there was no answer. She began bellowing down into the canyon periodically, but that too was met with silence.

S TANTON STRUGGLED MORE THAN ANYONE ELSE, as though all his past heroics had drained the sum total of his energies. Snow-blindness left him stumbling, and on the morning of the sixth day, December 21, he lingered by the fire smoking his pipe. One of the women asked if he was coming, and he responded that he would join them soon. Maybe they thought he really would follow. Maybe they knew he was finished and left him in peace. He didn't come into camp that night, and though they waited the next day, hoping that he might arrive, he never appeared. No one had the strength to go back and search.

Stanton had reached safety once, at Sutter's Fort back in the crisp days of autumn, and it would have taken a hard man to damn him had he chosen to stay and save himself. Instead, he kept his word and went back to aid a company in which he had no family or close friends. Now, in his hour of need, he had been abandoned to his fate. There was probably no other choice. A man can't be carried all the way out of the Sierra. Stanton, like the others, had to walk or die. But as he sat in the warmth of his dying fire, the irony must have struck him. In the spring, would-be rescuers found his bones.

B Y CHRISTMAS EVE THE SNOWSHOERS HAD GONE without food for three days, maybe four. Eddy found some bear meat in his knapsack, placed there secretly by his wife, but there is no evidence he shared it. For weeks, everyone had been on starvation rations, and combined with the rigors of their journey, the lack of food for even a few days put them in a desperate situation. The women were still fairly strong, but some of the men were fading.

Like so many stranded sailors before them, the members of the Forlorn Hope began to mull over the most extreme options. Someone proposed a fatal game of chance, casting lots to decide who would be killed and eaten. In a sign of their despair, at least some members of the group agreed, but it wasn't unanimous, and the idea was dropped. As an alternative, Eddy proposed that two men—it's not clear if he suggested specific candidates—each take a pistol and shoot it out, agreeing ahead of time that the loser would be consumed. But that plan too was rejected.

A blizzard roared down out of the sky, and they hunkered down to ride it out, too weak to keep moving even in good weather, let alone a screaming gale. Their fire went out, and in the raging storm they were unable to relight it. Eddy tried to use gunpowder, but the powder horn blew up and badly burned his face and hands. On Christmas, people started to die. The first was a Mexican laborer known only as Antonio. The next, a few hours later, was Franklin Graves, the man who helped make the snowshoes that brought them over the pass. There were stories for years afterward, perhaps true, that as Graves died he urged his daughters to use his body for food.

In a desperate attempt to find warmth, they created a makeshift tent by sitting together in a tight circle and laying blankets over their heads, letting the snow pile up above them. They avoided freezing to death, but the confined space was hellish. The blizzard howled relentlessly as they crowded together in their man-made snow cave, shoulder to shoulder, shivering and praying, blank and bony faces trading stares. Their only hope was to outlast the storm, to conquer nature's wrath with human patience, and so they sat there for three unending days, with nothing to do but try to stay alive. "Could not proceed; almost frozen; no fire," Eddy noted the day after Christmas.

In time the strain grew unbearable. Patrick Dolan, the bachelor who had traveled with the Breens, lost his head and stripped off his coat and hat and boots and ran out into the open weather, behavior that we now know might have reflected severe hypothermia. They wrestled him back into the circle, but he was too weak to recuperate. Sitting there among them, he died soon afterward. Next was Lemuel Murphy, the boy who had trudged on even when his younger brother turned back.

When the storm finally broke, Eddy climbed out of the huddle and managed to light a nearby pine tree on fire. Gathering around for the warmth, the other survivors sat there as if in shock, not even moving when burning branches fell from the tree. It was obvious they had to eat immediately if they were to survive. With the rapid succession of deaths, one of the earlier objections to cannibalism was now moot, since corpses were at hand and no one had to be killed. Still, the exact moment and manner of the decision remain a mystery. Relying on interviews with survivors, early chroniclers of the Donner Party glossed over the decision, perhaps out of a nineteenth-century sense of propriety. The first-person accounts offer a straightforward description of events, not a revelation of the emigrants' inner turmoil. Mary Graves, for example, said simply that after the snowstorm eased, the party traveled onward, "subsisting on human flesh."

The first ugly dilemma was who to eat. As a rule, people resorting to cannibalism almost always choose outsiders as their first victims, and, as much as possible, the Forlorn Hope followed form, trying to avoid the relatives of the living. Franklin Graves's body lay nearby, but his two daughters were still alive and present. One of Lemuel Murphy's older sisters was among the group. That reduced the choice to Dolan or Antonio, the Mexican laborer. Racial and ethnic minorities have often been the first victims of cannibalism, but in this case Dolan was selected, perhaps for a reason as gruesome as any that could be imagined. He had died more recently than Antonio, and in cases of survival cannibalism the relatively warm blood of the newly deceased is often the first thing consumed.

Deciding to eat Dolan's flesh was merely the beginning of a process that is almost as challenging physically as it is mentally. Human beings are large animals, and it is no easy job to butcher one. The captain of the *Mignonette,* forced to dismember the body of a dead crew member in a lifeboat, grew concerned that in the course of the arduous work he might actually puncture the hull of the vessel and sink it. To stay afloat, he used the boat's brass oarlocks as a cutting board. If Dolan's body was already starting to freeze, the work would only have been more difficult. In the case of a team of rugby players stranded by a plane crash in the Andes in the 1970s, the first man who tried to hack away some of the meat found that he could only slice off little strips the size of matches.

Once the butchering is begun, it often follows a grotesque pattern. A common first step is to disfigure the corpse, eliminating the grim reminders that survivors are about to eat a fellow human, perhaps a friend or relative. In lifeboats, the heads might be cut off and thrown overboard, sometimes the hands and feet too. If decapitation is not performed, the eyelids might be closed to avoid the disturbing blank "stare" of the dead. The heart and liver are often cut out and eaten immediately. Pieces of flesh can usually be cut from the arms or legs or torso, either to be cooked or consumed raw. To preserve the meat, thin strips are often dried, either over a fire or simply by laying them in the sun. Brain matter has been swallowed raw. Lungs have been eaten. Marrow has been sucked from bones cracked open with a rock.

The members of the Forlorn Hope cut pieces of flesh from Dolan's arms and legs and cooked them over a fire they managed to kindle. If their experience was like that of other groups forced to the same extreme, they ate the first small pieces haltingly, in silence, each person deep in private contemplation. The taboo dispelled, they moved to the other bodies after Dolan, eating some of the abominable meat and drying the rest so they could carry it with them. When they finally departed the camp on December 30, two weeks had passed since they walked away from the lake. Five members of their little band had died, almost all subsequently consumed as food. The Forlorn Hope was now reduced to just ten people, five men and five women.

By Eddy's estimate, they made four miles the day they broke camp and six the following day, which was New Year's Eve. They must have noted New Year's Day, but Eddy made no mention of it in his journal, recording only that they "passed a rugged canon," perhaps the deep crevice carved by the North Fork of the American River. At some point that day they had to climb the side of a gorge so steep that they grabbed plants growing from the near-perpendicular walls and pulled themselves up. They were wandering, heading generally to the west but uncertain exactly where they were or where they should go.

When their supply of human flesh ran out, they began eating the rawhide strings of their snowshoes. Then Luis and Salvador vanished, almost surely out of justified fears that the group might kill and eat them.

On January 5, Franklin Graves's son-in-law Jay Fosdick died and was cannibalized. His wife, Sarah, the oldest Graves daughter, forged onward through her grief. Eddy shot a deer the same day, but the venison seems not to have lasted long. They had been walking for three weeks, and now they were thoroughly lost, plodding through the confusing welter of canyons and ridges and ravines that constitute the Sierra's western slope. With Stanton dead and Luis and Salvador fled, no member of the group had ever been over the territory. About the only thing they could do was try to head both west and downhill. The result was agonizingly slow progress, and within days they once again faced the ultimate crisis: They were out of food.

THE LATE STAGES OF STARVATION ARE DIFFICULT to study, since obviously people cannot be denied food indefinitely purely to advance scientific research. Yet remarkably, some highly detailed observations about the effects of starvation have been made by individuals who were themselves starving. Jewish physicians in the Warsaw Ghetto, for example, produced an impressive study of the hunger they experienced and saw around them every day. So did British doctors held in Japanese internment camps.

Along with obvious physical changes such as weight loss, the doctors noticed striking psychological effects, among them a stark pattern of apathy and listlessness. Starving people simply lost their desire to act. They lay in bed, their faces pale, blank masks. Often, they were unable or unwilling to get up even to eat. In some cases, people died with food in their hands.

Ironically, enervation is often combined with irritability, as if starving people can find energy only for conflict. In a landmark study conducted in 1944 and 1945, thirty-two volunteers at the University of Minnesota agreed to lose about a quarter of their body weight over a six-month period. All were conscientious objectors who had already shown themselves to be "sincere and upright" in civilian public service projects before the experiment. But as the volunteers' hunger deepened, scientists monitoring their behavior found that minor differences led to major disagreements. The men "blew up" at one another or grew annoyed with the kitchen staff, suspicious that perhaps the cooks weren't measuring the rations correctly. Some men refused to sit with others at the dining tables. Once, when one man licked his plate of every last morsel, another man told him that he sounded like "a damn cow" and stormed off. To gauge their social skills, they were invited to parties, but their behavior grew boorish. To measure their motivation and abilities, they were asked to perform tasks, but their patience and commitment dwindled. One man quit his job of walking a small child to nursery school each day because he found her behavior so infuriating and worried about his own decreasing level of self-control. Some of the men began stealing food or, in one case, items associated with food: china coffee cups. Many of the men had hoped for spiritual enlightenment, but instead, according to a summary of the experiment, "Most of them felt that the semistarvation had coarsened rather than refined them, and they marveled at how thin their moral and social veneers seemed to be."

Desperate to keep moving and stay alive, the starving members of the Forlorn Hope fought off lethargy, but like the subjects of the Minnesota study, they fell prey to anger and division. Their cohesiveness as a group disintegrated. Near the beginning of their effort, they had waited, however briefly, for Stanton to rejoin them. They had also rejected the initial proposals for cannibalism, including those for a lottery or a fair fight. When they finally resorted to eating human bodies, it was only the flesh of those who had already died.

But now, suffering both the mental and physical ravages of extreme hunger, they began to contemplate murder. Accounts differ as to the precise plots, but it is clear that killing and eating each other seemed increasingly acceptable. The Graves family maintained for years afterward that Eddy had tried to lure Mary Graves away from the others so he could kill her, while Eddy insisted that the only other surviving man, William Foster, had suggested murdering three of the women for food. Eddy said he refused but threw Foster a stout club and then advanced on him with a knife, apparently trying to forcibly implement his earlier suggestion of a fight to the death, with the loser to be eaten. Some of the women separated the men before anyone was hurt.

When they came across tracks left by Luis and Salvador, all scruples vanished. Finding the two men collapsed and near death, Foster took the gun and advanced. He shot both men in the head, trying to justify the murders by insisting that the men would have died soon anyway, which might be true. No one intervened, and afterward the two bodies were butchered and eaten.

The deaths of Luis and Salvador were the only time during the ordeal of the Donner Party that anyone was killed to be eaten. The two Indians, about whom not much is known, probably had little choice but to accompany Stanton on his relief mission, but their courage is not lessened by that fact, and it is indisputable that they helped save the Donner Party before they were killed by one of its members. Several versions of the incident eventually appeared, including an account in an early Donner Party book almost surely based on Eddy's testimony, but in none of the stories was Foster condemned. He never faced legal punishment for his act, echoing the history of similar cases at sea.

The survivors had now lost enough altitude to be out of the snow, but even so it was difficult to keep moving. Eddy was shuffling so badly that when he came to a fallen tree, he couldn't find the energy to step over it. Instead, he bent down, put his hands on the log, and rolled himself across. They rested every quarter mile.

Finally they staggered across a trail and followed it to a small Miwok Indian village, where the startled residents provided acorn bread for these emaciated figures wandering out of the impassable mountains. Eddy could not tolerate the acorns, so he ate grass instead.

Even with help from the Indians, most of the group soon collapsed and could go no farther. Indomitable, Eddy willed himself ahead. Accompanied by Miwok guides, he walked eighteen miles in a single day, bloody footprints marking his path. A little before sunset, he approached Johnson's Ranch, the first American settlement on the western side of the mountains, and walked up to the small cabin of Matthew Dill Ritchie, who had brought his family over the mountains just a few months before. Eddy saw Ritchie's daughter and asked her for bread. She looked at him, registered his horrible condition, and burst into tears. It was January 17, exactly a month and a day after the members of the Forlorn Hope walked away from the lake camp.

Fighting the coming darkness, men from the little community at Johnson's Ranch rushed out to find the other survivors, sometimes backtracking along Eddy's bloody footprints. The others were fed and then, the following morning, brought down and reunited with Eddy.

Of the seventeen who started with the Forlorn Hope, only seven reached their goal. Two turned back the first day, and eight others died. The survivors included two men—Eddy and Foster—and all five of the women, Mary Ann Graves, Sarah Fosdick, Sarah Foster, Amanda McCutchan, and Harriet Pike. Among the women, McCutchan was probably the oldest, and she was only about twenty-three. The others were so young that today they would be college undergraduates.

Two and a half months had passed since the Sierra's brutal winter grabbed hold of the Donner Party. Now the emigrants had proven it was possible to break free.

A Low Situation

Four days after the Forlorn Hope walked away from the lake cabins, Milt Elliott appeared out of the snow like a specter from a wintry hell. More than a week had passed since Elliott and Noah James, another teamster, set off for the Alder Creek camp. A blizzard kicked up the day they left and blew for five straight days, so the logical conclusion was that they were dead. "Thinks they got lost in the snow," Patrick Breen wrote in his diary.

But now here was Elliott, stomping the snow off his boots and turning his backside before the fire. He and James had reached the Donner family tents the day of the blizzard and stayed ten days, and then somehow Elliott managed to hike all the way back to the lake by himself. He bore sad news, for people had started to die at Alder Creek. Jacob Donner was gone, along with three young, single men: Joseph Reinhardt, Sam Shoemaker, and James Smith. The rest of the Alder Creek group was doing poorly too, "in a low situation," as Breen phrased it.

The next day, December 21, Breen endured a severe attack of what he called "the gravel"—kidney stones. In his diary he mentioned his quick recovery, adding, "Praise be to the God of Heaven." Religion was becoming ever more present in Breen's account, perhaps because

Christmas was approaching, perhaps because he was seeking comfort and fulfillment amid the harshest of ordeals. Devoid of theology in the first few weeks, his little chronicle of events now turned to faith. "Tough times, but not discouraged," he wrote at one point. "Our hopes are in God, Amen." Two days before Christmas he began to read the Thirty Days' Prayer and then ended his diary entry with something approaching a benediction: "may Almighty God grant the request of an unworthy Sinner that I am. Amen." The next day, Christmas Eve, was warm, the wind blowing up from the south, and so rather than snow there was rain. "Poor prospect for any kind of Comfort Spiritual or temporal," Breen wrote, adding, "May God help us to spend the Christmass as we ought considering circumstances"

Christmas fell on Friday. The rain turned to snow, the most unwanted white Christmas in history. Breen was laid up with another attack of "the gravel" and had to rely on his two older sons, both barely into their teens, to gather wood for a fire. The family prayed together Christmas morning, but Breen couldn't shake a sense of doom. "The prospect is apalling," he wrote, "but hope in God, amen."

In the Reed cabin, the children stood wide-eyed at the fire, watching the boiling contents of a kettle. Margret Reed had secretly squirreled away a small stash of supplies, too small under normal conditions even to make a meal, but large enough now to constitute a feast: a few dried apples, a few beans, a little tripe, and one small piece of bacon. Thrilled, the children sat down to a Christmas dinner they had not dreamed of.

"Children, eat slowly," their mother told them, "for this one day you can have all you wish."

For the rest of her life, no banquet of turkey and mince pies and plum pudding ever tasted so good, Virginia Reed remembered later. "So bitter was the misery relieved by that one bright day, that I have never since sat down to a Christmas dinner without my thoughts going back to Donner Lake."

THREE-YEAR-OLD ELIZA DONNER GRIPPED her mother's hand as they approached a mysterious hole in the snow, smoke rising up like the sign of some menacing underworld. Eliza's mother, Tamzene, said reassuringly that they were there to see Aunt Betsy and Eliza's cousins, that there was a tent buried there much like Eliza's own, a little way away across the snow-filled meadow at Alder Creek, but when the little girl stooped down and peered into the chasm, she saw only darkness.

Eliza had not seen her cousins since the snows came and the wagons stopped rolling and her parents explained that they would stay in this cold and forsaken spot until spring. Afraid to go down into the unknown depths, she called out, but the hollow faces that peered up at her were hardly recognizable as the hardy playmates she had known only weeks before. "I was glad when my mother came up and took me back to our own tent," Eliza recalled, "which seemed less dreary because I knew the things that were in it, and the faces about me."

Both camps teemed with little ones in need of distraction, for the Donner Party was increasingly an assembly of juveniles. Most of the healthy adults departed in the Forlorn Hope, giving the hikers a better chance of reaching civilization and fetching aid, but leaving behind fewer adults to do the necessary work at the mountain camps. Then when Baylis Williams died and the sudden rash of deaths struck the Alder Creek site, the problem only worsened. There were now sixty-one people left at the two camps, two-thirds of them children. In the Graves half of the double cabin, Elizabeth Graves was alone in caring for eight youngsters. In the Murphy cabin, the only adults were Levinah Murphy and Eleanor Eddy. Between them, they were caring for nine children, five of whom were toddlers.

Childlike playfulness occasionally broke through the tragedy. Once, Eliza spied a sunbeam shining down into their hovel, spotlighting a little patch of floor. "I saw it, and sat down under it," she remembered, "held it on my lap, passed my hand up and down in its brightness, and found that I could break its ray in two." She let the delicious warmth play upon her head and face and arm, and then set her apron beneath this mysterious treasure to capture its glorious power.

She ran to show her mother, but when she carefully opened the folds of the apron, she was shocked to find that her little morsel of heat and light was gone. She looked back toward her play spot, only to see the sunbeam creep back up the stairs and, like so many other dashed hopes of the Donner Party, vanish.

FOOD SUPPLIES DWINDLED UNTIL PEOPLE began to eat what would normally have been considered inedible. The hides of the slaughtered cattle were cut into thin strips, which were laid atop the coals until the hair burned off. Scraped clean with a knife, the singed strips were then boiled until they reduced to a gelatinous paste invariably compared to glue. It could be gagged down, at least by the iron-gutted, although one survivor observed later, "That kind of living weakened my knees a little."

Chores grew ever more difficult. Gathering wood was especially laborious. When felled, tree trunks sank in the snow, requiring even more effort to heave them up and carry them to a cabin. Exhaustion and weakness deepened the isolation. Breen noted once that the weather would be delightful were it not for the maddening blanket of snow that blocked their progress and kept them prisoner, but even on sunny, clear days people were moving around less, stirring from the miserable cabins only when necessary. "Saw no strangers today from any of the shantys," he wrote on a day of cloudless mountain skies.

"Dutch Charley" Burger, the teamster who had turned back from the Forlorn Hope on the first day and was living in Keseberg's lean-to, deteriorated faster than most and at last, on an especially cold night, died. His few possessions were inventoried: $1.50 in cash, two handsome silver watches, a razor, a gold pin, three boxes of caps, the clothes on his back. His treasure was dispersed among the other members of the Donner Party's little German contingent. Spitzer took his coat and waistcoat, Keseberg everything else.

MARGRET REED PONDERED AN UNSPEAKABLY AUDACIOUS PLAN. Her family was once again almost out of food, and she had no way to get more. Few people had much left, and in any event she had nothing more to trade for beef or hides. She had already parted with the most valuable items she possessed—a fine watch that belonged to her husband

and a medal signifying his status as a Mason. It had been hard to part with mementos of a husband she might never see again, but she had done it. Now there was nothing more she could do to get food. So she decided that she, two of her employees, and her oldest child would walk over the mountains to California.

In a sense, the idea was preposterous. For all she knew, the Forlorn Hope had marched off to its death, yet that group had been far stronger than her own. The Forlorn Hope had included fifteen of the strongest emigrants, most of them young adults in the prime of their physical lives, and had been equipped with the best snowshoes that the mountain-born Franklin Graves could construct. The Reed party, by contrast, would include just four people, one of them barely a teenager, who would plod off into the implacable snow with virtually no equipment of any kind. Worse still, the Forlorn Hope had left almost three weeks before, three weeks during which the remaining families had subsisted on the most meager and insubstantial of diets. Margret Reed and her family, in other words, were three weeks closer to starving to death.

But anything was better than sitting around waiting to die, so Reed set about the unimaginable task of dividing her family. The three youngest children—eight-year-old Patty, five-year-old James, and three-year-old Thomas—were too small to go, so their mother made the rounds of the cabins to ask if someone could take them in. Nobody wanted more mouths to feed, but to their great credit the Breens and the Graveses consented. James simply moved across the dividing wall that ran down the center of the cabin in which he had been living, switching from his family's territory to that of the Graveses. Patty and Thomas hiked over to the Breen cabin.

That left the four who would make the attempt at crossing the mountains: Margret, thirteen-year-old Virginia, and two of the family workers, Milt Elliott and Eliza Williams. They dried the family's meager supply of remaining meat and then bid an anguished farewell to the three younger children. "We could hardle get a way from them but we told theme we would bring them Bread & then thay was willling to stay," Virginia remembered.

The little band trudged off late on a Monday morning, January 4, the weather so fine that it seemed the spring thaw might be coming. The hikers paralleled the flat lakeshore, then made the long climb up toward the pass. Like many people in mountain terrain, they soon experienced the leaden despondency that comes from climbing to the top of a ridge, then gaining the crest and realizing that it is followed not by a gentle downward slope but merely by more of the same terrain, ridge after ridge after ridge stretching away to the horizon. "It was so discouraging," Virginia Reed wrote. At night, they would bed down wherever darkness found them.

Eliza Williams gave out after only a day, returning alone to the lake cabins, but the other three forged ahead, Virginia at times crawling on her hands and knees. They finally stopped for a day in an overdue effort to make snowshoes, but eventually they too realized the hopelessness of the attempt and turned back. Virginia, by far the youngest of the group, had done well so long as the hope of salvation—and food—lay ahead, but once they began to retreat, her strength faltered. She nearly collapsed and one of her feet became badly frozen, but she persevered, and four days after they set out they once again reached relative safety at the lake.

But now they had no real place to live. There had been no time to build proper roofs when the company was first trapped, so the cabins had simply been covered with the hides of the butchered oxen. Cupboards bare, the Reeds had been forced to begin eating hides sooner than most families, and the only way to get them was to pull down their own roof. Margret Reed left a hide for her younger children to eat when she tried to escape, but it must have been one of their last, for by the time she returned the family's half of the double cabin was roofless, and thus uninhabitable. They had literally eaten themselves out of house and home.

Milt Elliott and Eliza Williams finagled housing where they could—Elliott with the Murphys and Williams with the Graveses—but the rest of the Reed clan took shelter in the Breen cabin. The family's separation during the escape attempt had taken its toll, and the reunion was cherished all the more. "We could sit by the same fire, sleep under the same roof, kneel on the ground togeather and pray," Virginia Reed wrote later. "I never even think of that Cabin but what I can see us all on the ground togeather praying, some one holding the little pine Candle. I was very fond of doing that, and while we we[re] giving him light we were receiving light."

The Breen cabin was now more crowded than ever, but occasionally camaraderie flowered. The two families chatted, sometimes passing "pleasant hours" that leavened the sheer horror of their lot. "We used to sit and talk together and sometimes almost forget oneself for a while," Virginia Reed recalled. The few books they possessed went from hand to hand, read again and again to stave off boredom. Occasionally, even food was shared. The Breens still had some meat, and while Patrick Breen was apparently determined to hoard the precious victuals for his family, his wife, Peggy, could not help but slip tiny nibbles to the Reed children. In at least one case she thought it a gesture of compassion rather than utility, a way to ease suffering rather than sustain life. She was so convinced of Virginia Reed's impending death that she took Margret Reed up out of the cabin and onto the snow, out of earshot of both women's children, to suggest that Margret prepare for her daughter's demise.

Taking the Field

18

As Margret Reed and her children fought for their lives, her husband was involved in a more literal fight. By the time James Reed arrived in California, the United States and Mexico were at war.

Beginning in the 1820s, American settlers hungry for cheap land poured into Texas, which was then a part of Mexico. The Mexican government, eager for growth in what had been a dusty backwater, welcomed the influx, but in time tension developed. The Americans chafed under Mexican laws that required Catholicism and prohibited slavery, provisos often ignored by the Protestant, slaveholding settlers. In turn, Mexican officials resented the truculent independence of the newcomers, who soon outnumbered the Mexicans. In 1830 the Mexican government prohibited further American settlement, angering the Americans who were already there. By mid-decade, the Americans were in revolt, and in 1836 they defeated the Mexican army at San Jacinto and won their independence.

For the better part of a decade the Republic of Texas trundled along, but the idea of American annexation loomed up inevitably, in part because the Texans were happy to be absorbed. Mexico had never recognized Texan independence, however, nor was there even agreement as to where the border lay. When negotiations on these issues faltered, President James Polk ordered American troops into the disputed border region, a provocative act sure to enflame Mexican sensibilities. In April 1846 a skirmish predictably broke out between Mexican and American troops, a minor incident that was seized on by Polk as justification for war.

Word of the outbreak of war reached the area around Independence, Missouri, in May, just as the Donner Party was setting out, but after that the emigrants had no way of getting news. They must have wondered what was happening, since their intended destination of California was part of Mexico, and thus as Americans they might be received as citizens of a hostile power.

When Reed reached Sutter's Fort in late October, he found that the war had in fact spread to California, and that newly arrived American settlers were organizing a volunteer military effort against the Mexicans. He and William McCutchan launched their valiant two-man rescue attempt, but when they returned to the fort and accepted the impossibility of an immediate winter rescue, Reed joined the war effort.

He rode south for San Jose, an old Spanish settlement below San Francisco, where he took time first for a little personal business. Optimistically laying the groundwork for his family's future life, he walked into the magistrate's office at the Pueblo de San Jose and forged his wife's name on a land claim. (He also submitted a forged claim for Baylis and Eliza Williams, two of his snowbound employees.)

By Christmas, as Margret was thrilling her children with their "feast" of dried apples and tripe, James was serving as the first lieutenant to a volunteer cavalry unit of American settlers. On January 2, as Margret was planning her desperate escape attempt, James and the other Americans engaged several hundred Mexican loyalists—probably themselves volunteers—in what came to be known as the Battle of Santa Clara. The Americans won the first skirmish, chasing the Mexicans from a grove of trees, although the Mexican cavalry soon regrouped and charged the Americans "in beautiful style." "They are, indeed, fine-looking horsemen," wrote Reed, who had so cherished his own acclaim as the owner of the best mount in the wagon train. The Mexicans alternately retreated and charged until finally the Americans found themselves at the bank of a small creek, their horses knee-deep in mud. "The enemy were popping away in fine style," Reed recalled, "and I do assure you we returned compliments without much delay." The Americans had the only artillery piece—"Every now and then the cannon would discharge at them," Reed said—and it seems to have made a difference. The Mexicans broke ranks, and that night sent a white flag into the American camp to ask for terms of surrender.

It was hardly the bloodiest engagement in martial history—the Mexicans eventually reported three dead and five wounded, while one American took a minor head wound—but it pleased the ever-proud Reed. "I am heartily glad that I had such an opportunity to fight for my country," he wrote ten days later to John Sutter. "I feel by so doing I have done my duty and no more, but I am still ready to take the field in her cause, knowing that she is always right."

More than pride, the little battle seems to have won Reed a promotion. In the wake of the victory, Reed was appointed by American naval officials to take command of the mission at San Jose. He took up his duties, but he also found time to improve his land claim by planting some pear and apple trees and even a little barley. Then he sat back and awaited what he hoped would be an early California spring. Warm weather would help the barley to sprout, of course, but far more important, it would give Reed another chance to try to reach his family.

19

Patrick Breen began the new year with a plea for divine relief: "We pray the God of mercy to deliver us from our present Calamity if it be his Holy will," he wrote in his diary on New Year's Day. But the failure of the Reed family escape attempt soon dimmed whatever flickering optimism the holidays had generated, and on Friday, January 8, the day after the bold little group returned to the lake camps, Breen summed up the company's situation with candid pessimism: "prospects Dull."

A new blizzard started cascading snow upon them, and by the fifth day of steady accumulation the threatening walls of white had climbed higher than the cabins. "Must be 13 feet deep," Breen wrote. "Dont know how to get wood this morning. It is dredful to look at."

Even the Breens' relatively bountiful supply of meat was coming to an end. Like other families before them, they resorted to increasingly desperate measures. Early in the entrapment, Patrick Dolan, who had lived in the Breen cabin until he walked away with the Forlorn Hope, threw his tobacco on some portion of his meat supply, a careless and foolish act that risked invaluable foodstuffs. In the month since Dolan left, the tobacco must have contaminated the beef in some indescribable way, but now the Breens were ready to eat nearly anything. They forced down the ruined meat but paid a price. The wretched fare sickened Peggy and Edward.

L ITTLE HARRIET McCUTCHAN SHRIEKED in agony. Lice. The hastily erected cabins and tents of the Donner Party had never offered comfortable accommodations, and as the entrapment lengthened, conditions worsened. The interiors were crowded and dank, redolent of sweat and smoke and mildew. Survivors sometimes referred to the "inmates" of a given cabin, and the analogy was apt. Weather trapped people inside for days. So did the weakness and lethargy of slow starvation. Bathing must have been a vanished luxury, and it would have been difficult if not impossible to wash the bedding and clothes, including the diapers of the babies.

Then there were the lice. Harriet, who was only a year old, suffered more than the others. Even decades later, Patty Reed remembered "the terrible screames of that poor little one." No parent could comfort the tot. Her father, William, had ridden ahead to fetch supplies from Fort Sutter and then been unable to return. Her mother, Amanda, had left with the Forlorn Hope, reckoning that the only way to save her child was to go and fetch help. The Graveses agreed to care for the little girl, but there wasn't much they could do about the lice. She scratched until she bled, so they tied her tiny arms straight by her sides. Then they tried to block out the fact that she was still screaming.

M ILT ELLIOTT DID NOT WANT TO DIE with strangers. As the days and weeks wore on after the aborted escape attempt with Margret Reed, he felt himself fading and thought the end might come soon. But he was living in the Murphy cabin and hardly knew the people there. Margret and her children were over in the Breen cabin, and Elliott felt a yearning to be with them. He was, after all, a Reed by feeling if not by blood, so close to his employers that he called Margret "Ma." And so he dragged his failing body over to the Breen shanty, where he lay down just to the left of the fireplace and dozed off.

But if Elliott wanted to die in the Breen cabin, that was the one thing Patrick Breen was determined to avoid. Watching a man die might demoralize his family. They might lose heart, and heart was one of the keys to survival. Breen insisted that Elliott return to the Murphy cabin that was now his home. Breen had already taken in Margret and her children. That was enough to ask.

Margret Reed roused Elliott and helped him toward the other cabin. Along the way, she gave him a pep talk.

L IKE ELLIOTT, ELIZA WILLIAMS ALSO ACHED at the separation from the Reeds, her employers and surrogate family. She had found shelter in the Graves cabin, but twice she walked over to the Breen shanty. She was sent away both times. "She wont eat hides," Breen recorded in his diary. "Mrs. Reid sent her back to live or die on them."

T WO HUNDRED MILES TO THE WEST, in the small coastal community of Yerba Buena, residents awoke to find the streets and sidewalks and lampposts glazed with ice almost a quarter inch thick. They pulled their collars tight as they hastened through their morning errands, the better to get back inside and sidle up to a fireplace or a woodstove. It was, the old-timers said, an unusually cold winter.

A T TRUCKEE LAKE, SNOW STARTED FALLING again a little after sunrise on Friday, January 22, the flakes ghosting down in the half-light of dawn. By 10:00 A.M. Breen had concluded that another blizzard was upon them. By nightfall the wind was screaming, the snow swarming down in a storm as horrific as any they had yet encountered. It kept up for the better part of four days, and when the storm finally broke for good, Philippine Keseberg walked over to the Breen cabin to say that her son, Lewis Jr., who had been born along the trail during the soft days of summer, had died three days before. If there was any comfort to be offered the grieving mother, it was that her daughter, Ada, was still alive.

O N THE NIGHT OF A FEROCIOUS BLIZZARD, Virginia Reed lay awake in her bed, listening to the howling storm. "I could not sleep," she recalled, "was lying there in that little dark cabin under the snow, listening to the pitiless storm, so cold and hungry." Physical measures suggested the hopelessness of their plight, so she turned to the spiritual.

Back in Illinois, she had been drawn to the local Catholic church, preferring its candlelit solemnity to what she regarded as the feigned and theatrical spiritualism of her family's tent-revival creed. The attraction deepened as she watched Patrick Breen read Catholic prayers by the glow of a lit piece of kindling, a visual echo of the luminous and shimmering Mass she remembered. Now, as the storm raged outside, she found herself on her knees, vowing that if the God to whom the Breens prayed so fervently would allow her to survive, she would join the Catholic church they cherished.

L ANDRUM MURPHY HAD BECOME THE MAN of his family. At the journey's beginning, he had been a mere teenager, two older sisters and their knowledgeable husbands above him in the family pecking order. But his brother-in-law William Pike had been killed in a firearms accident back on the trail, and then his two older sisters and his remaining brother-in-law, William Foster, risked everything with the Forlorn Hope. Landrum was left as the closest thing to an adult partner for his harried mother, now the caretaker for Landrum, three younger siblings, and three grandchildren.

Two weeks after the entrapment Landrum turned seventeen, an age when a boy's chief ambition is to become a man, and surely he took it upon himself to do what he could, to labor with the heaviest camp chores and comfort the smallest children. No longer a mere uncle to toddlers, he had become the surrogate father to a family.

The work wore on him. By mid-January, Breen noted in his diary that Landrum was "crazy last night." Two days later, the young man was "very low, in danger if relief dont come soon." A week after that, he was bedridden. His desperate mother walked over to the Breen cabin and pleaded with Peggy Breen for a little meat to give the boy.

Breen consented, but by the time Levinah Murphy returned with the precious morsel, her son was too far gone to eat. A little past midnight on the last day of January, just a week after the Keseberg baby's death, Landrum Murphy slipped away.

IT HAD BEEN THREE MONTHS since they were trapped, and deaths came now in rapid succession, like the steady striking of a clock. Every two or three days word went around camp of some new fatality: Landrum Murphy on January 31; the McCutchan baby on February 2; the Eddy baby on the 4th; Eleanor Eddy, grieving her baby's loss, on the 7th; Augustus Spitzer on the 8th; and then Milt Elliott, still amid the strangers with whom he did not wish to die, on the 9th.

Survivors struggled to dispose of the corpses. Proper graves were out of the question—digging down to soil was unimaginable—so instead the bodies were merely hauled outside and covered with snow. The baby Margaret Eddy's tiny body lay in the cabin for three days, surrounded by people who were barely alive themselves, until finally her mother died and someone decided they should be buried together. John Breen, a teenager who had himself been ill, roused the necessary energy and laid them to rest. Margret Reed told her children that when she and Levinah Murphy removed Milt Elliott's body from the cabin, they were so weak they had to drag it by the hair.

IT WAS SOMETHING OF A MYSTERY how the Reeds' little lapdog Cash had survived this long. He was the last of the family's five dogs, the same animals that saved their masters' lives by providing a warm-blooded blanket against the cold winds of the Great Salt Lake Desert. With food supplies dwindling, there was nothing to spare for the little creature, and yet here he was, still barking and panting and nuzzling against the youngsters on the cold nights. Patty Reed thought that perhaps he had survived by catching crickets in the vermin-infested cabins. But in time, the family was faced with the unavoidable necessity, and Cash himself was sacrificed for the greater good. "We ate his head and feet & hide & evry thing about him," Virginia Reed remembered later. The grim canine stockpile lasted a week, and then the ever-struggling Reeds once again faced starvation. At times they ate an unappetizing mush produced by taking the bones from which the Breens had gnawed their sustenance and boiling them for days on end.

The Breens still had a little meat, but by and large they refused to share it, understandably calculating that it would be needed for the paramount goal of their own survival. Peggy Breen ached with anxiety, "very uneasy for fear we shall all perrish with hunger," as her husband put it in his diary.

The Graveses worried too. Breen noted in his diary that Elizabeth Graves seized the Reeds' scanty remaining property as collateral against some unspecified debt, presumably Margret Reed's purchase of two cattle weeks before. The seizure probably didn't mean much, since the Reeds had virtually nothing left and were no longer occupying their half of the double cabin they had once shared with the Graveses, but it was plain evidence that collaboration had irreversibly dissolved, that the Donner Party was beset with the petty imbroglios that invariably afflict any group of people confined together amid trying circumstances. Elizabeth Graves eventually took her bickering to a ludicrous level, insisting to Breen that his predictions of warmer weather were a sort of jinx, an ironic guarantee of continued freezing. Apparently she meant this quite seriously, since the normally ungrudging Breen wrote succinctly, "she is a case."

Nobody could hold out much longer, as Patrick Breen clearly understood. For weeks he had been hoping for a thaw, whether to aid the arrival of the rescuers or the escape of the emigrants. Again and again he had recognized what he thought were the signs of a changing season— the chirping of birds, the caress of the sun—only to be disappointed when the blizzards returned. Now, as if in recognition of their perilous state, he seemed to lower his goal, to aim not necessarily for ultimate salvation but merely for a fleeting victory over the snow that had so long held them captive. "We hope with the assistance of Almighty God," he wrote, "to be able to live to see the bare surface of the earth once more."

Part 3

Salvation

Fellowbeings

20

In the modern world, rescue is often a relatively easy affair. Discover that some unfortunate band of adventurers is trapped in the wilds— isolated by the natural confines of mountain or island or jungle—and usually a helicopter can whirl down and disgorge medics and guides and helpers of every ilk. There are exceptions, of course. It has been said that the upper reaches of Mt. Everest might as well be the moon, for all the hope of sudden deliverance from afar. But most of the time, if sufferers can be found, assistance can be delivered with astonishing speed. Sailors are saved from turbulent seas; climbers are plucked from cliffs. Even if those in need cannot be reached, they can often be located, so that a crackly voice on the radio or the steady beep of a transponder can serve as the target for a parachuted cache of calories that preserves life until the motor-powered cavalry roars over the hill.

The nineteenth century presented more intractable dilemmas. In the case of the Donner Party, learning the precise location of the stranded party provided no guarantee of its salvation. The helpless travelers faced a mountain range all but impassable on foot or in the saddle, yet would-be rescuers shared precisely the same means of transport. And if getting in is just as hard as getting out, if you cannot reach them for precisely the

same reasons they cannot reach you—then how the hell do you save their lives?

A<small>T FIRST, EVEN THE POTENTIAL HELPERS</small> needed help. When the seven surviving members of the Forlorn Hope struggled down out of the mountains in mid-January, the little settlement they found at Johnson's Ranch was too small to mount a rescue mission. So the first task was not to head east to aid the victims, but south and west to summon men, equipment and supplies from Sutter's Fort, forty hazardous miles away.

Winter rains had deluged Northern California. Rivers strained against their banks, floodwaters surged over fields, mud seized hooves and feet and wagon wheels and held them with an unbreakable grip. The countryside, one man remembered, was "one vast quag mire."

The first obstacle was the Bear River, pounding along too high and too fast to ford. Two pine logs were lashed together with strips of rawhide, and the next morning the haphazard raft was shoved out into the roaring current, an Indian messenger named Indian Dick hanging on for dear life. The little vessel remained intact long enough to ferry its passenger to the opposite bank, where he took off his shoes, rolled his pants up above the knee, and set off on his lonely slog through the floodlands. Remarkably, he reached Sutter's Fort that night and raised the alarm about the desperate, trapped emigrants.

Heading into the Sierra in the dead of winter was a life-threatening enterprise, so recruiting participants posed a problem. With a war on, John Sutter had briefly lost control of his own fort, which was now under the command of an army lieutenant named Edward Kern. Kern had no authority to pay a rescue party, but he made a vague promise that the federal government would do something for the men, then fired off a quick letter to his superiors seeking retroactive approval and guidance. Kern's amorphous promise fell short. Only three men came forward, too few to even begin the journey. Then Sutter stepped in and proved that an established local man often has more credibility than the federal government. Along with John Sinclair, whose Mexican title of *alcalde* made him something akin to a mayor, Sutter said he would guarantee the rescuers three dollars a day, a hefty paycheck. With Sutter and Sinclair backing the finances, four more men volunteered, enough to make the core of an expedition.

Rescuers said later that money was not their incentive, and it's hard to discount their courage. "Finally it was concluded that we would go or die trying," wrote Daniel Rhoads, one of two brothers who agreed to go along. "For not to make any attempt to save them would be a disgrace to us and to California as long as time lasted."

Whatever their motivations, a party of about a dozen men was raised, many of them fresh emigrants who had themselves crossed the plains only months before. They gathered at Johnson's Ranch to make preparations. Sutter and Sinclair built on their earlier generosity by providing provisions and horses, but still it took days to ready the supplies. Cattle were slaughtered and the meat dried. Rawhide strips were cut so they would be ready later for making snowshoes. Saddles posed such a supply problem that two local women loaned sidesaddles for the rescuers' use.

By early February, a little less than three weeks after Eddy stumbled down out of the mountains, the party was ready to leave. Sinclair arrived to take down the names of the rescuers for the official record and to bid them farewell. They were doing a noble thing, he said, and should not sacrifice their own lives in the effort. But neither should they flinch. They were "never to turn their backs upon the Mountains until they had brought away as many of their suffering fellowbeings as possible." A few of the horses had gone astray, and by the time they rounded up the loose animals much of the day was gone, so they delayed their departure until morning. A forbidding sky hinted at a brewing storm, and that evening the clouds loosed a downpour, "one of the heaviest hurricanes ever experienced on the Sacramento." In the higher elevations the rain would be snow, and as the men of the rescue party drifted off to sleep, they must have wondered if the attempt to save other lives would cost them their own.

FROM THE SAFETY OF THE LOWLANDS, Caleb Greenwood raised his eyes to the seductive white peaks and the ominous winter skies, calculating the odds. Greenwood had spent a lifetime in the mountains of the West, as trapper, guide, hunter, explorer. He was in his eighties, but his sinewy strength and vigor suggested a younger man. His worn buckskins looked as though he had not taken them off for years. A Crow Indian wife shared his household. Grown sons, universally referred to in the ugly argot of the day as "half-breeds," joined in his adventures.

Greenwood had stayed alive by respecting the countless agents of death that populated the wilderness: beasts and disease and enemies and, perhaps most of all, ruthless winter. He knew what awaited a handful of men, mostly rubes fresh from the East, with no real guide, trudging off into the teeth of the Sierra in the dead of winter. Greenwood proposed a hard but realistic wager: None of the rescuers would ever be seen alive again. Nobody took the bet.

FROM THE MOMENT THE RESCUERS LEFT Johnson's Ranch, the squelch of mud served as the drumbeat of their march. The trail was so sodden that frequently they had to unburden the pack mules, drag them out of the muck, then reload the beasts and continue on. Within days, the men and equipment were so soaked that they needed an entire day of immobility just to dry out. There was no rain the next day, although they encountered a creek so swollen that the animals had to swim across. The provisions were tied to a log and floated over.

The little band reached the snow on Tuesday, February 9, six days and more than forty miles into their journey. Within hours, the mules were floundering "belly deep," and the next day William Eddy, who had somehow recuperated enough to join the rescue effort, was sent back with some of the exhausted animals. Two men were left with a cache of provisions, and the rest of the meat was divided into fifty-pound packs, a heavy load for men in deep snow.

They struggled on, but as they climbed higher the snow grew deeper every day. On Sunday, the 14th, three of the men simply refused to go farther. That meant only seven were left, and morale plummeted. There must have been some talk of a general retreat, for Reason Tucker, who had been named by Sinclair as one of two captains of the party, decided that a drastic step was needed. "Under existing circumstances I took it upon myself to insure every man who persevered to the end five dollars a day from the time they entered the snow." Tucker was taking on a significant financial risk, but perhaps he was motivated by a sympathetic compassion: He had crossed the plains himself the previous summer, even traveling briefly with the Graves family before they joined the Donner Party. The wage guarantee worked. "We determined to go ahead," Tucker wrote in his diary.

Each man took a turn at the head of the line, breaking trail by sinking knee-deep in the snow at every step. When the leader grew exhausted, he fell to the back, and the second man took over as pacesetter. To guide their return, they set fire to dead pine trees along their path. Every few days they hung a small bundle of meat from a tree, lightening their packs and providing a ready source of resupply on the trip home.

The hiking was fatiguing, brutal work, but when they made camp at night they somehow had to find the strength to fell saplings and make a platform for their campfire. Daniel Rhoads remembered that they usually roasted some meat for supper, "and then throwing our blankets over our shoulders sat, close together, around the fire and dozed through the night the best way we could."

They were extraordinarily exposed, and if a major blizzard hit, they could have been trapped as inescapably as the people they were trying to rescue. But for the most part, the weather held, and up they went, three miles on a bad day, eight miles on a good one. On the 17th, they reached the headwaters of the Yuba River, just beneath the pass, where they guessed the snow was thirty feet deep.

The following day they crossed the pass in the morning and descended the steep eastern slope of the range, the icy flatness of Truckee Lake spread below them. They reached the lake in the late afternoon, their long shadows reaching out as if to announce their presence. They trudged on to the far shore, at the eastern end, where they had been told the cabins lay. Well supplied and with some idea of where they were going, they had completed the journey in about half the time of the Forlorn Hope, yet still it had taken two weeks.

But where was everyone? No emigrants waved or danced or shouted gleefully to herald their arrival. In fact, no one could be seen at all. "No living thing except ourselves was in sight," Daniel Rhoads remembered, "and we thought that all must have perished." Probably they were just a little too late. Probably starvation or disease or despair had taken their ultimate toll. It was a reasonable assumption, but out of some desperate hope one of the rescuers let out a yell, "a loud halloo." Then they waited to see who, if anyone, was alive to answer.

From California, or Heaven?

21

The trapped emigrants had kept a yearning vigil westward, peering off toward the mountains and squinting their eyes against the blinding white glare of sun and snow. In his diary, Patrick Breen anticipated the arrival of help. "Expecting some account from Suiters Soon," he jotted down at one point. And then a few days later: "Expecting some person across the Mountain this week." At Alder Creek, Jean Baptiste Trudeau took a more direct approach. The young Donner family worker once climbed to the top of a tall pine tree near camp—an impressive and exhausting feat given his condition—so that he might catch sight of any arriving rescue party.

So it is ironic that when help finally arrived, no one was waiting. When the seven rescuers walked up to the lake cabins and let out their loud "halloo," the emaciated occupants were all inside their cramped and filthy quarters. As the rescuers stood waiting, hoping for a response and expecting none, Levinah Murphy finally emerged and climbed up the roughly hewn steps in the snow. She reached the surface and stared at these apparitions who had appeared in the midst of so unforgiving a wilderness. In a thin croak—"a hollow voice very much agitated," remembered one of the rescuers—she rasped out a question: "Are you men from California or do you come from heaven?"

Conditions staggered the rescuers. Emigrants whispered shallow breaths from gaunt frames, some unable to stand or walk. Bodies lay about, most buried as well as the waning strength of the survivors had allowed, though some merely covered with quilts. Inside, in the crowded cavelike cabins where the emigrants had passed three and a half months, the revolting glue of boiled hides and bones clung to grimy pots. Bedclothes reeked. Vermin flickered about. The stench overwhelmed.

Rescuers dug into their packs and doled out what little food they had to spare—jerked beef and biscuits "made out of the coarsest flour" but to the emigrants as sweet as any baker's delicacy. Then the rescuers posted a guard over their remaining larder to prevent the famished survivors from raiding supplies needed for the return trip.

The lake cabins were only the first stop, and the next morning three of the rescuers took advantage of warm, clear weather to set off for the Alder Creek camp. A few hours later they arrived, finding the tent-bound Donner families in conditions that were, if it was possible, even worse than those at the lake. The rescuers huddled with George Donner immediately, talking over hard decisions that had to be made almost instantly. A blizzard could roar over the peaks at any moment, dropping fresh sheets of snow that would rise up around both rescuers and victims like the walls of a prison. The return march had to begin that very day, right away in fact, but it was plain that some of the emigrants were too weak to travel. So yet again, as when the Forlorn Hope set out, families faced a horrifying and brutal triage, deciding who would make a harrowing bid for salvation and who would remain behind, very possibly to die.

Softening the blow as best they could, the rescuers claimed that fresh parties were being raised in California, something that Sutter had promised but they did not know with certainty. They feigned ignorance about the gruesome ordeal of the Forlorn Hope, whose true experiences of death and cannibalism would have disheartened the remaining emigrants. William Eddy survived, the rescuers said, for their own expedition had been outfitted in response to his pleas, but as for the rest of the party they claimed to know nothing.

Betsy Donner had no choice but to stay behind. Her husband, Jacob, had died weeks before, and now she was sole parent to seven children, some of whom clearly were too young for the journey. She kept her oldest son, fifteen-year-old Solomon, with her, presumably deciding to risk his life so that he might help care for his youngest siblings. The two next oldest children, twelve-year-old William and ten-year-old George, she sent along with the rescuers.

In the other tent, George Donner was plainly too sick to go. The laceration on his hand—the gash he had received while trying to fix the wagon clear back at the start of the entrapment—had grown infected, and the fetid wound had crippled him. Tamzene Donner, his wife, was healthy enough to make a try for safety, but she refused to leave her ailing husband. She sent away her two stepdaughters—fourteen-year-old Elitha and twelve-year-old Leanna, George's children by a prior marriage—but kept her own three toddlers by her side.

The rescuers felled a pine tree, so the remaining emigrants would have firewood, and then measured out the pathetically small rations they could leave behind for each of those staying at the tents—a tea-cupful of flour, two small biscuits, and a few thin pieces of jerked beef as long as a forefinger. Such scraps might suffice until another rescue party arrived, and in any event common decency required some sort of allowance, even if the recipients were doomed.

Then, within hours of their arrival, they departed, tramping off single file toward the lake, their charges trailing behind. Sparing what she could, Tamzene Donner took some string and tied a threadbare blanket around her stepdaughters' shoulders, hoping it would serve as a shawl in the daytime and a bedroll at night.

The drama was all so quick that it seemed a little unreal. For months the Donners, like every other trapped family, had prayed for the joyous arrival of help from across the mountains. But no trumpets heralded the great moment. Instead it was just three exhausted men bearing scant food, not much news, and precious thin hope. Tamzene's youngest daughter, three-year-old Eliza, didn't even understand what had happened. Only afterward did she comprehend the sad and brutal truth that the long-awaited rescuers had just come and gone.

Reason Tucker was a big, rangy Virginian with an uncompromising desire to help the stranded emigrants. When William Eddy first stumbled down out of the mountains, Tucker was among the handful of men who saddled up horses and rode out into the night to bring in the trailing members of the Forlorn Hope. And then, in the early stages of the rescue mission, it was Tucker who personally guaranteed the men's wages, a promise that preserved the whole expedition from collapse. Tucker had no relatives in the Donner Party, nor even, so far as we know, any particularly close friends, and yet he never balked at the dangerous business of deliverance.

But as Tucker led the survivors away from the Alder Creek camp and back toward Truckee Lake, the enormity of the experience overwhelmed him, and the vigor that had brought him so far sheered away like an avalanche sheeting down a mountainside. "On the road back I gave out," he confided to his diary, although he displayed characteristic pioneer stoicism and offered no more detailed explanation. In time, he recovered and trudged onward through the dimming light of late afternoon. He reached the lake cabins at sundown, narrowly avoiding the nocturnal cold that might have transformed him from rescuer to victim.

Trailing in Tucker's wake, twelve-year-old Leanna Donner struggled even more. Even at the start, she was so weak that others doubted she would reach the crest of the first hill. As the day wore on, she began to cry, then sat down on the snow, refusing to go farther. Her older sister, Elitha, urged her on, promising that the cabins of the lake camp were just over the next hill. Leanna struggled to her feet, plodded to the crest of the rise, and saw nothing. Again she collapsed and wept. Again Elitha pushed her forward. The cycle repeated until at last they saw the smoke curling upward from the cabin chimneys, a magical lure that drew them on. "When we reached the Graves cabin it was all I could do to step down the snow steps into the cabin," Leanna remembered later. "Such pain and misery as I endured that day is beyond description."

She had gone seven miles; now she had to cross the Sierra.

PATRICK BREEN PUT AWAY HIS DIARIST'S PENCIL, for the sudden presence of strangers in camp meant the first chance for fresh conversation in months. On the two days after Tucker and the others returned from Alder Creek, Breen scratched out the most meager of entries: "pleasant weather" the first day and "Thawey warm day" the second.

People were moving around again, rejuvenated by the knowledge that the snow and the mountains and the winter could be conquered. "The sight of us appeared to put life into their emaciated frames," one rescuer wrote. Yet there wasn't much to do. To rest the rescuers, it had been decided that they would not begin the return journey until Monday, four days after their arrival. In the meantime the survivors at the lake cabins filled the dreary hours with the same heartrending calculus that had already occurred at Alder Creek: families assessing the cold odds of life and death and deciding who would make the Herculean effort to escape and who would stay and wait.

Back in December, the Forlorn Hope had consisted almost entirely of adults, several of whom were parents with children back at the cabins. The remaining adults could care for the youngsters, and without provisions the trip was just too risky for the young. So the adults left and the children stayed.

Now it was the other way around. Most of the adults were dead, too sick to travel, or forced to remain in camp to care for children so young they could barely toddle. The new group would be led by relatively healthy adults—the rescuers—with at least some basic provisions, so the parents of the Donner Party took the opportunity to send away their older offspring. Patrick and Peggy Breen sent away two of their seven children. Elizabeth Graves chose the three oldest of her brood to go. Levinah Murphy dispatched two of her three remaining children and one of her two remaining grandchildren. Lewis Keseberg was still hampered by the injured foot that had rendered him a mule passenger during the futile assault on the mountain pass in the fall, but his young wife risked the attempt with her only surviving child, whom she planned to carry. Margret Reed, desperate as always to reach her banished husband, declared that she and all four of her children would flee.

The resulting roster was astonishingly juvenile. As the column marched out of camp, the seven rescuers were pursued by twenty-three skeletal emigrants, most of whom were fourteen or younger, a good many with no parent accompanying them. It was a procession that would today be considered a school parade: two fourteen-year-olds, two thirteen-year-olds, three twelve-year-olds, an eleven-year-old, a ten-year-old, two eight-year-olds, a five-year-old, and, carried in the arms of others, three three-year-olds.

Before long it was plain that two of the Reed children—eight-year-old Patty and three-year-old Thomas—could not go on. Aquilla Glover, along with Tucker a co-captain of the rescue party, recognized the hard truth and told Margret Reed that two of her children would have to go back. He would see them safely to the cabins, he said, then hustle back to catch up. Reed balked. She declared that she too would return to the lake and stay there with Patty and Thomas, letting her two other children go ahead with the party.

Glover took her gently to task, arguing that her return would only add to the number of mouths to feed at the lake. By forging on, she could help Virginia and James, her two other children, and she could effectively conserve the limited provisions that would have to sustain everyone at the cabins. Glover even promised that if they met no other rescue party, he would return and bring out the children, a courageous commitment that could have cost him his life. Reed pondered the unimaginable choice before her, then asked if Glover was a Mason like her husband, a distinction in which he took great pride. Glover said he was, and Reed asked him to back up his vow by tying his commitment to the honor of the fraternal society. Glover gave his word as a Mason, and Reed bent to bid two of her children farewell.

"Well, Ma," said Patty, "if you never see me again, do the best you can."

S TRUGGLING BACK TO THE LAKE CABINS, the two Reed children were hardly greeted with glee. They would have to return to the Breen cabin, where they had been living before they left with the rescuers, and the Breens were understandably reluctant to share their sparse provisions with two more hungry mouths. They had already housed the Reed family for weeks, and now it was presumed they would feed and shelter two of the children longer still. Resentment welled up, and initially they refused to let the children enter.

Two rescuers who had brought the youngsters back lobbied for the Breens' forbearance. Fresh relief parties would arrive shortly, they insisted, with more supplies and a renewed determination to pluck the remaining survivors from the mountain prison. Slowly, grudgingly, the Breens relented. Patty and Thomas padded down the snow steps they had climbed only that morning, back into the dark and wretched cabin they had briefly escaped.

M ARGRET REED MUST HAVE TURNED IT OVER in her head a thousand times. She had just walked away from two of her children, leaving them to a fate she could not fathom or predict, and now she had nothing to do, save walk and walk and walk.

The third day out from the lake, an Englishman named John Denton crumbled. Denton was a likable figure, a man who had proven himself handy around camp. When Sarah Keyes died back at the Big Blue River, it was Denton who hefted a chisel and carved her name on a tombstone. As the company endured its winter captivity, he bore up better than most of the other young single men, the majority of whom were long since dead. But the journey toward safety sapped his last reserve. He struggled to keep pace, pushing himself with desperation, but in time it became plain that he could not go on.

Not wanting to hinder the others, he asked to be abandoned, so they built a fire on a small platform of green logs, chopped some extra firewood, and left what food they could spare. Reason Tucker laid a crude bed of evergreen boughs next to the fire and provided a blanket to ward off the worst of the cold. Putting up a brave face for a man he was forced to abandon, Tucker vowed to send back help soon, but he knew it was a pointless promise. Denton knew it too. He gave Tucker a brace of pistols he was carrying and told him to keep them in case the worst happened. Tucker's bluffing confidence fooled little James Reed Jr., who asked to be left with Denton and the warmth of the flames. His mother refused, of course, and James and the others gathered up their meager provisions and moved on.

Alone, Denton made himself as comfortable as possible, then took out a pencil and a small journal. He began to write, revising as he went by rubbing out lines with a small India rubber eraser. Surrounded by endless white snow, his mind returned to verdant boyhood summers back in England: gazing at a brook, wandering through fields, sitting beneath "the old witch-elm that shades the village green"—joys now impossibly distant. He finished his composition, and waited.

Weeks later, rescuers found his body sitting against a snowbank, his head down upon his chest.

PHILIPPINE KESEBERG CARRIED HER DAUGHTER, three-year-old Ada, for as long as her arms had strength. She had already lost one child on the journey, Lewis Jr., who had not survived to see his first birthday. Her husband was back at the lake, his injured foot precluding any walking, and it was easy to suppose he would die there. Ada might be the only family Philippine had left. Aching for a respite, she offered a gold watch and twenty-five dollars to anyone who would carry Ada, but no one accepted. Philippine recentered her resolve and marched on, but it was the daughter rather than the mother who could go no farther. Sometime that night, Ada died, the latest victim of hunger and cold.

In the morning, the others discovered that Philippine literally could not let go of her child. She clutched the tiny corpse like a pilgrim with an icon. Her mind reeled back beyond her son's death, beyond even the beginning of the journey, all the way back to her homeland of Germany. Before the Kesebergs crossed the Atlantic, Philippine had given birth to twins, Ada and another little girl they named Mathilde Elise. The tots had barely been a year old when the family came to

America, and perhaps the journey proved too much for Mathilde, for she died two months after they arrived. Philippine must have been adamant that she would not lose Ada too, and yet now she had been helpless to prevent it, even as she held the child in her arms.

Reason Tucker stepped forward. They had to keep moving, and it was madness to carry a corpse. The child had to be left to a mountain grave. At last Philippine agreed and stumbled away with the others. Tucker bent to put the little body in the snow, covered it as best he could, and hurried to catch up. "Her sperrit went to heaven," he wrote of Ada, "her body to the wolves."

The grim band marched in single file, just as the rescuers had on the inbound trip, the leaders breaking trail with snowshoes and the others following in their tracks. Each morning they awoke to find their clothing frozen solid. Virginia Reed remembered that even her shoestrings hardened into immovable wires. They started the day's march the minute it was light, for it was easier to walk on the snow when it was still frozen hard rather than softening under the midday sun. Unexpectedly, the sun was in some ways a curse, its glare glinting off the snow until their eyes ached, its warmth melting their frozen clothes until they were soggy and dripping. Virginia, who was thirteen, tried to think of her wet smock as clinging like a fashionable dress.

Hunger deepened by the hour. Hopeful faces sank as they approached the food caches hung in trees by the rescuers on their way up the mountains. Animals had somehow reached many of the bags, gnawing them open and gorging on the contents. Tucker measured out what was left, dividing the rations as evenly as possible and urging his charges to be careful with the precious scraps, lest a lifesaving bite be wasted.

The last allotment was a double ration, two small strips of dried beef, each about the size of an index finger, meant to serve as both dinner that evening and breakfast the following morning. Leanna Donner could not muster the needed self-discipline, and she feasted on both meals at once. At dawn, she had nothing, so she sat in the half-light and watched the others nibble on their breakfasts. Her older sister, fourteen-year-old Elitha, who had kept Leanna going on the first day's fatiguing hike from Alder Creek to Truckee Lake, could not stand to see the girl sit by ravenously while others savored the precious taste of food. Elitha took her own small strip of meat and divided it neatly in two. Leanna, who remembered that the tiny morsels were then "more precious than gold or diamonds," never forgot her sister's help. "How long we went without food after that," she recalled, "I do not know."

The children scrounged desperately. Tucker's buckskin pants were frayed along the bottom, and so the youngsters began to cut off slices of the leather, crisping it in the fire and gnawing it down, in effect recreating the old meals of boiled hide that had sustained them at the lake. By their fifth day on the trail, the whole party was hungry enough to do the same. At noon, Tucker divided up some shoestrings, roasted them, and provided them to the marchers.

There was every possibility now that they all might perish, that they might, like John Denton and Ada Keseberg, survive the ordeal only to die amid the rescue. No one struggled more than little James Reed—at five the youngest of the children who were actually walking, as opposed to being carried by someone. He plunged down into the snow up to his waist, then propped his knee on the edge and struggled from the personal crevasse he had created, thrusting his foot forward to repeat the whole process. Every agonizing step, he told the others, brought him "nigher Pa and somthing to eat." To keep him moving, the adults surely promised him that it was true. Then they must have wondered if it was.

B ACK IN THE CAMPS, silent questions of conscience stole through the shelters like a rumor going around town. Even before the rescuers left, the Donners tamped down the inhibitions of taboo and broached an obvious, if forbidden, topic. If they could not find the bodies of their frozen cattle under the layers of snow, they told the rescuers, they would soon begin to eat the dead.

The same horrifying desperation seeped through the lake cabins. The day after the rescue party left, the Breens shot their dog, Towser, and dressed out the meager body. The butchering knives pried little meat from the bones, for the animal was hardly more than skeleton and hide, but even so small and fleeting a bounty drew envy from the other cabins, half-dead neighbors begging for a chance at survival. Elizabeth Graves hobbled over from her cabin to ask for meat. Patrick Breen, whose family had long held the richest larder of the company, could see the longing inspired by his provisions. "They think I have meat to spare but I know to the Contrary," he wrote of the other families. "They have plenty hides. I live principally on the same."

The nights turned especially cold—"froze hard last night," Breen wrote in his diary on four consecutive mornings—and the flagging emigrants could no longer guard the half-buried bodies of the dead against the wolves. The beasts edged ever closer to the cabin doors, and at night their howls rang through the shanties like the keening wails of ghosts.

Friday, February 26,dawned clear and warm after another arctic night, a brisk wind blowing out of the southeast. Patty Reed's jaw bulged with the swollen protrusion of a toothache, but Breen pondered more agonizing matters. Pulling out his pencil, he set to work on the day's diary entry with a fretful mind. Most families now recoiled at the disgusting boiled hides, he noted, although there were enough to go around. "We eat them with a tolerable good apetite," Breen wrote. "Thanks be to Almighty God, Amen." Then Breen turned to the real cause of his vexation. The day before, he confessed to the little diary, Levinah Murphy had come to his cabin and, like the Donner families before her, acknowledged the depth of their plight. Unless the wolves took it first, she intended to cannibalize the corpse of Milt Elliott, the Reed family's faithful helper. "Mrs Murphy said here yesterday that thought she would Commence on Milt. & eat him," Breen wrote straightforwardly. "It is distressing."

Threshold of Desperation

As Reason Tucker's initial relief party bulled its way up to the high camps and then started back down, James Reed was busy mounting a separate attempt at rescue, one that lagged behind Tucker's but ultimately would become intertwined with it. Discharged from his military duties after the Battle of Santa Clara, Reed rode north to the little town of Yerba Buena, which was about to shed its name for the more impressive San Francisco. He was armed with a petition informing the American naval commander that the Donner Party had been delayed "from unavoidable causes" and was now trapped. The signers, prominent local residents from San Jose, asked that the government dispatch rescuers on snowshoes immediately.

Ushered in to see the top-ranking naval officer on the scene, Capt. J. B. Hull, Reed encountered a mixed response. Hull promised to do what he could but rejected the idea that he mount the whole expedition himself, a reaction not unlike Lieutenant Kern's at Fort Sutter after the arrival of the Forlorn Hope. Hull insisted that if he agreed to outfit the entire operation during wartime, bureaucrats back at the War Department would balk at the expense. He was polite but firm. "His sympathy was that of a man and gentleman," Reed recalled.

So Reed turned to charity. Local leaders called a public meeting, and the men of the town gathered in the saloon of the best hotel. People asked Reed to speak, but when he rose to make his appeal the gravity of the moment overwhelmed him, and he was unable to go on. James Dunleavy, a Methodist minister who had also come west earlier that year, stepped in to take Reed's place. Trained by the weekly rigors of the pulpit, Dunleavy appealed to the crowd's basic empathy, describing what he guessed was the sad and deteriorating condition of the emigrants. He also mentioned his own journey, which was probably crucial in giving the San Franciscans, most of whom had arrived by sea, some sense of the rigors faced by overland emigrants.

It was a test of the mettle of the little community, and the response proved their pride. Collection jars filled with eight hundred dollars, and sailors on two American ships in the harbor pitched in three hundred more. Local leaders guessed that more money would come in soon. "This speaks well for Yerba Buena," one of the newspapers reported proudly.

Organizers agreed that the expedition would split in two initially. Reed would head for Napa and Sonoma, forty miles north, to raise more funds and recruit more help, while the bulk of the supplies would be sent up the Sacramento River on a donated schooner commanded by a young naval officer named Selim Woodworth, who volunteered for the job. The two parties would rendezvous at the confluence of the Sacramento and Feather rivers, and from there proceed on foot into the Sierra.

As Woodworth and Reed prepared to leave, a launch arrived from Sutter's Fort with the startling news that some of the trapped emigrants—the surviving members of the Forlorn Hope—had materialized from the wilderness. For the first time, San Franciscans learned that a preliminary relief expedition—the one led by Tucker—was already being mounted. But they also learned the true horror of the ordeal: starvation and death and cannibalism.

Surprisingly, given later coverage of the tragedy, these first public discussions were remarkably muted and sympathetic. The members of the Forlorn Hope apparently made no attempt to hide their cannibalism, and the first newspaper reports treated the issue as simply one component of the ordeal. Two papers broke the story on the same day, February 13. The *Californian* mentioned cannibalism in only one plainspoken sentence: "the survivers were kept alive by eating the dead bodies." The *California Star* said nothing of cannibalism until the middle of a long dispatch, and then the account was hardly sensationalistic. The paper noted calmly that members of the Forlorn Hope considered conducting a lottery to determine who should be killed for food, but also reported that a game of chance proved unnecessary. "But at this time the weaker began to die which rendered it unnecessary to take life, and as they died the company went into camp and made meat of the dead bodies of their companions." Far from portraying the Donner Party as a collection of ghouls, these early stories seemed designed to generate sympathy for the emigrants and support for the rescue efforts. Later, stories far different in tone would appear.

Aware that Tucker's initial relief was already on the way, Woodworth delayed his departure from San Francisco while fund-raisers worked the town for more cash. The idea now was not merely to rush ahead with food but to set up a base camp partway into the mountains and then to resupply the emigrants thoroughly. In the end, private contributors donated thirteen hundred dollars, and Captain Hull loosened his purse strings enough to add four hundred dollars in government support. Supplies of every type soon filled the hold of Woodworth's vessel: fifteen barrels of flour, four hundred pounds of sugar, seventeen pounds of tobacco, six frying pans, two axes, two hatchets, a shovel, a tea kettle, twenty-four blankets, forty-eight pairs of woolen socks, two pounds of thread, four packets of needles, twelve pairs of women's stockings, twenty-four pairs of pantaloons, thirty red flannel shirts, fifteen pairs of children's shoes, a dozen pairs of adult shoes, four pairs of mittens. Everything was finally stowed on Sunday, February 7, so, without waiting for the passing of the Sabbath, Woodworth weighed anchor, set a spread of sail, and coasted upriver toward the mountains.

Reed went north on his fund-raising and recruiting expedition, successfully rounding up horses and men. But when the party arrived at the confluence of the Sacramento and the Feather, Woodworth was nowhere to be found. The young naval officer had encountered headwinds, so he and his crew had to warp the vessel—attaching ropes for pulling, the lines spitting off water as they were heaved taut, the boat literally dragged upriver against the twin enemies of wind and current. Progress slowed, and when Reed arrived, Woodworth was still well downriver.

Flush with winter rains, the Sacramento ripped along its bank. Without Woodworth's boat, Reed had no way to cross, so he found an elk herd and had his men shoot two of the animals. He intended to stretch the hides over wooden frames to make skin boats, the quickest way to construct some sort of vessel that would float. Crossing a pounding river in the fragile boats would have been treacherous, especially with horses and equipment, and Reed and his men were saved the trouble when a small launch suddenly appeared and offered to help. Reed crossed first with his horse, climbed into the saddle, and hustled off to the last settlement before the mountains, Johnson's Ranch.

Reed started slaughtering cattle while Johnson ordered his Indian workers to grind flour in hand mills. They worked round the clock for two days, the crackle of the drying fire and the creaking of the flour mills keeping time with their labors. Reed's men soon arrived, and on February 23 they headed up into the mountains. Woodworth was somewhere behind, presumably coming on as fast as he could.

Hoping to keep the pack animals from floundering in the snow, Reed left behind spare equipment and supplies, trying to create the lightest possible loads. When they cinched the packs down, each animal carried a mere eighty pounds, less than the lightest of jockeys. Even so, when they reached the snow, hooves plunged downward like rocks tossed into a pond.

They broke camp early the next morning, hoping that the snow would still be frozen from the night and thus would bear up under the animals. But again, as the day before, the horses lurched and sank, every step a trial. After only two hundred yards, the animals heaved and sweated in the dawn chill.

Calling a halt to the barely moving column, Reed must have pondered a perplexing and challenging decision. He knew the first relief party led by Tucker had taken this same route more than two weeks earlier, but he had no way of knowing their fate. Perhaps they had never reached the cabins at the lake. It was entirely possible they had been caught in the open by a blizzard at the higher elevations and frozen to death. From the stories of the Forlorn Hope, Reed knew the desperate straits of the trapped emigrants, including his own wife and children, and if no relief had reached them, death could be imminent for all. But if the animals could not go forward and he pushed on without substantial supplies, how much help would he be? He might arrive at the lake cabins virtually without food. Or his own men might be stranded for days by a storm, with few provisions to tide them over. The last thing anyone needed was yet another party in need of rescue. Standing there in the snow and cold, looking at Reed and waiting for his decision, the men grew silent.

Faced with his staring troops, Reed accepted the bald fact that the animals could no longer negotiate the deepening snow. Resolving to push onward anyway, he decided to shift the loads to the humans and leave the horses behind. So after the initial and pathetic two hundred yards of the morning march, the men slid the packs off the animals and began rearranging provisions. When they shouldered the loads, the uncertain silence that Reed had noted melted away, the presence of a definite task lightening their spirits even as the packs weighed down their backs. "The hilarity Commenced as usual," Reed wrote in his diary.

The long upward miles stretched out into the afternoon, until at last they saw two figures coming toward them, spots against the snow. They hurried forward and discovered two members of the first rescue party, detached and sent ahead for supplies. Questions pierced the cold mountain air: Were there survivors among the emigrants? What were the conditions at the camps? Who was walking out? Reed learned that his wife and two of his children were among those on the trail ahead and quickly sent two men forward with provisions.

The two men Reed sent ahead reached the long file of marchers that afternoon, shortly after the Tucker party had been reduced to a noon meal of roasted shoestrings. With fresh provisions at hand, a fire was quickly kindled and a meal of dried beef devoured by the famished survivors. Two parties were now only a few miles apart and headed directly toward one another—Tucker and his rescued emigrants heading west, Reed and the other men of the second relief party heading east—but night fell before they could close the gap and find one another. As both parties pitched camp, they knew of each other's presence, though certainly not their exact location, and they also knew that a sudden storm could transform the smallest distances into the largest obstacles.

Reed passed what must have been a fitful night, then roused his men early so they could make good time on the still-frozen snow. After only four miles, they began encountering survivors strung out along the trail. Death-mask faces pressed around the rescuers, pleading paupers desperately chanting, "Bread, Bread, Bread, Bread." Bakers had been at work in anticipation of the moment, so the rescuers dug into their provisions and offered sustenance to the bony, grasping hands. In his diary, Reed referred to the survivors as "the poor unfortunate Starved people."

A shout went up for Margret Reed, and then another to promise that her husband was among the rescuers coming up the trail. She fell to her knees in joy and relief. Virginia Reed ran to embrace her father, fell again and again, then at last folded herself into his arms. Little James Reed Jr., who had vowed that every step brought him nearer to his father, must have celebrated his vindication. It was February 27, the first time the Reeds had seen each other since the patriarch's banishment from the Donner Party back in the russet days of autumn. "The meeting was very affecting," one witness wrote with nineteenth-century understatement.

But then Margret breathed horrifying news to her husband: Two of their children were still trapped. James Reed urged the survivors to keep going, then mustered his men and started back up the mountains. Within minutes of a reunion that ended almost five months of separation, Reed was off again, waving farewell to half his family in a frantic attempt to save the rest.

A T THE MOUNTAIN CAMPS, THE SURVIVORS were perched at a threshold of desperation. They had all endured the unendurable—months of hunger so sharp it twisted the belly, meal after meal of boiled leather, the slow deaths of comrades and family. Yet now there was hope. Rescuers had made it through once. Perhaps others would too. If only breath and blood could be kept active for a few more days, a lifetime might still stretch out ahead.

Out in the snow lay the food they needed, buried in the shallowest of graves and preserved by the icy cold. At last someone took a knife—perhaps it was one of the Donners, perhaps it was Mrs. Murphy making good on her vow to eat Milt Elliott, perhaps it was someone else. There may have been a conversation: arguments back and forth, tears and angst, the frank necessity pitched against the age-old taboo. Or it may have been a silent consensus, a sudden and collective acceptance of the unavoidable. Someone took a knife and went out into the snow.

I RONICALLY, PEOPLE WHO ARE STARVING can be killed by an overabundance of food. To survive a prolonged period of malnourishment, the body begins to consume itself, burning off fat and then eating through muscle. As the process accelerates, the body begins to plunder the tools it needs to process nutrients, so that eventually a person who is desperately craving food can be killed by a gluttonous feast. In recognition of such perils, modern relief workers are provided with guidelines for the gradual refeeding of famine victims.

The potential dangers of uncontrolled gorging by starvation victims was known even amid the primitive medical knowledge of the nineteenth century, and so when the survivors reached a camp where Reed had stationed one of his men with supplies, the emaciated emigrants were doled out only limited portions. The adults recognized the necessity of this restraint, but to twelve-year-old William Hook, it must have seemed a stubborn and perplexing denial. For months he had eaten almost nothing, had watched his family members wither and die for lack of food. Now an abundant larder was being kept cruelly beyond his reach.

As he lay awake at night, his stomach knotted with a ravenous hunger. His mouth watered at the memory of the meager meal he had been given. At some point, temptation overwhelmed obedience, and he wriggled from his bedroll and snuck quietly to the food cache. For the first time in months, he could eat as much as he wished, and he began inhaling food, gorging himself in a hushed, private feast. Within hours, he was deathly ill. He was given tobacco juice to make him vomit, but when the party was ready to move on, William was too sick to march, so he was left behind with an adult attendant and two other youngsters who could not go on. At one point, apparently sick, William went out on the snow and crouched down, resting on his hands and knees. He was approached by eleven-year-old Billy Murphy, who had been left behind with frostbitten feet. Billy put a hand on William's shoulder, speaking to him and urging him to come back into the camp. William fell over, already dead. Billy and the camp attendant took some biscuits and dried beef from William's pockets and then buried him under a tree where the snow had melted.

Billy's shoes had been cut off, and with no extra pairs on hand, he had no choice but to walk the rest of the way barefoot. They caught the main group of survivors three days later, and four days after that—on March 7—the whole party reached Johnson's Ranch, the end of their journey. After a winter of unending white, the lowland spring seemed a riot of colors and life: the green of the grass, the varied hues of early flowers. Even the soft brown of bare and unfrozen dirt was an enlivening change. "I really thought," remembered Virginia Reed, "I had stepped over into paradise."

Weeping

23

George Donner looked away and wept. His three youngest children, the three little girls who remained in the bedraggled tent at Alder Creek with their parents, had been so pitifully hungry, their sunken faces so heartbreaking. Yet George and Tamzene had been unable to satisfy their daughters' pleading. No more rescuers had come to help. No hunter had provided meat.

Out of options, they went out into the snow to dig up the shallow graves of loved ones. At first, the only body that could be found was that of Jacob Donner, George's brother, who had died back in December. His widow gave her permission, and the flesh of his limbs was sliced away.

The girls ate, but George could not bring himself to watch. He had uprooted his prosperous and settled family and dragged them across a desiccated continent in search of a better life, and the great endeavor had come to disaster. The girls ate, and noticed their father's tears.

THE NASAL HONKING OF GEESE sliced through the cold night air, and Patrick Breen lay in bed listening. It was early for the birds to be flying north. They might easily reach their summering grounds before spring loosed the grip of winter. They were at the forefront of their migration, as prompt as the Donner Party had been tardy.

FROM THE SHELTER OF THE FOREST, pitying eyes peered in toward Breen's cabin. During the months of their entrapment, the emigrants had assumed they were alone, seeing no other human presence until the first rescuers arrived from California. In fact, they had been watched ever since they first drove their ox teams up into the mountains.

The Washoe Indians lived in the eastern Sierra Nevada. They spent summers near Truckee Lake and winters at lower elevations, but hunting parties would have returned to the lake even in the colder months. The Washoe had no written language, but their oral traditions recount a long observation of the strange invaders from the east. At first, the Washoe watched the wagon trains wend up the river canyons and thought the long processions looked like some giant, monstrous snake. Most of the trains disappeared over the crest of the mountains, of course, but the Washoe saw that one group stalled just at the onset of winter and then settled in at makeshift camps. The Indians had heard tales of the Spanish missions in California, where Native Americans were essentially enslaved, and so they were understandably reluctant to contact whites. But as the condition of the Donner Party slowly worsened, the Washoe's fear turned to sympathy, and on the morning after Breen heard the geese flying over, one courageous ambassador approached the cabins.

He wore a heavy backpack and, so far as Breen could see, was alone. He approached from the lake, on snowshoes with strings made of bark. He said something the emigrants could not understand and left five or six small roots as an offering of food. Then he walked off toward the east. "Where he was going I could never imagine," remembered John Breen, Patrick's teenage son.

The roots looked like onions and tasted like sweet potatoes, but the texture was stringy, "all full of little tough fibres," Breen wrote. Still, the emigrants devoured the gift gratefully. The Washoe never approached again. By now, they had seen things that convinced them the strangers were inhuman.

Gruesome Sights

24

Climbing up into the higher elevations after leaving the members of the first rescue party, James Reed and his men began to plunge down to their waists in powder, the deep snow grabbing them like a demon from the netherworld. The men heaved themselves back to the surface, searched around for some firmer bit of footing, then launched another stride that would take them a yard closer to the summit and, almost surely, deliver them back into the depths.

By midday the sun simmered snowfields into mushy bogs, impossible to walk on. The men lay down to take what rest they could, then rose at midnight, thinking the dependable night chill had again hardened the snow. But still the surface gave beneath their feet, so they waited another two hours and then at last resumed their climb by stars and moonlight and the coming dawn. Reed estimated the snow at thirty feet deep, the same guess Tucker made while marching in with the first relief party.

Soft snow and exhaustion again forced them into an early camp, a delay that cornered Reed into a difficult decision. He and most of the others were spent and needed a full night's rest. But three of the men—Charles Cady, Nicholas Clark, and Charles Stone—somehow found a reserve of energy. They could keep climbing through the night, they insisted, although it was now their second night with almost no sleep. The risks of separation were obvious. A splintered party could more easily fall prey to some accident, and if caught by a blizzard would have fewer bodies for sharing warmth or chopping firewood. Already the saga of the Donner Party and its rescuers was a fractured tale, small groups scattered about like icebergs calved from a glacier: some safe in California, others at the mountain camps, still others in between. To split off a small group yet again might invite disaster.

Yet Reed also knew the desperation of those in the mountain camps, including two of his own children. He knew that for those still alive at the lake cabins and Alder Creek, the odds lengthened with each passing moment, the seconds ticking away until midnight on an executioner's clock. If Cady, Clark, and Stone could march through the night and reach the camps a few hours sooner, they might save lives. Reed told the men they could keep going, and so as he and the others bedded down on the snow, the tiny breakaway group hiked off into the dark.

They approached within two miles of the lake cabins but then spotted a party of about ten Indians. In fact, the Washoe had given aid to the Donner Party, but the three men quickly assumed the Indians were hostile, presuming they had killed those in the cabins. They huddled together and spent the remainder of the night camped without a fire, fearing that flames might attract the attention of the Indians and invite attack.

Morning dawned clear and pleasant, and for the second time a rescue party walked toward the cabins at Truckee Lake thinking that all those inside were already dead.

D ESCENDING THE CRUDE SNOW STEPS of the cabins, the rescuers found a gruesome sight. Some of the emigrants were still alive, but around their hovels lay partially butchered corpses, "fleshless bones and half-eaten bodies of the victims of famine." Limbs and skulls littered the ground, even the hair of those who had been consumed. When they moved on to the Alder Creek site, they found the children of Jacob Donner eating his heart and liver raw, the blood still on their chins.

At least that is the story that Reed and his men recounted in a version that first appeared in the *Illinois Journal* on December 9, 1847, nine months after the rescues, in an article based on Reed's notes, though written by someone else. In a later retelling, Reed made no mention of discovering cannibalism, but on the other hand he never refuted the *Journal* article.

Parts of the newspaper account seem exaggerated or melodramatic, as though they might have been added by a writer looking to make an extraordinary story even better. Skulls are said to have filled camp kettles, for example, although few people forced to resort to survival cannibalism actually eat the heads of their former comrades. But on the broader point—that cannibalism had occurred at both the lake cabins and the Alder Creek site—there is little reason to doubt Reed and his men. For one thing, it should come as no surprise that the survivors were eating human flesh. Cannibalism had already occurred in the saga of the Donner Party among the members of the Forlorn Hope, the survivors of which had been able to reach Johnson's Ranch only by eating the dead. Furthermore, people at both mountain camps had already acknowledged their plans for cannibalism. The Donners had told members of the first relief party that they would begin eating human bodies soon, and Levinah Murphy had told Patrick Breen of a similar strategy for survival. A week had passed since the departure of the initial rescuers, who had been able to leave few supplies, and yet no one had died.

Most important, some of the survivors later described their cannibalism, including Mary Donner, two weeks shy of her eighth birthday, and Jean Baptiste Trudeau, the teenager who was doing much of the work at the Donner camp. Perhaps most convincing of all is the unadorned candor of Georgia Donner, who had just turned five. It was Georgia who remembered her father crying and turning away, and she also recalled a macabre moment in which her aunt, Betsy Donner, asked, "What do you think I cooked this morning?" and then answered her own question, "Shoemaker's arm." Georgia seems to have resisted any temptation to embellish her tale, for she was frank in admitting what she did not know. "When I spoke of human flesh being used at both tents, I said it was prepared for the little ones in both tents. I did not mean to include the larger children (my half sisters) or the grown people, because I am not positive that they tasted of it."

Such plain and apparently reliable testimony later came into question as doubts were raised about the practice of cannibalism at Alder Creek. Chiefly, these came from Eliza Donner, who turned four in the midst of the events and who later developed an iron determination to disprove allegations of cannibalism by her family. She wrote her own account of the Donner Party's ordeal, and her great triumph came during an interview with Trudeau when he recanted his earlier testimony. But this occurred decades after the entrapment, and he was telling his interviewer exactly what she yearned to hear.

The controversy cropped up again recently, when an archaeological team excavated the Donner families' cooking hearth and tested some of the bone fragments found there. When none of the bones proved to be human, many casual followers of the tale concluded that this finding repudiated the possibility of cannibalism. But in fact, it would have been astonishing to find archaeological evidence of cannibalism at Alder Creek. In the acidic soil of the conifer forests of the high Sierra, uncooked bone disintegrates quickly. The only bones found by the archaeologists—the only ones still there to find—were cooked. But the likelihood is small that the families at Alder Creek would have cooked any human bones. In typical cases of survival cannibalism, the desperate sufferers slice flesh from the cadavers and cook only this gruesome "meat." Not until after the supply of flesh is exhausted are the bones boiled, so they too can be eaten.

But at Alder Creek, cannibalism would have occurred for no more than a week. There were four full-grown adult bodies at hand (although it's possible that one or two had been lost in the deep snow), and it is unlikely that the handful of survivors would have stripped away all the flesh, requiring the cooking of bone. This is even more true if Georgia Donner's account is correct, since she suggests that the adults may not have participated. It seems unlikely that a few small children and a single teenager would have eaten all the flesh off even a single body in less than a week. So there is a high probability that when the archaeologists scrutinized their diggings for physical proof of cannibalism, they were searching for something that no longer existed. And there is an equally high probability that when James Reed and the other men of the second relief party arrived at the high camps, they saw the plain evidence all around them.

W HEN REED EVENTUALLY REACHED THE MOUNTAIN CAMPS, he walked up to the Breen cabin to find his daughter Patty sitting on the roof, her feet dangling on the snow. In the shanty he found his son Tommy, and knew that at least for now all the members of his family were alive.

"Informed the people that all who ware able Should have to Start day after tomorrow," Reed wrote in his journal. "Made soup for the infirm . . . and rendered evry assistance in our power."

The next morning, Reed and three of his men hiked over to the Alder Creek camps, where agonizing decisions had to be made. Betsy Donner allowed the rescuers to buy the personal property of her late husband, Jacob, whose partially cannibalized body lay nearby. No one recorded her motive, but perhaps she thought that the money would help her children, especially if she too died and left them orphaned. Boots went for $4 a pair, cordovan shoes $3, silk handkerchiefs $1.25 each. Donner's knife, the one item that wasn't some sort of garment, brought $1. A careful record was kept—subtotals for each man, the sums accurate to the penny—and in all the sale raised $118.81, presumably to be paid when the party reached California.

The harder decision for Betsy Donner must have been to divide her family yet again. Two of her children had gone out with the first relief, but five remained with her. The two smallest, Samuel and Lewis, were too weak to go, as was their mother, but she sent the three oldest, Solomon, Mary, and Isaac.

In the other Donner tent, the decision was more vexing. The three little girls were in relatively good health—"Stout harty children," Reed called them—and so was Tamzene, their mother. But George Donner, beset by the infection from his injured hand, was too weak to move.

Tamzene would not leave her husband alone, and Reed told her honestly that he expected another rescue party shortly—the group led by Selim Woodworth, the naval officer whose well-supplied expedition had been moving toward the Sierra when Reed entered the wilderness. Promised that more help was on the way, Tamzene decided to stay where she was and keep her three children with her. Having done what he could, Reed bundled up Betsy Donner's children and hiked back to the lake, where his own two youngsters waited.

Since being sent back from the group that escaped with the first relief, Patty Reed had become something of a surrogate mother for her little brother Tommy, and her father seemed to recognize her new status. Before leaving for Alder Creek, he had told her that she could have flour from the rescue provisions to make bread. Patty, who had just turned nine, knew the value of the foodstuffs lugged in by the rescuers, knew that none could be wasted, knew that lives might depend on the wise use of every morsel, and yet now her father was trusting her with the precious stores. She thought herself "quite a little woman." She beamed with pride.

She also set to baking, and when the rescuers returned from Alder Creek, well after dark, the alluring smell of fresh-baked bread wafted from the Breen cabin, a stark contrast to the previous months of deprivation. The men came in—"cold and hungry and tired and heartsick," Patty recalled—and huddled around the fire for warmth. At one point, Patty promised everyone that all the bread was good—the portions she was serving to the strangers as well as those she gave to people she knew—and everyone laughed at her sweet pronouncement. "The laugh," she wrote later, "did almost as much good as the bread."

THE NEXT MORNING, REED AND THE OTHER RESCUERS led seventeen people toward the pass, once again most of them children. Elizabeth Graves took her four remaining youngsters, emptying out once and for all the big double cabin that had been built for her family and the Reeds. The Breens and their five children all left. Patrick Breen, who had so faithfully chronicled the travails of the party in his diary, ended with an astonished acknowledgment of the obdurate foe that had held them all captive. He had talked with old mountain hands among the rescue party, he noted. "They say the snow will be here untill June."

To help care for those unable to travel, Reed detailed three of his men to remain in the high camps—Clark and Cady at Alder Creek, Stone at the lake—assuring them that Woodworth would arrive soon with more help. Whatever meager provisions could be spared were left as well. Just fourteen survivors remained behind, most of them at the edge of death.

Those who walked away with Reed had endured more than four months of captivity, surviving numbing cold, debilitating disease, filth, boredom, and despair. They had divided their families in hopes that some might live while others died. They had watched their friends and family members starve, and at least some of them had been forced to cannibalize the bodies. Now their ordeal was about to get worse.

Terror, Terror

25

James Reed looked up into the sky and felt an abiding dread seize his heart. The sky was darkening, portentous clouds rolling up over the peaks. At this elevation, the clouds pressed close, looming down on a man like a monster from a nightmare.

They were three days out from the lake. Progress had been slow, and they had only surmounted the crest of the Sierra a few hours earlier. They were about as high—and about as exposed to the elements— as at any point on their journey.

Reed concealed his alarm in the confessional of his journal. "The Sky look like snow and everything indicates a storm, god for bid.... Night closing fast, the Clouds still thicking. Terror, terror. I feel a terrible foreboding but dare not Communicate my mind to any. Death to all if our provisions do not Come in a day or two and a storm should fall on us. Very cold, a great lamentation about the Cold."

In the entire ordeal of the Donner Party, no one ever revealed a more acute fear.

Perhaps they had been a little too generous with the food they left at the lake camp and Alder Creek, for their own supplies had run short, and now they were weakened from half rations. Three men had gone ahead in hopes of finding a cache left by the rescue party on the way in, but so far there was no sign of their reappearance.

At least there was work to do, something to pry the mind from the waiting. Wood had to be gathered for a fire. Without a fire they might not survive the night. So those who were able scrounged around for some downed branches, the thicker ones for the fire, the boughs for beds to provide a little insulation from the incessant snow. If they could get some food and start a decent fire, then maybe, just maybe, they could withstand the onslaught coming from the sky.

As they worked, they must have stolen glances to the west, longing for the return of their comrades, and to the sky, eager for some change, a shaft of blue, literally a ray of hope.

But all they could see was the clouds.

S NOW STARTED FALLING EARLY IN THE NIGHT, and with it the wind rose into what Reed remembered as "a perfect hurricane." They were camped amid a stand of tall timber in a shallow valley just beneath the summit. Rectangular, with one of the short ends facing the pass, the little depression funneled the winds so that they raked the campsite ferociously. Blown sideways, snowflakes and ice crystals turned into tiny pellets of buckshot. The wind screamed through the tree branches. The temperature plummeted.

In his diary, Reed noted that he tried to keep watch for the men returning from the cache, but that would quickly have proved impossible, and useless anyway. Given the conditions, the advance scouts were either dead or holed up somewhere. "My dreaded Storm is now on us," Reed wrote. "Crying and lamentations on account of the Cold and the dread of death from the Howling Storm." Children began to weep. Some of the men prayed for their lives.

They all circled the campfire, their backs outward, away from the flames, then piled up snow behind the circle, creating a windbreak that gave them at least marginal shelter. Peggy Breen was still nursing her youngest child, a daughter named Isabella, so she got down on her knees, pulled a blanket and shawl over her shoulders and head, and tried to let the baby take some nourishment.

The fire had been built on a platform of green logs, but still it had melted the snow beneath, forming a pit. At one point, fifteen-year-old John Breen collapsed—"I fainted or became stupid from weakness," as he put it—and would have fallen into the fire hole if a quick-witted companion had not caught him by the leg. His mother rushed over to revive him. His jaws had locked shut, but somehow she forced in a bit of lump sugar, which brought him back to consciousness.

With the temperature so low, the fire was an absolute necessity, but as conditions worsened some of the men gave out physically and could no longer feed the flames. Reed went blind, probably a delayed form of snow-blindness from reflected sunlight earlier in the day. Whatever the cause, he could not see the flames even when he stared straight into the campfire.

By default, the crucial job of tending the fire fell to William McCutchan and Hiram Miller. Like McCutchan, Miller had originally been part of the Donner Party but went ahead on the trail and thus avoided entrapment. In Miller's case, he joined a mule train early on during the journey and far outpaced the lumbering wagons. McCutchan and Miller fed the fire relentlessly, and there were those in the group who thought that if the two men had failed, everyone might have died. Years later, McCutchan gave the credit to his colleague: "Miller being a man of Herculean strengths and indurance was the life and savior of the party."

Morning brought no relief. The storm raged on, creating a white-out, snow as present in the air as on the ground. Looking into the wind, visibility stretched to less than twenty feet. The sky—"the light of Heaven," Reed called it—was an unknowable mystery.

Maintaining the fire grew ever more strenuous. The snow pit was now fifteen feet deep, although still the bare ground could not be seen. If the fire itself slid down into the hole, it would be too far away to give off much warmth, and so in addition to feeding the flames, men had to tend the platform of green logs laid across the pit. The supply of wood gathered the previous night was exhausted, so they had to go out into the storm and find nearby trees to fell, then drag the wood back. Even with the warmth of exertion, they could only work in ten-minute shifts before the cold forced them back into the fire circle to regain feeling in their hands and feet. Then they would head back out again.

Peggy Breen had a few seeds and a little tea and sugar, but for all practical purposes they were without food. So long as the storm continued, there was no chance of anyone arriving with supplies, and certainly none of hunting, so as their hunger deepened they could do nothing but bide time. In the lore of the Donner Party, the site became known as Starved Camp. "Hunger, hunger is the Cry with the Children and nothing to give them," Reed wrote. "Freesing was the Cry of the mothers with reference to their little starving freesing Children. Night closing fast and with the Hurricane Increases. . . . I dread the coming night."

T HE DROPS THRUMMED ON THE ROOF above Virginia Reed's head. She was safe now, down in the valley, in California, out of the endless winter, generously sheltered in a real house with a real roof, not a makeshift cabin topped with a hide. But lying awake at night, she listened to the steady patter. She knew that in the mountains above, the raindrops were snowflakes, an infinity of snowflakes piling up into inches and feet and yards. Earlier in the day, she had seen her mother standing in the doorway for hours, looking up at the mountains.

Somewhere up there, Virginia knew, her father and siblings struggled against the snow, struggled to reach, as she had done, bare earth and soft grass and a spring rain.

T HE BLIZZARD BELLOWED ON INTO ITS SECOND NIGHT at Starved Camp. The fire failed, snuffed out by wind and snow and cold. McCutchan jumped up and managed to rekindle it, piling up the driest pine logs he could find in their meager supply.

Reed slumped into some sort of half-coma, near death. McCutchan and Miller grabbed him and shook him back to consciousness, slapping and shaking and rubbing him until he stirred. Patty Reed lay in her blankets, unable to move, listening to the men screaming at her father, "Reed! Reed! Wake up man, speak! Reed! We will all die! Wake up! Great God, Reed! Come! Come! You must not die now!" At times, she recalled, they swore at him.

"The Hurricane has never Ceased for ten minuts at atime during one of the most dismal nights I ever witnessed," Reed wrote, adding that he hoped never to see such a thing again. "Of all the praying and Crying I ever heard nothing ever equaled it. Several times I expected to see the people perish by the extreme Cold."

At times, the wind was so strong that it seemed one of the nearby trees might topple and crush the little camp. "Snowing and blowing, hailing, sleet and so cold," Patty Reed remembered. "I have not words."

In the circle around the fire, five-year-old Isaac Donner was wedged in between his big sister Mary and Patty Reed. Sometime in the night he whispered a final shallow breath. Amid the noise and fear and confusion, the two girls did not notice his death until the morning.

With daylight came occasional breaks, a few minutes of calm before a resumption of the deluge, and as the day wore on, the storm slackened substantially. In time, the winds calmed and the snow stopped, and the sky made plain that the torrent was over.

At Alder Creek, Nicholas Clark, one of the relief party members left behind to care for the Donners, peered out of the tent and estimated that the storm had dropped six feet of fresh snow. Up near the summit, a thousand feet higher, there undoubtedly was more.

BY THE TIME THE STORM SUBSIDED, Reed's eyesight had returned, and he declared that the party must rise and walk. Another blizzard might strike at any moment. They were without food, and they had no idea if they would be resupplied any time soon. Their own advance party—the three men sent ahead to hunt for the cache—might easily have died in the storm (in fact, they had survived but had been forced to head toward civilization, not back to help the others), and the separate party led by Woodworth, though long expected, had yet to materialize. To stay where they were would be suicide.

But some members of the party simply could not go on. Elizabeth Graves was near death, and it was unclear how her four young children could continue without her. Mary Donner had burned her foot in the campfire and could barely walk. Peggy Breen was holding up well, but Patrick was sickly and spent, just as he often had been at the lake. Two Breen sons struggled. John, the teenager who had handled so many of the chores around the family's cabin, was still recovering from his near-fatal collapse into the fire. James, who was six, was already far gone.

Looking around him at all of this, Patrick Breen announced that his family would stay. It was better to die by a warm fire than collapse into the snow somewhere out on the trail, he said. Perhaps another relief party would come through with provisions. Or perhaps even Reed and his men might make it to safety and send someone back.

Reed began to argue. They must get up and walk, he exhorted. To idle was madness. It would mean certain death. Repeatedly Reed implored them to move. Repeatedly Breen said they would not. Finally, Reed called over the other rescuers and asked them to serve as witnesses to the fact that he was not abandoning his charges, that Breen and the others were staying behind voluntarily.

In fact, both men were merely doing what they had to do. Reed was right that those who were able should push onward. But Breen was right that much of the party was in no condition to do so. Between his family and the Graveses, there were at least five children too young or too weak to walk. Among the adults, it's likely that Elizabeth Graves was unable to go anywhere at all, and so it's difficult to know how one would have convinced her four children to simply abandon their mother to a lonely death.

Nor could Reed and the other rescuers help much. Miller, the strongest of the bunch, planned to carry Tommy Reed, but the other men were apparently unable to take another child. Patty Reed remembered that Mary Donner was willing to go, but with her injured foot was unable to walk. In a letter years later, Patty said that her father asked if any of the other men could help her, but apparently no one stepped forward, and Patty produces no evidence that Reed himself offered to carry Mary, although she consistently portrays her father in the most positive terms possible. If the rescuers were unable to carry the children, then Breen was doubly right to say that for his family and the Graveses, with so many small youngsters, a continued march would have been foolhardy. Perhaps it was only with time that Reed grew sensitive to the idea that he had abandoned people. His diary, which includes an entry for that day, never mentions it, but his later accounts place a greater and greater emphasis on his efforts to exhort Breen to move.

The departing marchers stacked up what wood they could, estimating it at a three-day supply. The party now included just three people rescued from the high camps: Patty and Tommy Reed and fifteen-year-old Solomon Hook, Jacob Donner's stepson. Behind them, lying about on the snow, were thirteen people, most of them children: the seven Breens, Elizabeth Graves and her four offspring, and Mary Donner. They had no shelter, no food, no expectation that they would regain enough vigor to walk to safety unaided. They could do nothing but wait, whether for rescue or death.

S ELIM WOODWORTH, THE MAN SO MANY PEOPLE were banking on, was heading toward the high country. After sailing upriver from San Francisco, Woodworth had reached Sutter's Fort in mid-February, then gathered supplies and made other preparations. On March 2, he was marching up the mountains when he encountered Tucker's first relief party coming down. He turned around and escorted them to safety, apparently arranging for their transportation to Sutter's Fort. Then he headed back into the wilderness. By now, the great blizzard was brewing, and it's likely that Woodworth spent the two days of the storm at Bear Valley, a well-known camping ground partway up the trail.

The reasons for his slow progress thus far would eventually become a topic of great debate. Defenders say he did the best he could with little help, manpower having been depleted by recruitment for earlier rescue parties and the absence of men who were fighting in the war with Mexico. Detractors claim Woodworth moved too slowly, perhaps from incompetence, perhaps indolence, perhaps even cowardice. Billy Graves, who was capable of getting things wrong, claimed that he saw Woodworth lollygagging around camp drunk.

Whatever the cause, the delay was over now. It had stopped snowing, and Woodworth and a precariously small party—just two or three other men—were on their way at last.

AT STARVED CAMP, THE BREENS SUFFERED through the cold and isolation. The history of the Donner Party owes much to Patrick Breen's diligence as a diarist, for his chronicle of the long months at the lake cabins is a unique and invaluable record. But once Breen and his family left the lake, Patrick abandoned his journalistic role entirely. Peggy Breen, on the other hand, is a silent figure at the lake but one who takes center stage during the rescue.

At Starved Camp, both before Reed's departure and after it, she appears to have been among the more energetic adults, attending to the children, including her own, with far more vigor than her husband. This heroic role eventually caught the eye of a writer named Eliza Farnham, who interviewed Peggy Breen about the sad days at Starved Camp. It is to Peggy Breen's account that we largely owe our knowledge of what happened.

The remnant faded toward death almost as soon as Reed and the others walked away. Elizabeth Graves died first, followed by her son Franklin. Almost as bad, the fire kept melting the snow, and the platform of green logs began to sink, so that with each passing hour the flames were a little farther from the skeletal figures in need of the heat. Without the chance to warm themselves, they would all surely perish.

JAMES REED PITCHED FORWARD INTO THE SNOW like a man felled by a gunshot. His snow-blindness had returned, and he stumbled along insensible to his surroundings, an incapacitated man who somehow kept moving. His feet were bleeding, the result of bad frostbite suffered during the storm.

Walking away from Starved Camp, Patty had done the best she could, but eventually she succumbed to her weariness and could go no farther. She was no toddler. At nine, she was heavy enough to constitute a substantial load for a man in good condition, let alone one who had almost died the night before. But there was no other choice, so her father bent down to a knee and took her on his back. To keep his hands free, he drew a blanket around her, then pulled the ends across his chest and tied them to a sturdy stick.

Soon Reed began to fall, although the indestructible Miller, who was already carrying Tommy Reed, heaved him back to his feet and sent him along the way. Even on her father's back, Patty weakened, until at last Reed realized that his daughter was dying, that she was almost gone already. At camp, Reed had taken a frozen, empty sack that once contained dried meat and held it over the fire. When it softened, he carefully scraped the inside seam, where a few tiny crumbs had clung to the fabric. He produced a teaspoonful, perhaps less, but even this was a treasure to be prized. Like a miser hiding a nugget of gold, he placed the tiny serving in the end of the thumb of one of his mittens, literally the last bite of food they possessed.

Now it was needed, so Reed carefully peeled off the mitten, plucked the frozen speck from its unorthodox storage bin, and placed it in his mouth to thaw. When it seemed edible, he took it from his lips and gently fed it to Patty by hand. She revived, and they went on, without even the smallest morsel in reserve.

PEGGY BREEN CHECKED ON THE SLEEPING CHILDREN one by one, holding a hand before every mouth and nose to wait for the soft exhale of breathy fog. But when she came to her James, who had been doing poorly, she felt nothing. Panic rose in her chest like a rush of rage. She called to her husband that his son was dying, pleading for his help.

"Let him die," Patrick replied. "He will be better off than any of us."

Even decades later, the memory of that instant was etched sharply in Peggy's mind. She said her heart stood still when she heard her husband's words. She sat stunned for a moment, then set to work, rubbing her son's chest and hands, trying to generate some circulation and breath once more. As she had when her eldest son, John, fainted and nearly fell into the fire, she broke off a piece of lump sugar and forced it into James's lips. He swallowed, moved his arms and legs a little, and then at last opened his eyes.

A Broken Promise

26

From the beginning of the relief effort, the rescuers marching into the mountains carried along motives as varied as their own lives. Some men strove to save their families. Some worked to fulfill a vow to old traveling companions. Some volunteered to save utter strangers. Some asked about the pay.

As time went on, intentions grew murkier, especially for Charles Cady and Charles Stone, two of the men whom Reed had detailed to stay at the camps and care for the survivors. The day after the main relief party walked away, Stone left his post at the lake cabins and hiked over to Alder Creek, where Cady had been stationed. Nicholas Clark, the third rescuer left at the camps, was out hunting.

Provisions were still plentiful, and there was every reason to believe help was on the way, but Stone and Cady decided they would flee. They struck a deal with Tamzene Donner, whose three little girls were still healthy enough to make it out. Stone and Cady agreed that in return for a fee, perhaps as much as five hundred dollars, they would take the girls. It was an offer that Tamzene had apparently already proposed to the members of Reed's now-departed relief party, who were too overburdened with survivors to accept.

When the deal was done, Stone and Cady took the three little girls up the steps and stood them on the snow. Tamzene emerged and put on their cloaks—red and white for Eliza and Georgia, blue and white for Frances—then pulled the matching hoods up around their ears.

"I may never see you again," she told them, "but God will take care of you." Georgia thought her mother seemed to be talking more to herself than to them.

STONE AND CADY TOOK THE GIRLS FIRST to the lake camp, where they were put in the cabin with Keseberg and Levinah Murphy and given an unwanted spot near the door. The big blizzard struck, and wind and snow blew in and chilled them. In the morning, it had to be scraped off their covers before they could get up.

But once they were out of bed, Stone and Cady made a shocking and shameful announcement. They had no intention of taking the girls over the pass, as they had promised Tamzene. Instead, they were leaving the youngsters in the cabin and going on without any survivors at all. Their decision to flee, suspect from the beginning, was revealed as a disgrace. They were supposedly there on a rescue mission, but now they were leaving without rescuing a soul. They would not stay and care for the sick. They would not carry out a child. They were just leaving.

TWO DAYS LATER, THE DESERTERS HAD CROSSED the pass and were walking through Summit Valley when they passed Starved Camp. Cady and Stone noticed the site, for Cady said later that they passed it at about two in the afternoon, something he would not have been able to pinpoint if they had walked by unknowingly.

But amazingly, neither man offered to help. They did not stop and share their provisions. They did not offer to carry a child or lead a sick adult. They gathered no firewood. So far as we know, they did not even stop to offer words of hope or encouragement. Both were in relatively good condition; they were two of the three self-described "young spry men" who had gone ahead of the second relief party to reach the lake camps early. (To be fair, at some point Cady suffered frostbite on his feet, but that was a comparatively minor matter.) They had been in the mountains a relatively short time, and thus were hardly in the late stages of starvation. They had not even spent a night in the open, since the previous day when they first left Truckee Lake they had been turned back by the blizzard and retreated to the relative safety and warmth of the cabins.

Cady and Stone had once displayed the admirable courage of all the rescuers, perhaps more. Their willingness to forge ahead of the rest of the party on the way into the mountains showed both physical stamina and personal bravery. But at some point, both men lost their moorings. Perhaps the horrors they saw at the camps overwhelmed them. For whatever reason, the same tenacity with which they first rushed into the wilderness on an errand of mercy was now displayed as they rushed out in a desperate bid for self-preservation. Maybe the real surprise is that the other rescuers didn't do the same.

Alive Yet

27

On a cold night, the mountains can be as quiet as a graveyard. Unless the wind kicks up, there is nothing to hear but the voices of your comrades and the crackling of the campfire.

Selim Woodworth and his men, however, turned their ears to something else—other voices, farther off. He sent emissaries to investigate and found the little party that had walked away from Starved Camp: James Reed and two of his children, William McCutchan, Hiram Miller, and the others. By chance, the two parties had almost literally stumbled into one another.

Reed and the others had mostly bedded down for the night, and they were too tired to move, but they asked that some food be brought over from Woodworth's camp, and for the first time in days, they went to sleep with the satisfying feel of a meal in the belly.

THE FIRE AT STARVED CAMP STILL BURNED, but it had fled from those it was intended to warm. Melting the snow, the flames had sunk so far down into a pit that the survivors felt little heat. Peggy Breen stared down into the hole, fifteen, twenty, perhaps even twenty-five feet deep.

At first she must have looked with despair, but then suddenly there was a tiny moment of joy. At the bottom of the hole, she thought she could make out bare ground. If so, if the fire had burned all the way through the winter's slow accumulation of snow, then it would sink no more. If they could descend to meet it, they would once again find some warmth.

She roused John, her teenager, and urged him to climb down. Using a felled treetop as a makeshift ladder, he did so, and then called up that she was right. He was standing next to the fire on warm, unfrozen earth.

She climbed down herself to investigate, then ascended once more and began to shake people from their slumbers. As they woke, she urged them down toward John, and in time everyone who was still alive was down in the pit. Eleven people had to crowd in, but at least they were out of the wind. At least they had the fire again.

WILLIAM EDDY AND WILLIAM FOSTER, BOTH OF WHOM had survived the brutal journey of the Forlorn Hope, bore a special determination to get back into the mountains. Each man hoped to save his own child. Eddy's wife and daughter had died back in early February, something he would have been told by the survivors who walked out with the first rescue party, but his son, James, might still be alive. Foster's wife had come down with him in the Forlorn Hope, but their only child, a son named George, was still back at the lake.

Eddy had briefly joined a previous relief effort, but he had been unable to keep up with the grueling pace. Now, both he and Foster were ready to attack the Sierra, so they borrowed horses at Johnson's Ranch and swung into the saddle. They rode hard until the snow was too deep, switched to hiking, and caught up with Woodworth about the same time Woodworth collided with Reed. By this time Cady and Stone were there too, so that with the exception of Nicholas Clark, the lone rescuer still at the high camps, all the rescuers were together, both those going into the mountains and those going out.

As the groups huddled together to decide what to do, Reed had good news: Eddy and Foster might be in time. When he had left the lake cabins about a week earlier, both their sons had been alive. The boys had been in dreadful condition, but Reed and his men had done what they could, bathing the youngsters and putting them in fresh clothes.

Suddenly Woodworth, who had never gone anywhere near the high camps, was being urged from all sides to mount another relief effort. There might still be people alive at three different locations—Starved Camp, the lake cabins, and Alder Creek.

But Woodworth would not move. He claimed to need a guide, although Reed noted that the tracks of his descending party were plainly visible. He warned Eddy and Foster of the dangers, although both men had walked out of the wilderness in the teeth of the winter with no guide, few provisions, and virtually no equipment. Both Reed and Eddy, and perhaps others too, thought Woodworth was a coward. Reed eventually provided some notes that were used as the basis for a newspaper story portraying Woodworth as a man who "quailed" in fear. Eddy told his story to one of the Donner Party's earliest chroniclers, who described Woodworth as a man who "had become tired from carrying his blanket."

Woodworth finally relented, to a degree. He would not go himself but promised that the government, which was funding his activities, would pay three dollars a day plus a fifty-dollar bonus for any man who carried out a child not his own. Eddy and Foster later claimed they paid two of the men themselves.

With the promise of pay, a little party came together. Remarkably, two of those who agreed to go back had just walked down with Reed: Hiram Miller, who was something of a bull, and Charles Stone, perhaps hoping to redeem himself for bypassing Starved Camp on the downward trip. Three other men said they would go too, so as soon as supplies were rounded up and stuffed into packs, seven men set out on yet another rescue effort, this one quite possibly the last. The money was an inducement, but it took real courage to go. They all knew what another blizzard could mean.

F OR ALL THAT PEGGY BREEN WAS THE MAIN FORCE of energy at Starved Camp, it was one of the children who first broached the obvious. Seven-year-old Mary Donner suggested that they should eat the dead bodies on the snow above them. She told the Breens that she had already eaten human flesh back at Alder Creek, perhaps lessening the strain of breaking the great taboo. Apparently the others agreed, and at some point Patrick Breen, who had regained a little strength, climbed up with a knife.

In an account of the story largely based on an interview with Peggy Breen, the writer Eliza Farnham maintained that only Mary Donner and the remaining Graves children actually ate from the bodies, but it is simply not believable that the Breens refused. Given the length of time of their entrapment and their condition, they must also have participated in the cannibalism, as much a necessity for them as it had been for so many others in their company.

They spent days there, enduring a gruesome tableau as awful as anything in the entire story: eleven people living in a hole, most of them children, unable to see anything but each other and the camp-fire and the sky above, someone occasionally climbing up to slice flesh from the bodies—family members to some of those below—and then returning to their claustrophobic world of ice and desperation.

By the end, when Peggy went up to fetch more wood, she had to crawl from tree to tree, then throw the cut branches along before her as she crawled back to the pit.

S HE HEARD THE RESCUERS BEFORE SHE SAW THEM. Her vision blurred by weakness, she had climbed up from the pit and sensed something coming toward her on the snow. She caught the undecipherable frag-ments of voices in the distance, and then at last heard someone say, "There is Mrs. Breen alive yet, anyhow."

On the snow lay three corpses, all crudely butchered. Survivors had begun by eating the bodies of the two dead children—Isaac Donner and Franklin Graves. From the body of Elizabeth Graves, they had eaten the breasts, heart, liver, and lungs.

The pit itself must have been appalling. Reed had departed five days earlier. Given their condition, most of the survivors had probably found it impossible to climb out unaided, and thus it's likely that one corner of the pit had been designated as a latrine. Although the depth of their fortress protected them from the wind and perhaps gave them some warmth, they were in other ways exposed to the elements. Snow must have sometimes cascaded down from the trees above. At night the cold would have seeped in. During the day the sun shone down mercilessly.

Still, in one sense it was a remarkable success story. When Reed and his men departed, there were thirteen people left alive at Starved Camp. The fact that eleven of them survived almost a week, essentially without shelter, in the middle of the Sierra, at high elevation, in winter, is astonishing.

There was no guarantee they would survive the trip out of the mountains, however. Most of them could not walk, and the deep snow made it impossible to bring in pack animals. Nor could all seven men of the relief party be expected to help. Eddy and Foster, understandably focused on plucking their own children from the high camps, kept going toward the pass, taking two other men along with them.

That left three rescuers staring down into the pit at Starved Camp. Charles Stone and Howard Oakley each picked up a child and started walking, arguing that given their party's limited manpower, the best they could do was save a handful of the survivors and abandon the rest. The third rescuer, however, balked at such a brutal triage.

John Stark's ancestors bequeathed him a streak of toughness. His father hewed a life from the wildlands of Kentucky; his mother was a cousin of Daniel Boone. Like many of those involved in the rescue efforts, he too had been an emigrant in 1846, going west with his wife and children and her extended family. His father-in-law and brother-in-law helped in the early stages of the relief effort, although neither ever made it to Truckee Lake. Stark was a big man—he weighed 220 pounds, a giant for the day—and stubborn in the best sense of the word.

As his colleagues walked away, he faced the seemingly impossible task of rescuing nine people single-handedly: all seven members of the Breen family and the two older Graves children, Nancy and Jonathan. Perhaps he pondered the strength of his pioneer ancestors. Perhaps he just refused to give up on a job. Perhaps he thought of his own overland migration and realized that with a little bad luck it might be he and his wife and his children looking up from the pit.

He decided he would not simply pick up a child and leave the others to die, as his comrades had. He would bring them all in. He would carry the little ones, encourage the older ones, bolster the adults, drag the whole party down out of the snow.

So he launched an extraordinary one-man relay. Already shouldering a backpack with provisions, blankets, and an axe, he picked up one or two of the smaller children, carried them a little ways, then went back for the others. Then he repeated the whole process. Again and again. To galvanize morale, he laughed and told the youngsters they were so light from months of mouse-sized rations that he could carry them all simultaneously, if only his back were broad enough. When they asked about his stamina, he said that once they were out of the snow he would eat something and take a rest. Somehow, he even coaxed or cajoled or bullied Patrick Breen down from the camp, although initially everyone thought that the family patriarch could not walk. In the end, all the survivors from Starved Camp made it down to safety.

The Breens treasured Stark's heroism, then and for the rest of their lives. When the party finally got down out of the snow, Peggy Breen was astonished to hear Woodworth take credit for the rescue. "I thank nobody but God and Stark and the Virgin Mary," she replied. Years later, Billy Graves, who heard the story, noted that she put Stark second, behind only God and ahead of the Madonna. "I think he deserved it," Graves wrote.

None for Tears

28

Nicholas Clark, the sturdy rescuer detailed by James Reed to stay with the Donner families, made sure he was out of earshot of the tents. He was outside with Jean Baptiste Trudeau, the teenager who had also been taking care of the Donners. Clark confided that he planned to leave, perhaps at the arrival of the next rescue party, perhaps even sooner. Nobody could blame him. George Donner was already half dead, and surely incapable of ever leaving the mountains. The three little Donner girls had been sent off with Stone and Cady, and Clark, who was at Alder Creek, had no way of knowing that the tots had been abandoned at the Truckee Lake cabins. The girls' mother, Tamzene, was healthy enough to go whenever she wanted. The only other people at Alder Creek were Betsy Donner and two of her children, Samuel and Lewis, but they too were all but dead. For Clark to stay any longer would be to risk his own life just so he could chop firewood for people who were going to die anyway. He admitted he was afraid he might starve to death, a reasonable fear given the struggles faced by the other rescuers in getting back down to civilization.

Trudeau had an even stronger case. He had been healthy enough to leave with either of the first two relief parties but had been prevailed upon to stay and help care for the Donners. Like Clark, there wasn't much more he could do by staying, so he vowed that he too would leave at the first opportunity. "I have been here four months," he told Clark, "and it is my turn if anybody's."

The two men set out for the lake cabins, and when they arrived were astonished to find the three little Donner girls. For days, Clark had been assuming that Cady and Stone had fulfilled their pledge to Tamzene Donner and taken her daughters over the mountains. Instead, here they were, stuck in a cabin with Keseberg and the Murphys. Clark stayed the night, then went back the next morning to Alder Creek to tell Tamzene that her daughters remained in danger.

Tamzene bent over the bed of the husband she had nursed for months. He drifted toward death every day now, weaker and weaker. She detested the idea of leaving, for it was obvious that he might die while she was away, but there was simply no choice but to go and make some arrangement for the girls. She bundled herself up in the warmest of the tattered clothes she had left, took one last look back toward George's sickbed, and headed for the lake.

THE LITTLE RESCUE PARTY LED BY William Eddy and William Foster burst into the cabin with the frenetic energy of adrenaline and emotion. Everyone was talking at once. "They came in like they were most wild," remembered Frances Donner. "We were frightened at first."

Eddy and Foster asked about their sons: three-year-old James Eddy and two-year-old George Foster, tots left behind when their parents fled with the Forlorn Hope or simply died. Both fathers had rushed back into the mountains determined to save their sons. That had been the justification for leaving children behind, after all—that the parents could summon help and return in time. Now Eddy and Foster wanted to know if they had made it. There must have been a mortified silence, eyes shifting downward, then perhaps a sad and subdued confession. Both little boys were dead, and yet that was not even the worst of it. Their bodies had been cannibalized by the survivors. By one account, Eddy grew so enraged with Keseberg over the cannibalism that he vowed to kill him later, a threat that was never fulfilled.

But the rescuers found four living children—Simon Murphy and the three little Donner girls—and resolved to save them all. Clark and Trudeau would go along too. Keseberg still refused. That left two women, Tamzene Donner, who had reached the lake cabins, and Levinah Murphy. Murphy had herded her extended clan on the great migration: herself, seven children, two sons-in-law, and three grandchildren. The family had slowly dwindled—some went out with the Forlorn Hope, some with the first relief parties, some died—while she herself had withered and weakened. But she kept Simon alive—he was her youngest—and she was kind to the Donner girls after they were abandoned at the cabins. Keseberg had ordered the girls to stay in bed, insisting that otherwise they were underfoot. Levinah enforced no such rule. When Keseberg left to gather wood, she let the girls get out of bed and play, a benevolence they would not forget.

She was far too weak for the journey out, a fact she recognized and did not protest, perhaps because she could reflect with pride that she had done all she could for her own children and the children of others. "As we were ready to start," remembered Georgia Donner, "Mrs. Murphy walked to her bed, laid down, turned her face toward the wall. One of the men gave her a handful of dried meat. She seemed to realize that we were leaving her, that her work was finished."

HAVING REACHED THE LAKE CABINS, Eddy and Foster had no intention of hiking the extra distance to Alder Creek. The warning of Starved Camp rang with clarity: Parties in the open could be trapped by a sudden blizzard and held for days, pushed to shocking desperation. The only sane thing was to keep moving, to get up the mountains and back down again as quickly as possible. Dawdling begged calamity.

From the standpoint of the rescuers, no real purpose would be served by going to the Donner family tents. Everyone there—George Donner; Jacob's widow, Betsy; and her two sons, Lewis and Samuel—was dead or dying. None would see spring. Better to turn around, leave now, and make it back down to Johnson's Ranch before another storm struck.

But Tamzene Donner was adamant. She would not leave her husband so long as he drew breath. There was no hope he would live, but she would not let him die alone. To check on her girls, she had been forced to come over to the lake briefly, but now she would return to Alder Creek. He might already be dead—she told her daughters as much—but she insisted that she go and see. If he was dead, she would return immediately and walk out with the rescue party.

But while Tamzene was still in sight, the rescuers, standing on the snow before the cabins with the children, yelled to her that they had no intention of waiting. They were going on, and she could come or not. It was her choice. She must have known that this was her last chance, must have realized that her choice wasn't merely about sacrificing herself but about choosing which members of her family would have to share the burden. Either she could let her husband die alone or let her children grow up without a mother.

She knew what her daughters would face; her own mother had died when she was young. But perhaps she thought back to her first family, to the long years of darkness after their deaths, to the new life she had found through her marriage to George. Perhaps she had simply made a promise she could not break. None of her daughters ever described a hesitancy, a pause, a flicker of irresolution. She just kept walking.

And then the parting was done, the rescuers hauling the children off toward the pass, toward safety and away from their mother. "There was hardly time for words or action," Georgia Donner remembered, "and none for tears."

It was the last time the Donner girls ever saw their mother. Years later, they could not remember what she looked like.

HEADING WEST, THE MARCHERS FOUND A SMALL PACKAGE on the snow, apparently dropped by Stone and Cady, containing silk skirts that Tamzene Donner had given to the men she thought were saving her daughters. The Donner girls were wearing the best clothes they had left—petticoats and linsey-woolsey dresses—but after months of entrapment they must have been sodden with snow and rich with vermin. The men pulled out knives and, as best they could, quickly recut the newly found clothes to fit the girls in makeshift ways, then tied them to the youngsters.

Before it had been killed and consumed, the Donner family dog had eaten Frances's shoes, and so now she was wearing a pair of her mother's, too big by far. They kept falling off as she tried to pull her feet out of the deep holes in the snow made by the adults' footsteps. Eventually a rescuer named Thompson, who was in charge of her, got tired of pulling the oversized shoes out of the snow and putting them back on her, so he left them and told her to walk in her stocking feet. After a time, he took pity on her and took off his mittens, using them as a pair of moccasins for her feet and going bare-handed himself. Later, he told her that if she walked up a hill he would give her some sugar. "The sugar was something to climb for so I got my prize," she recalled.

Some incentives were less generous. Frances was walking, but Eliza and Georgia were being carried. The men tired, put them on the snow, and told them they too must make their own way. The girls refused to budge, so the men reached down and gave them each a spanking. "There was a crying bee," Frances remembered.

But somehow the girls kept going, some of the smallest children to make the long journey without either parent present. Georgia said later that when she thought of the rescuers' efforts, the agonies faded. "I do not feel like I ought to complain."

JOHN BREEN AWOKE TO A WONDERLAND. His rescue and delivery from Starved Camp was complete, as was that of his family members, but they had arrived at Johnson's Ranch late at night, well after dark. In the morning, he found a world he had not seen for months:

> The weather was fine. The ground was covered with fine green
> grass and there was a very fat beef hanging from the limb of an

oak tree. The birds were singing from the tops of the trees above our camp and the journey was over. I stood looking on the scene and could scarcely believe that I was alive.

ONE LAST RELIEF EFFORT REMAINED. A small company set out in late March from Johnson's Ranch, mostly consisting of veterans of earlier rescue parties who found the will to try again. They reached the snow, but then quickly abandoned the effort. There were stories that the snow, touched by the first kiss of spring, was now so soft that progress was impossible. Another recollection held that a fresh storm blew in and blocked their way.

Or perhaps they just gave up. The only people who could conceivably be rescued were Keseberg and Tamzene Donner, and both of them had been healthy enough to travel when the previous party left the lake. Rescuers could be forgiven for a reluctance to risk their own lives to save people who had failed to save themselves. Whatever the reason, the last little party turned around and headed back down the mountains. If anyone was still alive at the high camps, they would have no rescue soon.

The Last Man

29

By mid-April, a month had passed since the last relief party had left the lake camp. Little hope prevailed that anyone remained alive. Survival on almost nothing but human flesh seemed an impossibility, nutritionally and psychologically, particularly since the handful of emigrants left behind would have had few comrades to bolster their morale.

The principal idea now was to bring in property rather than persons. John Sinclair, the local *alcalde* for the area around Sutter's Fort, cut a deal with a small group of would-be salvage agents led by a flamboyant mountain man named William Fallon, a giant known as "Le Gros" but also reputed to be so agile that he could pluck a sixpence from the ground while riding a galloping horse. The men would be allowed to keep half the property they collected from the camps of the two Donner families, including gold and silver. Sinclair, acting as an ad hoc child welfare agency, would take the other half and use it for the benefit of the orphaned Donner children. The contract specifying the terms of the deal made no mention of survivors until after the financial details were spelled out at length, and even then the treatment was perfunctory, addressing the issue of survivors' property rather than their lives. So when, about two weeks later, Fallon reemerged with a last surviving member of the Donner Party in tow, the small communities around Johnson's Ranch and Sutter's Fort buzzed with curiosity: How had anyone stayed alive so long? What had happened up there?

S IX WEEKS LATER, the *California Star* landed on the newsstands of San Francisco with an answer, courtesy of Fallon's diary. Fallon and his men had arrived to find the lake cabins deserted—at least by the living. The bodies of the dead lay everywhere, "terribly mutilated, legs, arms, and sculls scattered in every direction." A woman's body, thought to be that of Eleanor Eddy, lay near the entrance, "the limbs severed off and a frightful gash in the scull." Most of the flesh had been eaten from the bones, and "a painful stillness pervaded the place."

At the Alder Creek camps, the mood proved equally eerie. Jacob Donner's tent had been ransacked. Household goods—books, calicoes, shoes, furniture—lay everywhere. The bloody evidence of cannibalism presented a gruesome scene:

> At the mouth of the tent stood a large iron kettle, filled with human flesh cut up, it was from the body of Geo. Donner, the head had been split open, and the brains extracted therefrom, and to the appearance, he had not been long dead, not over three or four days at the most.

The carcass of an ox lay nearby, apparently preserved—and perhaps hidden—for much of the winter in the snow, yet almost wholly uneaten.

They spent a day packing—camping and working amid the dreadful scene—and then half the group started back for the lake cabins, the other half staying to cache whatever property they could not carry. When they returned to the lake, they were surprised to find Lewis Keseberg alive, lying next to "a large pan full of fresh liver and lights."

Keseberg said he was the lone survivor. Tamzene Donner, relatively healthy when the previous rescuers departed, had lost her way trying to hike from Alder Creek to the lake cabins, spent a night on the snow, and died soon after reaching Keseberg's wretched hovel. He seemed almost enthusiastic about his own resourcefulness—Tamzene Donner's flesh was "the best he had ever tasted"—but evasive about the property of the other emigrants. "He appeared embarrassed, and equivocated a great deal," then insisted that he had no property from any of the other families. But when the rescuers searched him, they found silks and jewelry worth two hundred dollars, and a brace of pistols that had once belonged to George Donner. Hidden in his waistcoat, they found $225 in gold.

They began threatening him, insisting that the other rescuers would hang him unless he came clean. A rescuer named John Rhoads decided to play the good cop and took Keseberg off to one side. If he owned up to everything, Rhoads said, he would be well treated and given help in getting down to the settlements. Through it all, Keseberg maintained his innocence.

The interrogation continued the next day, this time reinforced by the other rescuers. Fallon asked about a large amount of gold that George Donner had reportedly been carrying, and then grabbed a rope and threatened to hang Keseberg if he kept feigning ignorance. He fashioned a noose and threw it around Keseberg's neck, then pushed him to the ground and yanked the rope tight. At last, Keseberg relented and led them back to a spot near Alder Creek where he had buried the Donners' money.

The rescuers took him down to the settlements, but before the whole party left the mountains, they asked Keseberg why he had not eaten the ox meat. He replied that it was too dry. Humans made better eating. The brains made an excellent soup.

THAT WAS THE TALE TOLD IN FALLON'S DIARY, although Keseberg offered a different story. Left alone when Levinah Murphy died, he resisted the idea of cannibalism for four days after his provisions gave out, finally resorting to the grisly option so that he might live to support his family:

> There was no other resort—it was that or death. My wife and child had gone on with the first relief party. I knew not whether they were living or dead. They were penniless and friendless in

a strange land. For their sakes I must live, if not for my own.... I can not describe the unutterable repugnance with which I tasted the first mouthful of flesh. There is an instinct in our nature that revolts at the thought of touching, much less eating, a corpse. It makes my blood curdle to think of it! It has been told that I boasted of my shame—said that I enjoyed this horrid food, and that I remarked that human flesh was more palatable than California beef. This is a falsehood. It is a horrible, revolting falsehood. This food was never otherwise than loathsome, insipid, and disgusting.

Too weak to move the bodies of the dead, Keseberg lay in his cabin surrounded by corpses, and at times became so unnerved that he put his pistol in his mouth and fingered the trigger.

Late one night, Tamzene Donner arrived, cold and fatigued, her clothes frozen into ice. She said that George had died, and now she was intending to walk over the mountains alone, for she had to reach her children. She refused Keseberg's offer of human flesh, so he put her into bed and covered her as warmly as possible. By morning she was dead, and Keseberg was again alone.

He had promised Tamzene that he would retrieve the family's money and use it for her children, so when he felt strong enough he hiked over to Alder Creek. He buried the silver in a spot marked by a low-hanging tree branch and packed the gold back toward the lake cabins. Halfway there, the snow gave way beneath his feet, and he plunged down into a stream running beneath the snow. As he fell, he threw out his arms and managed to fall no deeper than his armpits, and then eventually managed to hoist himself from the hole. By the time he reached his cabin, he was half-frozen.

The next morning, he awoke to human voices. He rushed outside and saw the rescuers coming toward him, the relief that had seemed an impossible dream. But to his astonishment, they did not greet him with joy but with a simple and gruff demand: "Where is Donner's money?"

Worried about keeping his promise to Tamzene that the money would go to her children, Keseberg would not answer, begging instead for a bit of food. The men refused and threatened to kill him if he failed to hand over the money. With no other choice, he gave them the gold and told them where to find the buried silver. Heading down the mountains to safety, they offered no help to the pathetic, weakened fellow. Instead they concentrated on shuttling down two packs, each filled with booty, and left Keseberg to struggle into camp on his own.

WHOSE VERSION TO BELIEVE? In the common lore of the Donner Party, then and for 150 years to follow, Fallon's picture of Keseberg as a bloodthirsty ghoul held sway, perhaps because it intermingled with and reinforced an image already in the public mind. Even before Fallon's journal appeared, a newspaper account claimed that one of the survivors—unnamed but obviously Keseberg—took a child to bed with him and ate the youngster before morning, then ate another before noon the next day. Such yarns obviously involved scurrilous exaggeration if not outright falsehood, but Fallon's diary echoed the theme. Almost as soon as Keseberg came down from the mountains, the stories blossomed into the most damning rumor possible: He had murdered Tamzene Donner so that he might eat her body.

Surely the Fallon diary is, at best, half true. Donner Party scholars have long observed that the language—"evinced confusion" and "evident reluctance" and the like—is too refined for Fallon's rough-hewn life. And there is a lyrical quality at points that seems foreign to a mountain man's pen: "A painful stillness pervaded the place." Nor was it long before little pieces of the story began to crumble: A newspaper retracted the claim that it was Eleanor Eddy's body near the cabin door, and a summertime traveler found George Donner's body months later, apparently not mutilated. Furthermore, it seems incredible that Keseberg would have praised human flesh as moister and more succulent than beef.

And yet the diary must be right in describing Keseberg and the camp in hideous terms. By the time the final rescuers arrived, Keseberg had been alone for days, perhaps weeks, surviving on nothing more than human flesh. He had no choice but to crudely butcher the bodies, and probably had little energy to dispose of the remains. Indeed, a more sober and less biased source suggests precisely such a scene, without attributing to Keseberg the morbid enthusiasm reported by Fallon. More than thirty years after the tragedy, Reason Tucker, who led the first relief party and participated in the last, wrote of bones scattered about and skulls opened to get at the brains. It was a place, he said, of "Death & Destruction."

O N ONE POINT, THERE COULD BE NO DISPUTE. When Keseberg and the final group of rescuers arrived at Johnson's Ranch in the closing days of April 1847, the ordeal of the Donner Party was over. Of the eighty-one people who had been trapped by the early autumn snow at the eastern edge of the Sierra, thirty-six had died and forty-five had survived. No one remained at the high camps. For the Donner Party, the journey was finished.

30

The warmth of spring seeped through the rich riverbed land of the Napa Valley as surely as the cold had penetrated the huts at Truckee Lake. Barely two months after her rescue, Virginia Reed's mind was already turning to gentler matters. She wrote her cousin back in Illinois and boasted of her new homeland as a hunting ground for husbands:

> Tel Henriet if she wants to get Married for to come to California. She can get a spanyard any time.

It was only mid-May, but beef and bread had fattened the survivors' once-skeletal forms. "We are all verry fleshey," Virginia reported, as though this were an astonishing fact. Her mother weighed 140 pounds, or, as Virginia styled it, "10040 pon." In all, California had proved a worthy haven, a land of warm days and cool nights, of wide valleys and stout horses. "It is a beautiful Country," she wrote. "It aut to be a beautiful Country to pay us for our trubel getting there."

Not that the tragedy had vanished from Virginia's mind. Her letter gave a long, detailed account of much that had happened—one of the most valuable versions among all the Donner Party records—and then added a declaration that even greater horrors lay unstated:

O Mary I have not wrote you half of the truble we have had but I hav Wrote you anuf to let you now that you don't now what truble is. But thank the Good god we have all got throw and the onely family that did not eat human flesh. We have left every thing but i dont cair for that. We have got through.

Still, she wanted no part of hopelessness, harbored no desire to discourage those who might follow: "Dont let this letter dishaten anybody." She offered a single piece of advice, an admonition that might have served as the motto not only for the grand migration west but also for much of life: "Never take no cutofs and hury along as fast as you can."

THAT SUMMER, GEN. STEPHEN WATTS KEARNY, who had commanded the American armies in California during the brief war with Mexico, left Sutter's Fort to return east. When he reached Truckee Lake, he stopped to inspect the cabins, snowless now and surrounded by the natural hustle of a short mountain growing season—wildflowers and green grass, does nursing fawns, the flutter of butterflies and the buzz of mosquitoes where once could be heard only the murmured prayers of the starving.

Human remains lay about, the flesh mummifying in the dry mountain air and the bones scattered in the cabins. Edwin Bryant, the newspaper writer who had traveled the first part of the westward journey with the Donners and who was now going east with Kearny, described the scene as "human skeletons . . . in every variety of mutilation. A more revolting and appalling spectacle I never witnessed."

Kearny ordered a pit dug in one of the cabins and the bones thrown in, "melancholy duties to the dead," as Bryant phrased it. The cabin was torched, the men standing around hatless and solemn as they watched this impromptu pyre in the wilderness.

At Alder Creek, Kearny found George Donner's body, and with it the final evidence of Tamzene Donner's steadfast devotion. Before leaving for the lake cabins, she had wrapped her husband's remains in a sheet, the closest approximation of a decent burial she could provide.

F OR A FEW OF THE SURVIVORS, the tragedy of the Donner Party proved an unshakable ghost. Nancy Graves, Elizabeth's daughter, married a Methodist minister and had nine children but was haunted by the knowledge that she had participated in the cannibalism of her own mother at Starved Camp. As a girl, she burst into tears at the memory.

Decades later, she refused to help the writer C. F. McGlashan, who was working on a history of the party. "I have no information to impart," she wrote in her only postcard to him, "and do not wish my name mentioned. I hereby notify you not to use my name in that connection." She signed her name as Mrs. R. W. Williamson, omitting any use of Graves, the maiden name that would identify her as a member of the cursed emigrant contingent.

Eliza Donner, by contrast, cherished her place in history. She married a promising young attorney named Sherman Houghton—he went on to serve two terms in Congress—and later she took up a vigorous correspondence with McGlashan. In her late sixties she published her memoir, *The Expedition of the Donner Party and Its Tragic Fate*. On the cover and title page, she identified herself as Eliza P. Donner Houghton, embracing her maiden name as much as Nancy Graves had spurned hers.

Most survivors reflected neither Graves's reluctance toward the past nor Donner's enthusiasm for it. Most simply moved on, constructing new lives and displaying the remarkable resilience of the human soul. They married, reared children, tilled farms or built businesses, cherished advances and rued setbacks. They stopped by a saloon on Saturday and a church on Sunday. Some died young. Some saw their dotage.

James Reed never lost his on-the-make optimism and eventually touted the Gold Rush with the same heedless confidence that had once led him down the Hastings Cut-Off. "The gold is still plenty, plenty, plenty, and will continue plenty through this century and the next, and the next!" he wrote to his brother-in-law in 1849, after the family had settled in San Jose. "You find it in the big hills, you find it in the little rivers, you find it in the little branches, you find it in the little narrow indentations made on the surface of the earth during brief showers."

Nor did the capacity for boasting desert him. Real estate was booming, and he was glad to say he had shown the wisdom to invest. "As for myself I have a share and a fair share, too, after all my misfortunes."

Margret Reed, who had worked so diligently to keep her children alive, never found the robust health that California seemed to promise and died at forty-seven, fifteen years after the tragedy. Virginia eloped at sixteen and eventually had nine children. Her sister, Patty, had eight. Neither of the Reed sons had children. For a time, they both lived with Patty. Virginia Reed fulfilled the personal pledge she had made in the mountains and, against her parents' wishes, became a Roman Catholic.

The Breens repaired to the Mission at San Juan Bautista, where they were feted as conquerors of the harsh mountains, ensconced in the best house in town and bathed in Mexican hospitality. "Nothing that could add to the comfort of the sufferers was left undone," James Breen wrote later. In time the family prospered. Edward Breen, the boy whose fall from the saddle broke his leg so badly that it was nearly amputated, grew into a strapping man of more than six feet tall. He was an excellent horseman.

By some weird coincidence, three of the other Breen sons—Patrick Jr., Simon, and James—died within three months of each other in 1899.

The Donner orphans found homes where they could. Two of the three little daughters of Tamzene Donner were taken in by a German couple who lived near Sutter's Fort. The Reeds took some of the others.

The Murphy and Graves children were orphans too. Mary Murphy eventually married a prominent local man named Charles Covillaud. When a town sprang up near their home along the Yuba River, it was named Marysville in honor of Covillaud's wife. Simon Murphy, one of the last children rescued, returned to his home state of Tennessee and later served in the Civil War. So far as is known, he never returned to California.

Two of the Graves girls married men who assisted in the rescue efforts, although neither ever actually reached the high camps. Sarah married William Dill Ritchie, who six years later was caught with stolen mules and lynched. Mary, the belle of the train, froze her feet so badly during the journey of the Forlorn Hope that for three months she could not wear shoes. She married a rescuer named Edward Pyle Jr., who was murdered in 1848. After the trial Mary cooked meals for the murderer. She did not want him to die before the hanging day.

Billy Graves went east the next summer, where he soon grew weary of incessant questions about his titillating ordeal. He told the story "so many thousand times," he remembered later.

William Eddy, who lost his wife and two children in the tragedy despite his own heroic efforts, married twice more, the first ending in divorce. He died in 1859, on Christmas Eve.

Jean Baptiste Trudeau, one of the few single men to survive, never forgot the suffering of the mountains. Years later, when he was a poor man scraping out a hard and dangerous living as a fisherman, he said that even if he were offered half the state of California, he would refuse to spend another winter like the one he endured with the Donner Party.

Lewis Keseberg suffered more than anyone else, although in many ways this had more to do with public perceptions than actual events. On his arrival at Sutter's Fort, whispering rumors painted him a ghoul. The gossip compounded until, motivated by an especially wagging and malevolent tongue, Keseberg sued one of his own rescuers for defamation. The jury found in Keseberg's favor but concluded that his slanderers had broken tarnished goods: Damages totaled one dollar. In time he became a public caricature, the demented ogre who had relished his cannibalism. Business setbacks pushed him into poverty. Even the lottery of biology struck against him: Two of his daughters were born with disabilities that rendered them, in the language of the day, "idiots." Keseberg came to see himself as Job, singled out by God for afflictions designed to test his soul. He died a poor man, his burial unrecorded.

For brief periods in the years after the Donner Party, though, Keseberg enjoyed business successes. During one of them, he ran a Sacramento hotel, the Lady Adams. It might be strange enough that the putative fiend chose to enter a business where he would host weary travelers, but public fascination with the Donner Party was such that even that irony was insufficient. It may or may not be true, but the accepted lore of the tale came to be that the most notorious cannibal of the Donner Party eventually opened a restaurant.

THE FATES OF THE RESCUERS PROVED AS MIXED as those of the survivors. Selim Woodworth overcame the inauspicious start to his career as a naval officer. He commanded a supply ship during the remainder of the Mexican-American War, winning the respect of his men, and during the Civil War rose to the rank of commodore.

Hiram Miller remained a friend of the Reed family for decades, settling near them in California. Smallpox eventually swept through, infecting Miller, and after a time of quarantine in the local "pest house" he moved to the Reed home, where he was an invalid for the last five years of his life. They buried him in a cemetery nearby. Patty Reed, the little girl who had baked him bread when he arrived as a member of the second relief party, and to whom Miller had been kind, tended his grave for years.

William Fallon, the mountain man who led the last relief party, eventually went east but was traveling back to California in 1848 when he grew frustrated with the slow pace of the train and, with one other man, rode ahead. They were attacked and killed by Indians. Weeks later the main party found their bodies.

John Stark never got the public acclaim he deserved for his heroic rescue of the Breens from Starved Camp. In his report about the relief effort, Woodworth omitted Stark's name entirely, taking credit for those Stark saved. But his fine qualities drew recognition in other ways. He was the sheriff of Napa County for six years and even served in the state legislature. In 1875, when he was fifty-eight, the body that had sustained him through his remarkable performance in the mountains finally gave out. While pitching hay from a wagon, he had a heart attack and died.

Reason Tucker, the leader of the first relief party to reach the high camps, later spent two years in the gold fields, one with luck, one without. He built a fine home of split redwood near Calistoga, the back commanding an ostentatious view of the verdant Napa Valley, but later lost his estate in a dispute growing out of the settlement of Mexican land claims. A marriage collapsed amid uncertain circumstances, and in time he moved to Goleta, near Santa Barbara, where he lived out his days amid the gentle swells of coastal hills and ocean breakers. When he died, in 1888, he was buried beneath a white marble marker that reached back more than forty years to a moment of valor: "An honest candid worthy man—one of the heroic rescuers of Donner Party." Tucker would have liked the epitaph. He never forgot the scenes that greeted his arrival at the Truckee Lake cabins, an appearance that put the survivors in mind of angels. Years later, he could still see the rude huts and hear the emigrants' shouts of joy.

LANSFORD HASTINGS DREAMED HIS DREAMS to the end. The man who had envisioned a magical shortcut to California served as a delegate to the state constitutional convention in 1849 and then moved to markedly bigger stages. During the Civil War he hatched a fruitless scheme to conquer Arizona for the Confederacy. When he died a few years later, he was trying to plant a colony of former southerners in Brazil, as though his former efforts to lure midwesterners to California had been insufficiently grand.

Other parties stumbled along the Hastings Cut-Off, the chimera that had so worsened the Donner Party's woes. But the route never became a main channel of the great migration, and a single bald fact testifies to the rigors of the inhospitable terrain: So far as is known, no one ever traveled it twice.

AS SHE TRIED TO WALK OUT OF THE MOUNTAINS, before she died and her body was cannibalized, Elizabeth Graves had carried a heavier load than most. The Graves family wagon featured secret grooves in the middle of the bed—hiding places for the profit from the sale of the family farm back in Illinois. Before leaving the lake, rescuers helped Elizabeth pry up the coverings and recover the gold and silver, said to be eight hundred dollars in all. She lugged it along as best she could but eventually concluded she would have to stash it, perhaps because the rescuers were bantering about who would take the cash when she died, talk that was later dismissed as joking but must have seemed sinister to Elizabeth. So she hung back from the march one morning and buried the money, marking the location in her mind as best she could. So far as we know, she failed to tip off her children to the secret spot before her death a few days later, and so it seemed that the youngsters had lost their inheritance.

Then, on a spring day in 1891, almost half a century later, a miner named Edward Reynolds was digging for quartz on a hillside near Truckee when the glint of coin sparkled in his shovel. None of the pieces was dated after 1845, and the Graves children, now grown and graying adults, identified bite marks on a coin that had once been used as a family teething ring. Billy Graves, eighteen when his mother died, claimed the money.

In one of the last acts of her life, Elizabeth Graves had succeeded. She had saved the family inheritance for her children.

B Y THE TIME THE COINS WERE FOUND, Truckee Lake had become Donner Lake. Today, the surrounding countryside is rife with other imprints of the great drama. The notch in the mountains above the lake is Donner Pass; a nearby summit is Donner Peak.

Men tamed those tormenting heights with remarkable speed. Less than a quarter century after the tragedy—well within the lifetimes of most survivors—workers laid the tracks of the transcontinental railroad across the pass. In time, a two-lane road followed for automobiles, then at last a superhighway that bears the brunt of winter and remains open through all but the fiercest storms. Donner Lake is surrounded by vacation homes. The little valley near the summit where the Breens passed their hellish ordeal in the snowpit is now a ski area, chairlifts shuttling skiers upward with ease, all to be followed by a hot chocolate and a cozy drive home.

Even a century ago, survivors marveled at the transformation. In 1892 Virginia Reed read a description of Donner Lake as a "pleasure resort" and sensed in the phrase strange evidence of all that had changed:

It seems ages since I was there yet I can feel the cold and hunger and hear the moan of the pines. Those proud old trees used to tell me when a storm was coming and seemed to be about the only thing there alive, as the snow could not speak. And now the place is a pleasure resort. The moan of the pines should cease.

Yet still the Sierra winter can rise and growl. Lay yourself open to the elements, and you may suffer as the emigrants of old. In 2004 a sudden blizzard in late October—about the same time of the year that the Donner Party was trapped—left thirteen hikers temporarily stranded. Two climbers in Yosemite National Park died.

FROM THE BEGINNING, ONE PLAIN TRUTH of the Donner Party saga stood out against the sexist assumptions of the age: Women toughed it out far better than the men. The first book to tell the tale, J. Quinn Thornton's *Oregon and California in 1848*, included a crude chart outlining the different survival rates for men and women. Thornton noted that twenty-eight men died compared to only eight women. Even accounting for the greater number of men in the party, Thornton found that men tended to die while women tended to live. Nineteenth-century sensibilities admitted no explanation for this outcome, and Thornton hazarded no guesses.

One plausible theory was that, in effect, manliness killed the men. Much of the hard physical labor, both on the overland journey and during the entrapment, fell to the males. Men broke trail, drove the wagons, hitched and unhitched the teams. So far as we know, hunting was an exclusively male chore. Perhaps, therefore, the men were already weaker than the women when the party arrived at the Sierra, and then weakened still more as the taxation of masculine camp duties conflicted with a steadily diminishing diet.

But in the nineteenth century, female work was hardly for the frail. Women hauled water for cooking and washing. They produced the meals using cumbersome iron skillets and bulky Dutch ovens. Female arms and shoulders stirred the butter churn and rasped the family clothes across the washboard. At least on the open prairie, gathering firewood was more a woman's job than a man's. And walking was everyone's lot, especially as the draft animals deteriorated. The women, in other words, may have been just as exhausted as the men after months of travel.

That suggests that the greater male death rate may have been due to biology as well as behavior, a supposition buttressed by modern science. On average, women have a higher percentage of body fat than men. Fat acts as a storehouse for energy, meaning that as women starve, they have greater reserves on which to draw. Men, by contrast, begin to burn valuable muscle much faster. That difference only exacerbates another female advantage: Since women are, on average, smaller than men, they need fewer calories. The men confronted a dual curse. They needed more food than the women, and once their bodies began the internal process of self-consumption, the women were better equipped to endure it. Bravado aside, masculinity proved a deadly disadvantage.

Age intermingled with gender as a determinant of survival. In fact, statistical analyses have found that age trumped other factors. The young and the old, beset with too little exposure to life's abrasions and too much, always die first and most in tragedies. In the Donner Party, children under five exhibited a high death rate, as did adults in their forties and over. Of those who were trapped in the mountains, only two older adults survived, Patrick Breen, thought to be fifty-one, and Peggy Breen, about forty, both of whom benefited from their family's relatively plentiful hoard of beef. The three other couples who were over forty—George and Tamzene Donner, Jacob and Betsy Donner, and Franklin and Elizabeth Graves—all died.

In the prime of life, the gender disparity was especially pronounced, so pronounced that it may in fact suggest another cause altogether. Among those who were in their twenties, only one woman died (Eleanor Eddy), while only one man lived (William Eddy). The other seven men in their twenties, men presumably in the best physical condition of their lives, all died, many of them early in the entrapment.

Most of these men were distinguished, however, not only by their age but also by their life circumstances: They were traveling alone, typically as hired hands. The young women, by contrast, were all married, most with children, many with extended families.

To gauge the value of human connection, modern researchers have studied the health effects of social networks. Their findings buttress the common intuition that people are good for people. Those with interconnected lives—people who are married or have large families or many friends or whose lives in some way bring them into contact with others—enjoy longer, healthier lives. They sniffle through fewer colds, suffer fewer heart attacks, recover faster from the debilitating effects of strokes. Even the incidence of cancer is reduced. One study followed participants for nine years and found that those who were low in "social capital"—the strings that bind us to others—were two to three times more likely to die than those with interwoven nets of human contact. Nor is this solely a modern phenomenon, alien to the Donners' day. An analysis of records from Andersonville, the notorious Confederate prison camp during the Civil War, reveals that Union captives were more likely to survive if they were imprisoned with friends, and that the closer the familiarity the greater the benefit.

The reasons for these benefits are less scientifically demonstrable but seem in many ways obvious. People draw tangible assistance from others—someone comes to check on them when they are old, for example—but they are also succored by the emotional support of love and friendship. Human beings are social creatures.

The Donner Party demonstrated anew this age-old truth. Those who were traveling with their families, especially the larger extended families, survived at rates far higher than those who were alone. Of fifteen people who were trapped in the mountains without a relative, only two survived: the Donner family employees Noah James and Jean Baptiste Trudeau. Many of the single people were among the first to die. Of the four men who died before Christmas at Alder Creek, three had no kin in camp: Sam Shoemaker, Joseph Rheinhard, and James Smith. Jacob Donner, sickly even before the trip, was the only family man among the four. Had the Donner Party been miraculously plucked from their misfortune on February 1, almost no one with a family, save those who had gone with the Forlorn Hope and thus exposed themselves to incalculable additional danger, would have perished. The Donner Party is not merely a story of how hard people will struggle to survive, but of how much they need each other if they are going to succeed.

Survivors recognized that some of the young, single men lacked the incentive or tenacity to cling to life. A few months after the tragedy, James Reed wrote to a relative back east and told of the early passing of James Smith, one of his family's teamsters. "He gave up, pined away, and died," Reed wrote. "He did not starve."

ONLY TWO FAMILIES SURVIVED INTACT, the Breens and the Reeds. This was especially remarkable for the Reeds, since James Reed's banishment left the couple's four children solely in the care of their mother, a woman who had once been so frail she had been unable to rise from her sickbed for her own wedding. Her afflicting headaches returned at least once during the winter, perhaps more. Because they had been forced to abandon so much during the crossing of the Great Salt Lake Desert, the Reeds began the entrapment with virtually no food or supplies, a penury that forced Margret to begging. Against all that, she somehow kept her four children alive.

Even her own husband, who had seen the pallor of his children's faces firsthand, could not quite seem to grasp the straits to which his family had been reduced, or the magnitude of his wife's accomplishment. Once, after the ordeal was done, the Reeds were discussing the fact that at Truckee Lake, the Reed children had found what they thought were flakes of gold. James asked his wife why she had not saved some. She could have been forgiven for punching him in the nose. Instead she looked at him with disbelief and told him that at the time, finding something to eat had seemed more important than all the gold in the world.

A Day of Renown

31

Sometime in early April 1847, shortly after most of the survivors had been brought down from the mountains, an editor in the San Francisco offices of the *California Star* peered through a green eyeshade and a wafting helix of cigar smoke and approved a story for that week's paper. Typesetters bent over their trays, and ink-stained fingers soon began laying down the metal letters that would spell out the horrors of the Donner Party. "A more shocking scene cannot be imagined," the piece began, "than that witnessed by the party of men who went to the relief of the unfortunate emigrants in the California Mountains."

> ...Bodies of men, women, and children, with half the flesh torn from them, lay on every side. A woman sat by the body of her husband, who had just died, cutting out his tongue; the heart she had already taken out, broiled, and eat! The daughter was seen eating the flesh of the father—the mother that of her children—children that of father and mother.

Worse still, survivors had lost their most basic humanity. Once they would have "shuddered and sickened" at the thought of cannibalism, but now they "coldly" calculated which of their comrades would make future meals. Family members no longer cared for one another. Some preferred human flesh to the provisions of the rescue parties.

Earlier newspaper stories had described desperation and even cannibalism, but none had sketched so vivid a picture of depravity. Most of the details were false, or at least wildly exaggerated. Of the forty-five survivors, for example, only about half tasted human flesh. Perhaps another half dozen people resorted to cannibalism before dying. A precise count is impossible, nor would one matter. The abiding mark of the Donner Party was an act of desperation, nothing more. Faced with imminent starvation and death, the pioneers did what was necessary to survive. Eating the flesh of people who had already died wasn't barbaric or animalistic. It was the only logical and reasonable course of action open to those left alive.

But such caveats made no difference. Two weeks after the *Star* story the yarn was repeated in a paper in Monterey, this time embellished even more richly: Mothers had refused food to their famished children, then eaten the youngsters once they starved.

The mold was set. The story of the Donner Party went from paper to paper and mouth to mouth, spreading across the country in a titillating admixture of exaggeration, half-truth, and lie. The tall tales worsened in the retelling, as tall tales always do. Occasionally, even the survivors themselves spread bizarre and incredible anecdotes. Frances Donner once insisted that Eleanor Eddy "died deranged:"

> In the forenoon before she died she got the benches and arranged them in the floor in imitation of people and danced the cotilliion and other dances untill she was exosted and then died.

Such sagas found purchase in the public mind for several reasons, perhaps including, ironically, the fact that the Donner Party represented no great turn of history. For a story that has fascinated the national psyche for decades, it was an evanescent affair. Like the survivors, history trudged ahead. Migration to California plummeted the next two years, but almost surely that had more to do with the uncertainties of the

Mexican-American War than with the distant travails of a few families. When gold glittered, the allure washed memories clean. A renewed flood of humanity started marching across the continent to California, willing to risk anything for a chance at life's mother lode.

Indeed, the Donner Party was far more anomalous than typical. During the twenty years at the heart of the great overland migration—from 1840 to 1860—a quarter of a million people crossed the continent, few with a result similar to that of the Donner Party. The best estimates are that perhaps 4 to 6 percent of emigrants died on the route, and of course some of those would have died back at home. Gauging the number who gave up and turned around is almost impossible, but it is clear that the great majority of those who loaded a wagon and steered westward reached their destination in safety. In the end, of course, the migration peopled California and Oregon with astonishing speed, and thus helped spread the reach of the nation toward the "manifest destiny" in which so many emigrants fervently believed. Thus the tale of the Donner Party is mismatched with its broader context, for it is a cautionary warning about an enterprise that was largely, from the standpoint of the participants, a splendid success.

Early newspaper accounts often seemed at pains to make the point that most travelers had no trouble. The *California Star* noted that some companies reached the golden shore in less than four months. Even with time to spare for resting the cattle, no more than four and a half months was needed. All "candid persons" knew as much. Mere "ordinary industry and care" ensured a crossing of the Sierra before the first snow.

The real trouble with the Donner Party, according to this line of argument, was not the inherent risks of the journey west but the company's own sloth and foolishness. Even before the first rescuers reached the cabins, the *Star* blamed the party's delay on "a contrary and contentious disposition." Everyone would have completed the trek safely, the paper claimed, if only "the men had exerted themselves as they should have done."

It would be specious to claim insight into the motives of long-dead editors, but it's worth noting that this focus on the alleged shortcomings of the Donner Party suited the interests of the emerging American establishment in California, which was eager for more emigrants. If the Donner Party could be at least partly blamed for its own travails, other prospective newcomers might not be discouraged. The last thing anyone in California wanted to suggest publicly was that a harrowing catastrophe was simply an intrinsic—if highly unlikely—risk of westward migration.

In the early years, therefore, the public imagination took on a twofold perception of the Donner Party—first that they were ghouls, second that they bore a substantial responsibility for their own misfortune. Together, these two ideas intertwined into an ugly and depressing perception of the emigrants. Some survivors rarely spoke of the events, almost as if they were hiding a shameful family secret.

But in time, a new tableau emerged. In 1879 the editor of the newspaper at Truckee, near the site of the tragedy, published a history of the Donner Party, downplaying the occurrence of cannibalism and justifying almost everything the emigrants did. The book proved popular and began to change the public perception. By the early years of the twentieth century, the Native Sons of the Golden West were ready to erect a monument to the Donner Party, a grand statue of a pioneer family striding boldly into the future. It was set atop a massive pedestal said in popular legend to reflect the height of the winter snows of 1846. No longer were the men and women of the Donner Party the sad and incompetent counterpoise to the success of the westward migration; now they were the avatars of its glories, symbols of the Pioneer archetype. The Native Sons wanted "to acknowledge the Donner Party to be typical of the entire race of pioneers, strong, resourceful, self-reliant, fearless, unconquerable spirits—who even in their death added luster to California's name." Where once "there was reproach heaped upon it," now the party's name enjoyed "a day of renown." Eventually the head of the society's monument committee went well beyond that, declaring that the Donner Party reflected not only the best of the pioneer spirit but the best of human endeavor generally. The great edifice, he declared, would "charge the minds of all who behold it with a reverence for those characters who 'gird their armor on,' who square their shoulders to the world and who take the brunt of life."

If a single day typified the rehabilitation of the Donner Party name, it was the dedication of the monument, on a hot June day in 1918, more than seventy years after the tempest. Eight survivors were still alive, three of them at the dedication: Patty Reed and Frances and Eliza Donner. Eliza had become something of a celebrity, having written a book about the Donner Party in which she attempted to disprove her family's cannibalism, and so she was seated at the head of the honored guests, just to the right of the speaker's podium. There had already been a reception the previous day, an event at which Eliza, attempting to say a few words, had choked up with uncontrollable emotion. At the dedication ceremony, she looked out over the crowd, but the faces dissolved into ghosts. She could see her mother walking away from the cabins at Donner Lake, back toward her dying husband, "her small figure moving in and out among the pine trees." Her gaze shifted, and she could see herself and her two little sisters climbing up the massive escarpment hanging above the lake.

The sharp rap of the master of ceremonies' gavel snatched away her reverie. She flashed back to the present, a time when an automobile or a train or even an airplane could carry one across Donner Pass in less time than it might take to walk to the far end of the lake. Two girls dressed in white drew away cords, and a veil fell from the monument.

WAS THE DONNER PARTY, AS THE MONUMENT builders believed, composed of heroes? In the traditional sense of the word *hero*, some members qualify. Stanton's willingness to return to a company in which he had no family members, especially when McCutchan's illness offered him a ready excuse, offered a sterling example of commitment. Eddy's leadership of the Forlorn Hope notified the California settlements of the party's dire condition and summoned help without which the entire company might have died. Rescuers displayed much valor, especially Stark, whose bullheaded insistence pulled the Breens from certain death.

But more than gleaming heroism or sullied villainy, the Donner Party is a story of hard decisions that were neither heroic nor villainous. Often, the emigrants displayed a more realistic and typically human mixture of generosity and selfishness, an alloy born of necessity. The Breens hoarded their larger supply of meat when they deemed it necessary and shared it when they thought they could. Amanda McCutchan abandoned her daughter to the care of near-strangers when she left with the Forlorn Hope, but ultimately it was the Forlorn Hope that summoned help. Jean Baptiste Trudeau stayed to help the Donners as long as he could and left when he thought he might die. Tamzene Donner orphaned her daughters to comfort a husband sure to perish. Margret Reed left behind two of her children to care for the other two. To judge such decisions from the comfort of modern life is a fool's errand. The members of the Donner Party did the best they could, which is a form of Everyman's valor.

And therein lies the true lesson and attraction of the tale: They were Everyman. Often, adventure stories feature larger-than-life figures, grand Victorian explorers or indomitable generals or pith-helmeted naturalists resolutely seeking some wondrous discovery. They are tales of men seeking the South Pole or the North, or hunting the fortune of a lifetime at sea, or climbing to the top of the world. Such quests have much to teach us, but so too does the drama of the mundane gone madly wrong. The Donner Party is a narrative of merchants and farmers, of middle-aged parents with children and young couples with dreams, of infants and toddlers and teenagers on the cusp of adulthood. It is a story of American families doing what they have always done—moving west in search of a better life. It is a story of extraordinary deeds born of ordinary devotion.

That is why the most resonant moments of the Donner Party saga are often the quietest, the times when we can see glimpses of normalcy in lives torn asunder. There is no plainer exhibition of that fact than the day Patty Reed finally escaped the interminable snows. She had ridden down out of the mountains on her exhausted father's back and been taken ahead to the camp of one of the relief parties. She was fed a meal such as she had not eaten in months—rich California beef and soft fresh bread, even the almost-forgotten taste of sugar—and then led to a seat by the fire.

No one knew it, but months before, when the family had been forced to abandon one of its wagons on the harsh deserts of Utah, Patty had saved a precious artifact. Her parents told her that nothing could be preserved, but when adult heads were turned, she snuck from the wagon bed a doll that her grandmother had made for her—a tiny wooden figurine three or four inches tall, perfect for the grasp of a small hand, with a white dress and a red shawl and a bun of black hair painted on its head. Patty hid the treasured little item in the folds of her dress, secreting away the talisman through long months of fear and heartbreak, a private friend through an ordeal that called forth from Patty the courage and stamina of an adult more than the playfulness and gaiety of a child.

But now, at the relief camp, the nightmare was over. She pulled the doll from its hiding place and sank back into the lighthearted amusements of youth. She let the firelight shine off the wooden face. She smoothed the dress with her fingers. She laughed and chattered and listened to her companion's imagined replies. "Oh, what a pleasant little hour," she remembered decades later. Writing about the ordeal, it was that memory she seemed to treasure most, not her triumph over tragedy, but her return to the commonplace.

"Little Dolly looks old now," she wrote, "but she is appreciated by Patty as much today in April 1879 as she was in April 1846. You thought Dolly handsome, did you not Mr. McGlashan, when you seen her in San Jose a few weeks ago? My fine daughters and two sons look upon Dolly with feeling and respect for that little piece of wood, for their Mama had it to play with when she was a little girl, and carried it through all her troubles too."

Author's Note

This is a work of nonfiction. The story is true. In any piece of history, however, a writer must weigh conflicting and uncertain sources and make decisions about which are to be credited, and I have done so throughout the book. The events of the Donner Party story occurred in extremely difficult circumstances, involved many people, and often were not recorded immediately. Naturally, perceptions and recollections differed, and frequently the sources do not agree. As a general rule, I have relied most heavily on primary sources written at or near the time of the events, such as journals and letters. Second, I rely on memoirs and letters written years later by individuals who were directly involved. I have tried to place relatively little emphasis or reliance on third-hand accounts.

As with all writers who have recounted the Donner Party story, I created a chronology and at times had to choose among competing sources in selecting specific dates. Although I believe all the dates included in the book are accurate, I recognize that other Donner Party historians might reach different conclusions about specific dates. To preserve the narrative, assumptions must be made.

In places, I have relied on reasonable and obvious speculation to flesh out the narrative. Some things can be assumed. Parents fret about the safety of their children. Little girls smooth the dresses of their dolls. People wave farewell. At other points, I have relied on my own observations or experiences. During my research, I traveled the route of the Donner Party, and often one can still see today what one would have seen then: the heft of Independence Rock looming in the distance, the flat crawl of the Humboldt River across Nevada, the intimidating eastern face of the Sierra. I drew on personal experiences in other ways as well. I know, for example, the feel of a Sierra blizzard—the force of the snow against your face or the staggering, almost fearsome height of the drifts.

Readers familiar with the Donner Party story will note that some names are spelled differently in this book than in most others. In particular, I use Tamzene Donner instead of Tamsen, but also William McCutchan instead of McCutchen and Margret Reed instead of Margaret. Given that nineteenth-century spellings must be deduced from handwritten documents that are often unclear, the exact spelling of a name is sometimes open to dispute. I have reviewed countless original Donner Party documents and have tried to use the same spelling used by the person involved. I thank Kristin Johnson for her excellent research into the spelling of Donner Party names, on which I have also relied, and her willingness to share her knowledge with me.

The same caution should apply to the ages of Donner Party members, many of which are also imprecise. Again, I have tried to select the most likely date of birth for each character.

In quoting letters, journals, and other materials written by survivors, I have preserved the original spelling, some of which is, to say the least, unorthodox. Often I have, however, added punctuation for ease of readership.

One last logistical matter. Many of the letters, journals, and other original source materials about the Donner Party have been reprinted over the years. In most cases, I have read the original version of the documents during archival research. However, as a general rule I cite the published versions, since they are more accessible for readers who may wish to track my research. Indeed, by purchasing two anthologies—Dale Morgan's two-volume *Overland in 1846* and Kristin Johnson's *Unfortunate Emigrants*—interested readers can gain access to most, though certainly not all, of the key primary documents. I also cite two secondary sources as they are excerpted in *Unfortunate Emigrants,* since they are extremely difficult to find in their original form. They are J. Quinn Thornton's *Oregon and California in 1848* and Eliza Farnham's *California, In-Doors and Out.*

In the notes, a few sources are referred to in abbreviated form, as follows:

"Miller-Reed Diary" refers to the diary kept by Hiram Miller and James Reed, as reprinted in Morgan, *Overland,* 256–68.

"Breen Diary" refers to the diary kept by Patrick Breen, as reprinted in Morgan, *Overland,* 310–22.

"Reed Pacific Press" refers to an account written by James Reed and published in the *Pacific Rural Press* on 3-25-71 and 4-1-71, as reprinted in Johnson, *Unfortunate,* 184–200.

Acknowledgments

For assistance of many varieties, I thank the following librarians and archivists: Susan Snyder, Erica Nordmeier, and the entire staff at the Bancroft Library at the University of California, Berkeley; Kim Walters and Liza Posas at the Braun Research Library at the Southwest Museum of the American Indian/Autry National Center in Los Angeles; Romaine Ahlstrom at the Huntington Library in San Marino, California; and John Mark Lambertson at the National Frontier Trails Museum in Independence, Missouri.

Experts in various components of the story provided assistance. Several are thanked in the notes, but my particular gratitude to Mark McLaughlin for his help in understanding Sierra Nevada weather and to Penny Rucks for helping me to understand the history of the Washoe Indians, especially their oral traditions regarding the Donner Party.

My agent, Deirdre Mullane at The Spieler Agency, was a constant source of support and assistance from proposal to final manuscript. At Oxford University Press, Cybele Tom edited the book with a sure hand. Among others at Oxford, I thank Furaha Norton, who acquired the project, production editor Joellyn Ausanka, and copy editor India Cooper, whose fine reading saved me many an error or sloppy sentence.

On a more personal level, thanks for various reasons to Dan Borenstein, Yvonne Condes, Sonia Krishnan, Mike Lewis, Anthony Loveday, and Ellen Quain, as also to my brother and his family—Jeff, Patty, Micah, and Carl Rarick. Last, my thanks to two remarkable women: My daughter, Ellie, is a joy and inspiration, while Allison Ellman provided constant love and support, not to mention great patience when I was absorbed with the countless tasks of book writing.

Notes

Chapter 1

7   scene around Tamzene: She does not describe the scene around her in great detail. The portrait here is based on various emigrant accounts.

8   "I can give you" and other material from Tamzene's letter: letter from Tamzene Donner to Elizabeth Eustis, 5-11-46, Sherman Otis Houghton Papers, HOU 13, Huntington Library.

8   "Farewell, my sister": letter from Tamzene Donner to Elizabeth Eustis, 5-11-46, Sherman Otis Houghton Papers, HOU 13, Huntington Library.

9   "the *wunderkind* nation": McPherson, *Battle Cry,* 6.

10   agricultural prices: North, *Economic Growth,* 137.

10   time and cost of land vs. sea trips: Unruh, *Plains Across,* 340–41.

10   "any person would dare": Unruh, *Plains Across,* 1.

11   "excavated by the": Unruh, *Plains Across,* 2.

11   general history of public opinion about westward migration: Unruh, *Plains Across,* 1–33.

11   "palpable homicide": Unruh, *Plains Across,* 11.

11   Bidwell Party: Unruh, *Plains Across,* 76–83; McLynn, *Wagons West,* 49–91; Morgan, *Overland,* 14–20; Bean and Rawls, *California,* 65–66; Bidwell, *Echoes,* 5–65.

12   "We knew that": Bidwell, *Echoes,* 15.

13   Stephens-Townsend-Murphy Party: Rose, "Sierra Trailblazers."

14   "very good road": Morgan, *Overland,* 19.

15   "a heap better": Morgan, *Overland,* 498.

15   "The word is": Morgan, *Overland,* 509.

15   "Weep with me": letter from Tamzene Donner to Elizabeth Eustis, 1-26-32, Sherman Otis Houghton Papers, HOU 8, Huntington Library.

15   "Sister I could die": letter from Tamzene Donner to Elizabeth Eustis, 11-22-32, Sherman Otis Houghton Papers, HOU 9, Huntington Library.

15   "Wasting with sickness": letter from Tamzene Donner to Elizabeth Eustis, 4-21-33, Eliza Poor Donner Houghton Papers, HM 58154, Huntington Library.

15   "Think not I am unhappy": letter from Tamzene Donner to Elizabeth Eustis, 4-14-36, Eliza Poor Donner Houghton Papers, HM 58156, Huntington Library.

16   "I am abundantly able": letter from Tamzene Donner to Elizabeth Eustis, 9-13-36, Eliza Poor Donner Houghton Papers, HM 58157, Huntington Library.

16 "Think you that" and other quotations this paragraph: letter from Tamzene Donner to Elizabeth Eustis, 1-16-38, Sherman Otis Houghton Papers, HOU 11, Huntington Library.

16 "Our neighbors": letter from Tamzene Donner to Elizabeth Eustis, 4-3-42, Eliza Poor Donner Houghton Papers, HM 58158, Huntington Library.

17 "Things have turned" and "I am as happy": letter from Tamzene Donner to Elizabeth Eustis, 4-3-42, Eliza Poor Donner Houghton Papers, HM 58158, Huntington Library.

17 "Who wants": Morgan, *Overland,* 491; see also 502.

17 advice to Reed: letters from James Maxey to James Reed, 11-10-45 and 3-9-46, box 8-3-308, folders 45–47, Reed Lewis Papers, Sutter's Fort.

Chapter 2

19 portrait of Margret Reed: letters from Virginia Reed to McGlashan, 5-24-79, 5-26-79, and 6-10-79, all in folder 48, McGlashan Papers, Bancroft Library; handwritten account from Patty Reed, box 8-11-308, folder 22, Reed Lewis Papers, Sutter's Fort; Reed family roster page, "New Light on the Donner Party," www.utahcrossroads.org/DonnerParty.

20 "Don't be puny": letter from James Maxey to James Reed, 11-10-45, box 8-3-308, folders 45–47, Reed Lewis Papers, Sutter's Fort. See also Morgan, *Overland,* 474–76; Reed Murphy, *Across the Plains,* 11–16; and Mullen, *Chronicles,* 54–57.

21 "We are all": letter from James Reed to James Keyes, 5-20-46, Reed Papers, Bancroft Library.

22 "mortal carear": letter from James Reed to James Keyes, 5-20-46, Reed Papers, Bancroft Library.

23 Keyes death and funeral: Morgan, *Overland,* 207–9, 278; Johnson, *Unfortunate,* 18–19; Reed Murphy, *Across the Plains,* 16; Bryant, *What I Saw,* 58–65.

24 "excessively oppressive": Bryant, *What I Saw,* 92. See also Morgan, *Overland,* 210–11, 554–57; and Bryant, *What I Saw,* 65–93.

25 elk hunt: Bryant, *What I Saw,* 71–73, 79–80, 84–85.

25 "If we had found": Rawls, *New Directions,* 106.

25 "perfect 'stars'" and other Reed quotes and descriptions of the buffalo hunt: letter from James Reed to James Keyes, 6-16-46, in Morgan, *Overland,* 274–77.

Chapter 3

27 "vexatiously slow": letter from William Russell to the *Missouri Statesman,* 6-13-46, in Morgan, *Overland,* 557–59.

27 wagons: Bryant, *What I Saw,* 37–40; Stewart, *California Trail,* 106–26.

28 advantages of oxen: Unruh, *Plains Across,* 74–75.

29 "I am beginning": Bryant, *What I Saw,* 57.

29 "All are so friendly" and other quotations from the same letter: Morgan, *Overland,* 557–63.

Chapter 4

32 "I wonder what": undated, handwritten account by Virginia Reed, folder 100, McGlashan Papers, Bancroft Library.

32 "An ideal pleasure trip" and the description of Virginia's rides: Reed Murphy, *Across the Plains,* 16.

32 daily routine of wagon trains: Many sources describe the routine of wagon trains. For two sources specific to the story of the Donner Party, see Bryant, *What I Saw,* 75–76; and Morgan, *Overland,* 557, 563. For an example of mosquitoes so thick that they threatened stock, see Bryant, *What I Saw,* 134–35. For Donner riding a pony about camp, see letter from William G. Murphy, 5-26-96, Eliza Poor Donner Houghton Papers, HM 58173, Huntington Library. For "Chain up, boys!" see letter from Tamzene Donner, 6-16-46, in Morgan, *Overland,* 561–63. The lunch is described in a letter from Virginia Reed to McGlashan, 6-10-79, folder 48, McGlashan Papers, Bancroft Library.

33 sparing livestock: letter from Edwin Bryant, 6-16-46, in Morgan, *Overland,* 559–61; letter from Nathan Putnam, 6-17-46, in Morgan, *Overland,* 564–66.

33 Keseberg wagon accident: Bryant, *What I Saw,* 71.

34 "And from their": Miller-Reed Diary, 258. This diary is useful for the basic chronology of this portion of the trip and is reproduced in Morgan, *Overland,* 256–68.

35 "rugged and sterile": Bryant, *What I Saw,* 98.

35 "knobs, or hills": letter from Charles Stanton, 6-28-46, in Morgan, *Overland,* 577–79.

36 "Our journey": letter from George Donner, 6-27-46, in Morgan, *Overland,* 576–77.

Chapter 5

37 Beaver Creek description: letter from Charles Stanton, 7-5-46, in Morgan, *Overland,* 586; Bryant, *What I Saw,* 119–21.

38 "How this important event": Bryant, *What I Saw,* 40–45.

38 July Fourth: letter from Virginia Reed, 7-12-46, in Morgan, *Overland,* 278–79; letter from Charles Stanton, 4-5-46, in Morgan, *Overland,* 582–87; Bryant, *What I Saw,* 120–21.

38 keeping the Sabbath: letter from Charles Stanton, 7-5-46, in Morgan, *Overland,* 582.

39 Reed and buffalo: letter from Charles Stanton, 7-12-46, in Morgan, *Overland,* 612.

39 temperature: letter from Virginia Reed, 7-12-46, in Morgan, *Overland,* 278–79. See also letter from Charles Stanton, 7-12-46, in Morgan, *Overland,* 611–15.

40 "We miss her": letter from Virginia Reed, 7-12-46, in Morgan, *Overland,* 278–79.

40 Wind River Mountains: Miller-Reed Diary, 256–68; letter from Charles Stanton, 7-19-46, in Morgan, *Overland,* 615–20.

41 "more barrier than portal": Morgan, *Jedediah Smith,* 92. For history of South Pass, see Morgan, *Jedediah Smith,* 90–95.

42 "old Balley": Miller-Reed Diary, 260. For details of approaching and topping the Divide, including the wind at the crest, see Miller-Reed Diary, 256–68; and letter from Charles Stanton, 7-19-46, in Morgan, *Overland,* 615–20.

43 "active, busy life": letter from Charles Stanton, 5-12-46, in Morgan, *Overland,* 531–33.

44 "Thus the great day-dream": letter from Charles Stanton, 7-19-46, in Morgan, *Overland,* 615–20.

Chapter 6

45 the path for all westward travelers: Technically, there was another westward route—the trail to Santa Fe. But this was traveled almost exclusively by traders, not settlers, and certainly not those going to California and Oregon.

46 "an aspiring sort of man": Lovejoy, "Founding of Portland." See also Crawford, *Journal,* passim. For more general information on Hastings's career, see Andrews, "The Ambitions" and "The Controversial"; Cumming, "Lansford Hastings' Michigan Connection"; and the sketch of Hastings by Charles Henry Carey in Hastings, *Emigrants' Guide,* 1932 ed., vii–xxii.

47 "A new era": Korns, *West from Fort Bridger,* 25. For Hastings's talking of independence, see Hastings, *Emigrants' Guide,* 1932 ed., introduction by Carey, xix,; Cumming, "Lansford Hastings' Michigan Connection," 20–22; and Andrews, "The Ambitions," 477.

48 biographical details on Clyman: Camp, *James Clyman, Frontiersman,* 5–6, 264–66, 313; Hasselstrom, *Journal,* 49–55; Korns, *West from Fort Bridger,* 23–29.

48 "my beleef": Camp, *James Clyman, Frontiersman,* 213, 216, 218.

48 "In fact": Camp, *James Clyman, Frontiersman,* 213, 216, 218.

49 Clyman-Reed conversation: This is recounted twice, although only once in detail. Clyman mentioned such a meeting in his journal, although he did not cite Reed by name. Years later, he described the conversation in detail and said it included Reed. See Camp, *James Clyman, Frontiersman,* 225, 266.

49 "Deliberate" and physical description of Clyman: Hasselstrom, *Journal,* 49–55.

49 people changing their minds: Morgan, *Overland,* 630.

50 Hastings would wait for the wagons up ahead: Johnson, *Unfortunate,* 23.

51 Sweetwater River split: letter from Charles Stanton, 7-12-46, in Morgan, *Overland,* 614.

52 "eulogizing himself": letter from James Frederick Breen to C. F. McGlashan, 3-21-79, folder 6, McGlashan Papers, Bancroft Library. For the story about the axletree, see Bryant, *What I Saw,* 76–77.

52 Keseberg biographical details: McGlashan, *History,* 205–15; Lienhard, *Pioneer at Sutter's Fort,* 69, 170; letter from James Frederick Breen to C. F. McGlashan, 3-29-79, folder 7, McGlashan Papers, Bancroft Library; Mullen, *Chronicles,* 62–63; Reed Murphy, *Across the Plains,* 28; "Keseberg and the Buffalo Robe," *Crossroads* 7, nos. 2, 3 (Spring/Summer 1996).

53 Wolfingers biographical details: McGlashan, *History,* 53–54. Hardcoop biographical details: Johnson, *Unfortunate,* 39.

53 Dolan biographical details: letter from James Frederick Breen to McGlashan, 3-29-79, folder 7, McGlashan Papers, Bancroft Library; letter from John Breen to McGlashan, 4-5-79, folder 11, McGlashan Papers, Bancroft Library.

54 "When I was forced": Reed Murphy, *Across the Plains,* 12–14. The exact date and place of Billy's abandonment is unclear, but it seems likely that he was left on the trail somewhere in modern-day Wyoming.

Chapter 7

56 "Our situation": Bryant, *What I Saw,* 142–44. For other information about Bryant's letters, see Reed Pacific Press, 186.

56 arrival at Fort Bridger and experiences there: Miller-Reed Diary, 256–68; Bryant, *What I Saw,* 142–48; Morgan, *Overland,* 620–23; Lienhard, *From St. Louis,* 95.

58 "fine level road": letter from James Reed, 7-31-46, in Morgan, *Overland,* 279–80.

58 Walker's presence and views: Bryant, *What I Saw,* 143; Lienhard, *From St. Louis,* 94; Morgan, *Overland,* 372–73.

58 "excellent and accommodating gentlemen": letter from James Reed, 7-31-46, in Morgan, *Overland,* 279–80.

Chapter 8

60 Edward Breen's fall and recovery: letter from Harry Breen, his son, 2-12-1947, in Stookey, *Fatal Decision,* 189–94; letter from Virginia Reed to McGlashan, 4-11-79, folder 48, McGlashan Papers, Bancroft Library.

61 "We take a new rout": Morgan, *Overland,* 620.

61 buffalo skulls: Bryant, *What I Saw,* 79–80.

61 Harlan-Young Party: Technically, there was no such thing as the Harlan-Young Party. There were several independent parties led by Hastings ahead of the Donners, including one captained by George Harlan and one by Samuel Young. But they were all traveling more or less together along the cut-off, and the term Harlan-Young Party is traditional in the Donner Party literature. I adopt it for ease of reference.

61 "most consumate folly": diary of pioneer James Mathers, quoted in Morgan, *Overland,* 229–30. For other details of the Weber Canyon passage, see Lienhard, *From St. Louis,* 90–103. Lienhard was traveling just behind the Harlan-Young Party but also took the Weber Canyon route. Also see the excellent annotations to the Lienhard journal in Korns, *West from Fort Bridger,* especially 140–42.

62 scouting expedition to find Hastings: There are three principal versions left by Reed: Miller-Reed Diary, 262; a version published in the *Illinois Journal* quoted in Morgan, *Overland,* 289; and Reed Pacific Press, 186–87.

62 "He gave me": Reed Pacific Press, 187.

63 "fair, but would take": Reed Pacific Press, 187.

63 Applegate Cut-Off: letter from William Edgington to the Rev. Thomas Allen, 1-24-47, quoted in Morgan, *Overland,* 694–98.

64 "reported in favour" and "induced the Compay": Miller-Reed Diary, 262.

64 "Only those": Reed Murphy, *Across the Plains,* 21. For the journey through the Wasatch, the best source is the Miller-Reed Diary, 256–68, but also including the footnotes in the version of the diary published in Korns, *West from Fort Bridger,* 197–239. Other sources used here include Donner Houghton, *Expedition,* 34-37; McGlashan, *History,* 31–33; Morgan, *Overland,* 289; Reed Murphy, *Across the Plains,* 19–21; Johnson, *Unfortunate,* 24–28, 141–43; Reed Pacific Press, 186–88.

65 Stanton and Pike found: McGlashan, *History,* 33.

65 "It gave us": Johnson, *Unfortunate,* 143. For Virginia Reed's memory, see Reed Murphy, *Across the Plains,* 20–21.

66 thirty-five miles: The distance of the Wasatch crossing is from Mormon measurements in 1847, which presumably were true to the Donner trail. Morgan, *Overland*, 434. It took a few days after leaving Fort Bridger to reach the base of the Wasatch, so in all, the Donner Party had been on the road a little more than three weeks since leaving the fort and had covered roughly a hundred miles.

66 "worn with travel": Reed Murphy, *Across the Plains*, 21.

Chapter 9

67 Graves family background: "Mr. Graves and Family," *Donner Party Bulletin*, no. 10, March 2000, and Graves family roster page, both available at "New Light on the Donner Party," www.utahcrossroads.org/DonnerParty; and "Eleanor Graves McDonnell," "Eleanor Graves McDonnell Letter 1850," and "When Did the Graves Family Join the Donner Party?" all in *Crossroads* 7, nos. 2, 3 (Spring/Summer 1996).

68 Lake Bonneville, the Great Salt Lake, and the Great Salt Lake Desert: Utah Geological Survey Web site, www.ugs.state.ut.us/online/Pl-39. See also Morgan, *Great Salt Lake*, 17–31; Stegner, *Mormon Country*, 33–51; Redfern, *Making of a Continent*, 128–29; and Hassibe and Keck, *Great Salt Lake*, passim.

70 Halloran biographical details: "Luke Halloran" and "Looking for Luke in All the Wrong Places," both in *Crossroads* 7, nos. 2, 3 (Spring/Summer 1996).

70 "2 days": Donner Houghton, *Expedition*, 39–40; McGlashan, *History*, 31; Johnson, *Unfortunate*, 31.

71 "soapy slime": Kelly, *Salt Desert Trails*, 164–65. See also Hawkins and Madsen, *Excavation*, 43–62.

71 desert crossings: Donner Houghton, *Expedition*, 39–53; Bryant, *What I Saw*, 169–82; Lienhard, *From St. Louis*, 111–22; Hawkins and Madsen, *Excavation*, 36–38; Kelly, *Salt Desert Trails*, 11–18.

72 "The hiatus" and "unearthly": Bryant, *What I Saw*, 173–75.

72 Reed family ordeal in desert: Miller-Reed Diary; letter from Virginia Reed, 5-16-47, in Morgan, *Overland*, 281–88; Reed Pacific Press, 184–91; Johnson, *Unfortunate*, 29–32; Korns, *West from Fort Bridger*, 223–29; McGlashan, *History*, 36–39.

74 different views about hunting for cattle: see John Breen's version as told to Eliza Farnham, in Johnson, *Unfortunate*, 143, and Reed Pacific Press, 190.

75 "Here our real": Johnson, *Unfortunate*, 143.

75 "made the mothers": Johnson, *Unfortunate*, 144.

75 Stanton and McCutchan leave on resupply mission: McGlashan, *History*, 39–40; Reed Pacific Press, 190–91.

76 Edward Breen's fall and recovery: letter from Harry Breen, his son, 2-12-1947, in Stookey, *Fatal Decision*, 189–94; and letter from Virginia Reed to McGlashan, 4-11-79, folder 48, McGlashan Papers, Bancroft Library. The Breen letter describes Edward returning to the saddle, although not the specific scene.

77 Mad Woman Camp: Korns, *West from Fort Bridger*, 106, 231. For a good physical description of the area, see Paden, *Prairie Schooner Detours*, 99–100.

77 "We came into a valley": Lienhard, *From St. Louis*, 126–27.

79 "Hastings Longtripp": Lienhard, *From St. Louis*, 137. For the precise spelling, see the version of Lienhard's diary in Korns, *West from Fort Bridger*, 184.

79 delays on the Hastings Cut-Off: Lienhard, *From St. Louis,* 137–38; Johnson, *Unfortunate,* 248.

79 lost time: For an excellent comparison of travel times for parties that took the main route, see log entry for Sept. 26, 1846, available on Dan Rosen's Donner Party Web site, www.donnerpartydiary.com. See also Lienhard, *From St. Louis,* 137–38; Johnson, *Unfortunate,* 248.

Chapter 10

80 "very bad ridge": Morgan, *Overland,* 157.

80 "one bad hill": Morgan, *Overland,* 233.

81 "more a succession": Bryant, *What I Saw,* 200. The description of the trail across Nevada, here and throughout this chapter, is based on several sources. The Reed-Miller Diary covers the early days. Curran, *Fearful Crossing,* provides excellent detail about trail specifics. Two sources—Bryant, *What I Saw,* and Lienhard, *From St. Louis*—are particularly useful in assessing conditions specific to 1846.

81 "as cadaverous": Bryant, *What I Saw,* 202.

81 Reed-Snyder fight: McGlashan, *History,* 44–50; Johnson, *Unfortunate,* 36–37, 217–18; Reed Murphy, *Across the Plains,* 27–31; Donner Houghton, *Expedition,* 45–50; statement of Patty Reed, box 8-11-308, folder 35, Reed Lewis Papers, Sutter's Fort; exchange of letters between Patty Reed and Eliza Donner, 3-6-12 and 3-18-12, Eliza Poor Donner Houghton Papers, HM 58164 and HM 58169, Huntington Library; and the following documents in the McGlashan Papers, Bancroft Library: letter from Frances Donner to McGlashan, 4-17-79, folder 5; letters from James Breen to McGlashan, 1-9-79, folder 5, and 3-7-79, folder 6, and 3-29-79, 4-6-79, and 4-22-79, all in folder 7; letter from Mary Ann Graves to McGlashan, 4-16-79, folder 14; letter from Patty Reed to McGlashan, 4-11-79, folder 38; letter from Virginia Reed to McGlashan, 5-4-79, folder 48; statement of James Reed Jr., folder 102.

82 legal procedures in wagon trains: Reid, *Policing,* passim, but see especially 73–132.

82 Russell Company bylaws: letter from George Curry, 5-11-46, in Morgan, *Overland,* 520–23.

83 Snyder portrait: letter from James Breen to McGlashan, 3-7-79, folder 6, and letter from William Graves to McGlashan, 3-30-79, folder 16, McGlashan Papers, Bancroft Library.

84 Reed-Keseberg feud: Reed Murphy, *Across the Plains,* 28; letter from James Breen to McGlashan, 3-29-79, folder 7, McGlashan Papers, Bancroft Library.

84 "unleashed antagonisms": Mattes, *Great Platte River Road,* 78. For a general discussion of punishments on the trail, including a specific discussion of the Reed case, see Reid, *Policing,* 171–228.

85 "because he would": letter from Mary Ann Graves to McGlashan, 4-16-79, folder 14, McGlashan Papers, Bancroft Library.

86 "as true as steel": letter from William Graves to McGlashan, 3-30-79, folder 16, McGlashan Papers, Bancroft Library.

86 "We do hereby": Hall, *Donner Miscellany,* 31.

Chapter 11

89 Reed-Herron journey: Reed's map, reproduced and described in Morgan, *Overland,* 264–73; Reed's account in the *Illinois Journal,* contained in Morgan, *Overland,* 289–301; Reed Pacific Press, 184–200.

91 Indian-emigrant interaction: For the best general summary, see Unruh, *Plains Across,* 117–58.

93 "Since I could": Lienhard, *From St. Louis,* 134.

93 "Preparing to make": Munkres, "Plains Indian Threat," 214–15.

93 "They had not": Unruh, *Plains Across,* 151.

94 hiding Winnemucca Hopkins: Winnemucca Hopkins, *Life Among the Piutes,* 10–12.

94 "the wretchedest type": Malinowski and Sheets, *Gale Encyclopedia.*

94 "physically decadent": DeVoto, *Year of Decision,* 347. For DeVoto on insufficient Indian knowledge, see Trigger and Washburn, *Cambridge History,* pt. 1, 10–11.

94 Great Basin Indians: For good summaries, see Waldman, *Encyclopedia,* 82–83, 180–82; Leitch, *Concise Dictionary,* 341–47, 428–29, 493–95, 506–8; and Malinowski and Sheets, *Gale Encyclopedia,* passim.

95 Virginia Reed Indian stories: Reed Murphy, *Across the Plains,* 11–16.

95 losses on the Humboldt: Miller-Reed Diary, 268; Johnson, *Unfortunate,* 35–40, 217; McGlashan, *History,* 51–52.

Chapter 12

96 "as thick as": Curran, *Fearful Crossing,* 129. The description of this portion of the trail is based largely on Curran, *Fearful Crossing,* passim, but see especially 125–43.

96 "a veritable sea": Curran, *Fearful Crossing,* 136.

96 "the most thirsty": Camp, *James Clyman, Frontiersman,* 210.

97 "like the mouth": Curran, *Fearful Crossing,* 145.

97 "every few yards": Curran, *Fearful Crossing,* 151.

97 general crossing of the desert: Johnson, *Unfortunate,* 40–42.

98 "We beheld": Curran, *Fearful Crossing,* 152. General description of approaching the Truckee is based on many sources; for two accounts from 1846 that describe the general conditions the Donner Party would have encountered, see Bryant, *What I Saw,* 219–20, and Lienhard, *From St. Louis,* 164–65.

98 "We had to cash": Morgan, *Overland,* 282. For other information on Nevada caches, see Johnson, *Unfortunate,* 38–42, and Donner Houghton, *Expedition,* 56.

100 "more than tongue": Johnson, *Unfortunate,* 43.

100 "there has been several": Lewis, "Argonauts," 294. Other incidents in Munkres, "Plains Indian Threat."

100 death rates: Unruh, *Plains Across,* 345.

100 life insurance: Brayer, "Insurance."

101 "I don't know when": letter from Frances Donner to McGlashan, folder 54, McGlashan Papers, Bancroft Library.

101 "not fur": letter from Virginia Reed, 5-16-47, in Morgan, *Overland,* 283.

Chapter 13

105 Sierra Nevada geology: Hill, *Geology,* especially 66–67, 83, 154–57, 179–209.

106 snowfall and snow depth data: These were provided by Randall Osterhuber at the University of California's Central Sierra Snow Laboratory, which is located at Donner Pass and inherited the duty of regular weather observations from the Southern Pacific.

107 Alaskan storm: The exact origin, timing, and path of the storm that would eventually loose a dreadful snowfall just as the emigrants were trying to clear the pass are obviously unknowable. The description here is typical of a winter storm that would strike California.

107 frost and ice: The description of these conditions is actually from Bryant, *What I Saw,* 223–24. Bryant approached the Sierra two months before the Donner Party, so conditions would have been even colder when they arrived. Clouds on peaks: Johnson, *Unfortunate,* 145; John Breen, "Pioneer Memoirs."

108 attempts at crossing the pass: The general description is based on many sources, including a letter from Virginia Reed, 5-16-47, in Morgan, *Overland,* 281–88; Breen Diary, 310; Johnson, *Unfortunate,* 43–44, 144–47, 220–21; Sinclair statement in Bryant, *What I Saw,* 251; John Breen, "Pioneer Memoirs": and Keseberg statement in McGlashan, *History,* 208–9. It should also be noted that, ironically, it is not altogether obvious that the Donner Party attempted to cross the pass that would bear its name. A few weeks before, another emigrant train had discovered a different pass a little to the south, requiring a climb that was longer but more gradual and thus easier for wagons to surmount. It is possible that Stanton learned of this alternate route during his earlier crossings or at Sutter's Fort, and after his return tried to point the Donner Party toward the newfound trail. It makes no real difference. The alternative route is near enough to Donner Pass to experience the same climate, and either way, the emigrants were faced with climbing straight up into one of the continent's most rugged mountain ranges.

108 Foster note: Hall, *Donner Miscellany,* 33.

108 "We were compelled": Johnson, *Unfortunate,* 146.

108 Keseberg too lame to walk: "Lewis Keseberg's Testimony: Villain or Victim?" *Dogtown Territorial Quarterly,* Summer 1996, 64–67.

109 "One wanted": McGlashan, *History,* 208–9.

109 "Springing up": McGlashan, *History,* 209.

110 "The rest": McGlashan, *History,* 209.

110 "We had to go back": letter from Virginia Reed, 5-16-47, in Morgan, *Overland,* 283.

Chapter 14

111 "was low down and heavy": Reed Pacific Press, 193.

112 Reed rescue attempt: Reed's arrival at Sutter's Fort and his subsequent attempt to return to the emigrants is principally chronicled in two accounts, both of which have been republished. The *Illinois Journal* carried a story based on Reed's notes, 12-9-47, which is reprinted in Morgan, *Overland,* 289–301. The other version is Reed

Pacific Press, 184–200. For other details, see Johnson, *Unfortunate,* 80–87, 204–6; and Bryant, *What I Saw,* 346–50.

112 "Raising the lid": Reed Pacific Press, 194.

113 "I state": Johnson, *Unfortunate,* 204.

113 Sutter calculations: Reed Pacific Press, 195.

115 "where they could": letter from George Tucker to McGlashan, 4-5-79, folder 51, McGlashan Papers, Bancroft Library.

115 "We arrived here": "William G. Murphy's Lecture and Two Letters to Mrs. Houghton," *Dogtown Territorial Quarterly,* Summer 1996, 48.

116 "leaving a few chinks": handwritten account from Patty Reed, box 8-11-308, folder 22, Reed Lewis Papers, Sutter's Fort. See also letter from Patty Reed to McGlashan, 4-15-79, folder 38, and letter from Mary Ann Graves to McGlashan, 4-16-79, folder 14, McGlashan Papers, Bancroft Library; and William Graves account in Johnson, *Unfortunate,* 221.

117 who lived where: letter from Patty Reed to McGlashan, 4-15-79, folder 38, McGlashan Papers, Bancroft Library; Johnson, *Unfortunate,* 44.

117 "Father built": letter from Mary Graves to McGlashan, 4-16-79, folder 14, McGlashan Papers, Bancroft Library.

117 "he, & all of his family": letter from Patty Reed to McGlashan, 4-15-79, folder 38, McGlashan Papers, Bancroft Library.

117 "You would not": King and Steed, "Newly Discovered Documents."

117 Donners at Alder Creek: letter from John Breen to McGlashan, 5-18-79, folder 11; letter from William Graves to McGlashan, 4-1-79, folder 17; letter from John App, dictated by Leanna Donner, to McGlashan, 4-1-79, folder 1; letter from Rebecca App on behalf of Leanna Donner to McGlashan, 4-27-79, folder 1; letter from Georgia Donner to McGlashan, 3-27-79, folder 2; and letter from Eliza Donner to McGlashan, 11-22-84, folder 22, all in McGlashan Papers, Bancroft Library; King and Steed, "Newly Discovered Documents," 23; King and Steed, "Jean Baptiste Trudeau," 168.

118 nursing babies: It's possible there were seven infants. Nineteenth-century ages are notoriously imprecise.

118 ox carcass: Johnson, *Unfortunate,* 44. For the price in Independence, see Unruh, *Plains Across,* 79. Eddy never said he was being gouged, but surely, given the price difference, it must have crossed his mind.

118 Margret Reed trading for food: letter from Viginia Reed, 5-16-47, in Holmes, *Covered Wagon Women,* 77; William C. Graves account in Johnson, *Unfortunate,* 221.

119 Eddy and the bear: Johnson, *Unfortunate,* 45–46.

120 bear tooth: Hardesty, *Archaeology,* 117–19.

120 mules and the escape attempt: Johnson, *Unfortunate,* 47; Bryant, *What I Saw,* 251.

Chapter 15

122 Breen Diary: The original diary is in the Bancroft Library, although it has been transcribed and reprinted many times, often inaccurately. The quotations here and throughout this book are taken from an admirable transcription in Morgan, *Overland,* 310–22.

123 blizzard: In addition to Breen Diary, see Johnson, *Unfortunate,* 47.

124 mules missing: Breen Diary, 311.

124 starvation symptoms: various sources, principally focusing on accounts of a starvation experiment at the University of Minnesota and the conditions in the Warsaw Ghetto, both during World War II. See Russell, *Hunger,* 51–58, 89, 100–103, 118–23; Roland, *Courage,* 98–119; and Tucker, *Great Starvation Experiment,* 128–62.

124 "housed up": Breen Diary, 312.

124 Spitzer: Breen Diary, 312. General information on Spitzer is available at the teamsters roster page at "New Light on the Donner Party," at www.utahcross roads.org/DonnerParty.

125 "Stanton trying": Breen Diary, 312.

125 Donner accident: King and Steed, "Newly Discovered Documents," 18; King and Steed, "John Baptiste Trudeau," 168.

125 Alder Creek conditions: letters in McGlashan Papers, Bancroft Library, as follows: from Frances Donner to McGlashan, 4-17-79, folder 54; from Georgia Donner Babcock to McGlashan, 3-27-79, folder 2; from Eliza P. Donner Houghton to McGlashan, 11-22-84, folder 22; from Eliza P. Donner Houghton to McGlashan, 11-11-84, folder 21. Also King and Steed, "John Baptiste Trudeau," 168–69; Johnson, *Unfortunate,* 48; King and Steed, "Newly Discovered Documents," 17-19; Reed Murphy, *Across the Plains,* 37–38.

126 snowshoes: Breen Diary, *Overland,* 311.

126 "It is our only choice": Steed, *Donner Party,* 12.

126 "Stanton & Graves": Breen Diary, 311.

126 Stanton note: Hall, *Donner Miscellany,* 45.

127 Graves expecting to die: Johnson, *Unfortunate,* 46.

127 the Williamses: General information on Eliza and Baylis Williams is available on the roster page at "New Light on the Donner Party," www.utahcrossroads.org/DonnerParty.

128 "was insane": letter from William Graves to McGlashan, 4-1-79, folder 17, McGlashan Papers, Bancroft Library.

Chapter 16

129 Anasazi: Hardcastle, *Survive,* 98. See also Farb and Armelagos, *Consuming Passions,* 136.

130 "normal": Simpson, *Cannibalism,* 121.

130 maritime cases: Examples are taken from many sources, including Simpson, *Cannibalism,* 114–32; Leslie, *Desperate Journeys,* 182–99; Petrinovich, *Cannibal Within,* 50–52; Huntress, *Checklist,* 68–69; and Philbrick, *In the Heart of the Sea,* 174–76, 207–12.

133 Forlorn Hope's departure: letter from Mary Ann Graves to C. F. McGlashan, 4-15-79, folder 14, McGlashan Papers, Bancroft Library. For general details of the Forlorn Hope, see Stewart, *Ordeal,* 122–50; Bryant, *What I Saw,* 251–55; Johnson, *Unfortunate,* 49–65; McGlashan, *History,* 64–88, 105–12; and Morgan, *Overland,* 293–95.

135 "some Norwegian fur company" and other Graves quotes: McGlashan, *History,* 71–72.

135 "Storm continued": This and other quotations from Eddy's "journal" throughout this chapter are from the version later produced by Reed, included in Morgan, *Overland,* 293–95.

135 Graves sees smoke: McGlashan, *History,* 79.

138 "subsisting on human flesh": Johnson, *Unfortunate,* 130.

138 oarlocks: Petrinovich, *Cannibal Within,* 62.

138 Andes: Read, *Alive,* 85.

139 butchering pattern: The typical procedures of butchering and eating are recounted in many sources on cannibalism. Among others, see Askenasy, *Cannibalism;* Gzowski, *Sacrament;* Hardcastle, *Survive;* Leslie, *Desperate Journeys;* Petrinovich, *Cannibal Within;* Philbrick, *In the Heart of the Sea;* Read, *Alive;* and Simpson, *Cannibalism.*

140 starvation studies: Harrison, *Famine,* 61, 77–80.

140 Minnesota experiment: summarized in Guetzkow and Bowman, *Men and Hunger.*

Chapter 17

145 "So bitter": letter from Virginia Reed to McGlashan, 4-11-79, folder 48, McGlashan Papers, Bancroft Library; Reed Murphy, *Across the Plains,* 37.

146 "I was glad": Donner Houghton, *Expedition,* 70–72.

146 sunbeam: Donner Houghton, *Expedition,* 70–72.

147 "That kind of living": Johnson, *Unfortunate,* 222.

147 "Saw no strangers": Breen Diary, 313.

147 Burger biographical details: Breen Diary, 314.

148 Reed escape attempt: see especially letter from Virginia Reed, 5-16-47, in Holmes, *Covered Wagon Women,* 74–82; handwritten account from Patty Reed, box 8-11-308, folder 22, Reed Lewis Papers, Sutter's Fort; letters from Virginia Reed to McGlashan, 5-4-79 and 6-13-79, folder 48, McGlashan Papers, Bancroft Library; letter from Patty Reed to McGlashan, 4-15-79, folder 38, McGlashan Papers, Bancroft Library; Breen Diary, in Morgan, *Overland,* 306–22; and Johnson, *Unfortunate,* 156. See also William Graves's account, in Johnson, *Unfortunate,* 222, in which he claims to have gone along, a dubious claim that conflicts with other accounts.

148 "we could hardle": letter from Virginia Reed, 5-16-47, in Holmes, *Covered Wagon Women,* 74–82.

149 "It was so": letter from Virginia Reed to McGlashan, 6-13-79, folder 48, McGlashan Papers, Bancroft Library.

150 "We could sit": letter from Virginia Reed to McGlashan, 5-4-79, folder 48, McGlashan Papers, Bancroft Library.

150 "pleasant hours" and "We used to sit": letter from Virginia Reed to McGlashan, 5-4-79, folder 48, McGlashan Papers, Bancroft Library.

150 Virginia's possible death: letter from Virginia Reed to McGlashan, 5-4-79, folder 48, McGlashan Papers, Bancroft Library.

Chapter 18

152 land claims submitted by Reed: Hall, *Donner Miscellany,* 40–43.

152 Battle of Santa Clara: "An Unpublished Report of the Battle of Santa Clara," *San Francisco Chronicle* Sunday magazine, 9-4-10, 2.

153 Reed planting crops: Hall, *Donner Miscellany,* 42–47.

Chapter 19

155 ruined meat: Breen Diary, 317.

155 "the terrible screames": letter from Patty Reed to McGlashan, 4-15-79, folder 38, McGlashan Papers, Bancroft Library.

155 Milt Elliott visit: letters from Patty Reed to McGlashan, 4-11-79 and 4-15-79, and undated material, folder 38, McGlashan Papers, Bancroft Library.

156 Eliza and hides: Breen Diary, 316–17.

156 Yerba Buena weather: California Star, 2, 1-23-47.

157 Virginia and Catholicism: typed manuscript titled "V.R.M.S. Personal History," MS 543, folder 3, Braun Research Library, Southwest Museum of the American Indian, Autry National Center; letter from Virginia Reed to McGlashan, 11-3-80, folder 43, McGlashan Papers, Bancroft Library.

157 Landrum Murphy: Quotes are from the Breen Diary, 306–22. The story about the meat is in McGlashan, *History,* 102–3.

158 Eddy burials: Breen Diary, 319.

158 Elliott's burial: letters from Patty Reed to McGlashan, 4-11-79 and 4-15-79, folder 38, and letter from Virginia Reed to McGlashan, 5-4-79, folder 48, McGlashan Papers, Bancroft Library; handwritten account by Patty Reed, box 8-11-308, folder 22, Reed Lewis Papers, Sutter's Fort; Reed, *Across the Plains,* 41; "William G. Murphy's Lecture and Two Letters to Mrs. Houghton," *Dogtown Territorial Quarterly,* Summer 1996, 14–15, 48–53; Breen Diary, 320.

158 "We ate his": letter from Virginia Reed, 5-16-47, in Holmes, *Covered Wagon Women,* 74–82. For crickets, see handwritten account by Patty Reed, box 8-11-308, folder 22, Reed Lewis Papers, Sutter's Fort.

159 eating mush: letter from Virginia Reed, 5-16-47, in Holmes, *Covered Wagon Women,* 74–82.

159 "very uneasy": Breen Diary, 318–19.

159 "she is a case": Breen Diary, 318–20.

159 "We hope": Breen Diary, 320.

Chapter 20

164 "one vast quag mire": letter from George Tucker to McGlashan, 4-5-79, folder 51, McGlashan Papers, Bancroft Library.

164 journey from Johnson's Ranch to Sutter's Fort: The details are taken from a letter from George Tucker to McGlashan, 4-5-79, folder 51, McGlashan Papers, Bancroft Library, although Tucker says the messenger was John Rhoads. I accept a variety of other sources that say the messenger was an Indian. Among the most convincing of

these, and the source of the name Indian Dick, is a letter from Reason Tucker to McGlashan, undated but 1879, folder 53, McGlashan Papers, Bancroft Library. It's also possible that the messenger first went to the home of John Sinclair rather than Sutter's Fort, which was nearby. For general information on the preparation of the first relief party, see especially George Tucker's letter of 4-5-79; the handwritten comments of Sinclair appended to the end of the Diary of the First Relief, in Morgan, *Overland,* 334–36; and the account dictated by Daniel Rhoads for H. H. Bancroft, BANC MSS C-D 144, Bancroft Library,

165 issues regarding rescuer pay: letter from Edward Kern, Jan. 1847, Eliza Poor Donner Houghton Papers, HM 21355, Huntington Library; petition to Congress for compensation for Riley Moutry, Sherman Otis Houghton Papers, HOU 36, Huntington Library; Kern payroll records in Morgan, *Overland,* 452; Johnson, *Unfortunate,* 71.

165 "go or die trying": letter from Daniel Rhoads to Jesse Esrey, 1847, in Steed, *Donner Party Rescue Site,* 23–30.

165 sidesaddles: Sinclair notes to the Diary of the First Relief, in Morgan, *Overland,* 335.

166 "never to turn": Sinclair notes to the Diary of the First Relief, in Morgan, *Overland,* 335.

166 "one of the heaviest": Sinclair notes to the Diary of the First Relief, in Morgan, *Overland,* 335.

166 Greenwood wager offer: statement of Daniel Rhoads to H. H. Bancroft, BANC MSS C-D 144, Bancroft Library.

166 first relief party: The general description of the first relief party's progress is based principally on the so-called Diary of the First Relief, kept by Ritchie and Tucker, and available at Morgan, *Overland,* 331–36. Other details are from Daniel Rhoads's statement to H. H. Bancroft, BANC MSS C-D 144, Bancroft Library. As many Donner researchers have noted, the Ritchie-Tucker Diary conflicts with the Breen Diary in terms of the date. George Stewart suggested many years ago that the Ritchie-Tucker Diary is actually one day late, that the trip began on the 4th but Ritchie mistakenly wrote down the 5th. I agree that this is the most likely scenario, so I have adjusted the dates accordingly, although it is also possible that the error is elsewhere or even that the Breen Diary is one day off. Ultimately, we will never know, nor does it matter.

167 "belly deep": Diary of the First Relief, in Morgan, *Overland,* 332.

167 "Under existing": Diary of the First Relief, in Morgan, *Overland,* 332.

168 "throwing our blankets": statement of Daniel Rhoads to H. H. Bancroft, BANC MSS C-D 144, Bancroft Library.

Chapter 21

169 "Expecting some": Breen Diary, 306–22.

169 Trudeau climbing: Donner Houghton, *Expedition,* 74.

170 "Are you men": Daniel Rhoads's statement to H. H. Bancroft, BANC MSS C-D 144, Bancroft Library. The woman is identified as Levinah Murphy in a letter from Reason Tucker to McGlashan, 5-16-79, folder 53, McGlashan Papers, Bancroft Library.

170 "made out of": letter from Virginia Reed to McGlashan, 7-18-79, folder 48, McGlashan Papers, Bancroft Library.

170 Forlorn Hope comments: Donner Houghton, *Expedition*, 76; Daniel Rhoads statement to H. H. Bancroft, BANC MSS C-D 144, Bancroft Library. William Graves remembered the rescuers saying that the entire Forlorn Hope had made it through alive, but with feet too badly frozen to return (Johnson, *Unfortunate*, 222–23). Graves might be right, but I find it more likely that Donner Houghton is correct and the rescuers feigned ignorance, so as to avoid a blatant lie they would soon have to acknowledge.

171 blanket for shawl/bedroll: letter from Rebecca E. App to McGlashan, 4-27-79, folder 1, McGlashan Papers, Bancroft Library.

172 "When we reached" and the story of Leanna's struggle: letters from Rebecca E. App on behalf of her mother, Leanna Charity Donner, to McGlashan, 3-4-79 and 4-27-79, folder 1, McGlashan Papers, Bancroft Library.

174 Patty and Thomas turn back to the lake: handwritten account from Patty Reed, box 8-11-308, folder 22, Reed Lewis Papers, Sutter's Fort.

174 "Well, Ma": letter from Virginia Reed, 5-16-47, in Holmes, *Covered*, 79.

175 Patty and Thomas arrive back at lake: Johnson, *Unfortunate*, 75.

175 Denton left behind: Johnson, *Unfortunate*, 76–78, 223; Reed Murphy, *Across the Plains*, 43; letter from Reason Tucker to McGlashan, 1879, folder 53, McGlashan Papers, Bancroft Library; McGlashan, *History*, 149–51.

176 death of Ada: "The Missing Keseberg Child," *Donner Party Bulletin*, no. 14. Philippine never described her thoughts at this moment, but it seems impossible that she did not think of Ada's lost twin.

177 "her sperrit": letter from Reason Tucker to McGlashan, 1879, folder 53, McGlashan Papers, Bancroft Library.

177 Virginia Reed's dress: letter from Virginia Reed to McGlashan, 5-14-79, folder 48, McGlashan Papers, Bancroft Library.

178 Leanna and Elitha Donner: letter from Rebecca E. App on behalf of her mother, Leanna Charity Donner, to McGlashan, 3-4-79, folder 1, McGlashan Papers, Bancroft Library.

178 "nigher Pa": letter from Virginia Reed, 5-16-47, in Holmes, *Covered*, 79. See also Reed Murphy, *Across the Plains*, 43.

178 Donner cannibalism comments: Breen Diary, 321.

179 "they think": Breen Diary, 321.

Chapter 22

180 "from unavoidable causes": A copy of the petition is in Hall, *Donner Miscellany*, 76. Reed mentions the petition in Reed Pacific Press, 196.

180 "His sympathy": Reed Pacific Press, 196.

181 "This speaks": *California Star*, 2-6-47, in Morgan, *Overland*, 700–701.

181 word of the first relief: We know this was included on Sutter's launch because of McKinstry's letter in Morgan, *Overland*, 703–5.

182 *Californian* and *California Star* stories: Both are reproduced in Morgan, *Overland*, 701–5.

182 For general information on the raising of the second relief expedition, see various documents and press accounts in Morgan, *Overland*, 292–95, 323–40; Johnson,

Unfortunate, 65–70; Reed Pacific Press, 196–97; *San Francisco Chronicle* Sunday magazine, "An Unpublished Report of the Battle of Santa Clara," 9-4-1910, 2; and Hall, *Donner Miscellany,* 48–59.

183 warping boat: Soule, *Annals,* 796–97.

184 "[T]he hilarity": Reed Diary of the Second Relief, in Morgan, *Overland,* 344.

185 "Bread, Bread": Reed Diary of the Second Relief, in Morgan, *Overland,* 345.

185 "The meeting": Diary of the First Relief, in Morgan, *Overland,* 333. For general scene of the Reed family reunion: Diary of the First Relief, in Morgan, *Overland,* 333–34; Reed Diary of the Second Relief, in Morgan, *Overland,* 345; Reed Pacific Press, 197; the Merryman/Reed version, in Morgan, *Overland,* 296; Reed Murphy, *Across the Plains,* 45; letter from Virginia Reed, 5-16-47, in Holmes, *Covered Wagon Women,* 74–82; letter from Virginia Reed to McGlashan, 5-14-79, folder 48, McGlashan Papers, Bancroft Library.

187 death of William Hook: told principally in two places, each a slightly different version. See McGlashan, *History,* 155–56, and Johnson, *Unfortunate,* 79. For other details, see letter from Rebecca App to McGlashan, 3-4-79, folder 1, McGlashan Papers, Bancroft Library; and Diary of the First Relief, 334, and Reed Diary of the Second Relief, 345, both in Morgan, *Overland.* The idea that the boy lay awake before his feast is speculative but seems reasonable.

187 "I really thought": letter from Virginia Reed to McGlashan, 7-1-79, folder 48, McGlashan Papers, Bancroft Library.

Chapter 23

188 Donner girls eating: letter from Georgia Donner to McGlashan, 6-15-79, folder 3, McGlashan Papers, Bancroft Library. A letter from Georgia on 5-2-79, folder 2, identifies Tamzene as crying while the children ate, and it is very possible both parents were distraught.

188 geese flying overhead: Breen Diary, 321–22.

189 general information on the Washoe: Nevers, *Wa She Shu,* passim. The Washoe's oral traditions regarding the Donner Party in particular are recounted on 44. Also, I was helped to understand the Washoe by interviews with Penny Rucks, 2-21-2006.

189 "Where he was going": Johnson, *Unfortunate,* 154.

189 "all full": Breen Diary, 322.

Chapter 24

190 story of the second relief, led by Reed: Reed Diary of the Second Relief, in Morgan, *Overland,* 345–46; Reed Pacific Press, 197; Johnson, *Unfortunate,* 88. For the weather on the morning of their arrival, see Breen Diary, 322.

192 *Illinois Journal* article: Morgan, *Overland,* 289–301.

192 quotes from Georgia Donner: letter from Georgia Donner to McGlashan, 6-15-79, folder 3, McGlashan Papers, Bancroft Library. For an excellent and accessible summary of the historical evidence surrounding cannibalism at Alder Creek, see Kristin Johnson, "Cannibalism at Alder Creek: The Historical Sources," *Donner Party Bulletin,* no. 15, available online at www.utahcrossroads.org/DonnerParty.

194 "Informed the people": Reed Diary of the Second Relief, in Morgan, *Overland,* 346.

194 list of auctioned items: Hall, *Donner Miscellany,* 80–81.

194 "Stout harty children": Reed Diary of the Second Relief, March 1. Beginning with the first day of March, Reed confused his dates in the diary. Events that actually occurred March 1 he recorded as Feb. 29, although 1847 was obviously not a leap year. Thus, the events of the "March 1" diary entry actually occurred on March 2, the "March 2" entry actually represents March 3, and so on.

195 "the laugh": letter from Patty Reed to McGlashan, 4-16-79, folder 38, McGlashan Papers, Bancroft Library. Patty on the cabin roof when Reed arrives: Merryman, in Morgan, *Overland,* 298.

196 "They say": Breen Diary, 322.

Chapter 25

197 "The Sky look": Reed Diary of the Second Relief, March 4, in Morgan, *Overland,* 347.

198 blizzard: The most detailed account of the blizzard is in Reed Diary of the Second Relief, in Morgan, *Overland,* 347–50. It is the basis for much of the account of the blizzard here and in the pages that follow. For other sources, see the handwritten account by Patty Reed, box 8-11-308, folder 22, Reed Lewis Papers, Sutter's Fort; Johnson, *Unfortunate,* 158–67, 204–6; Morgan, *Overland,* 289–301; Reed Pacific Press, 198–200; King, *Winter,* 100–106; and the following letters in the McGlashan Papers, Bancroft Library: Patty Reed to McGlashan, 4-26-79, folder 38; John Breen to McGlashan, 4-20-79, folder 1; William McCutchan to McGlashan, 6-1-79, folder 39; and George Tucker to McGlashan, 4-5-79, folder 51.

199 "Miller being": letter from William McCutchan to McGlashan, 6-1-79, folder 39, McGlashan Papers, Bancroft Library.

200 Virginia listening to the rain: letter from Virginia Reed to McGlashan, 5-14-79, folder 48, McGlashan Papers, Bancroft Library. Virginia remembers this scene as occurring at John Sinclair's house, but by most traditional timelines she did not reach that house until after the great storm. Yet no other subsequent blizzard struck before James Reed reached safety, so either Virginia and her mother reached Sinclair's before the storm, or, more likely, the incident occurred somewhere else, perhaps at Johnson's Ranch. According to Tucker's account in Diary of the First Relief, they should not even have reached Johnson's Ranch in time, but I suspect his chronology may be off by a day. In any event, Virginia's fretful night must have occurred during the blizzard.

201 "Snowing and blowing": letter from Patty Reed to McGlashan, 4-26-79, folder 38, McGlashan Papers, Bancroft Library.

201 Clark remembers snow depth: letter from Nicholas Clark to McGlashan, 11-16-79, folder 13, McGlashan Papers, Bancroft Library.

202 Reed asks about help for Mary Donner: letter from Patty Reed to McGlashan, 4-26-79, folder 38, McGlashan Papers, Bancroft Library.

203 Reed sensitive to the idea of abandonment: The 1847 Merryman account, based on Reed's notes, mentions the exhortations only in passing. Reed's 1871 account in the *Pacific Rural Press* goes into greater detail. The Merryman account is in Morgan, *Overland,* 289–301. The 1871 version is Reed Pacific Press, 181–200.

203   debate about Woodworth's performance: Johnson, *Unfortunate,* 224.

205   Patty Reed's near-starvation: letter from Patty Reed to McGlashan, 4-16-79, folder 38, McGlashan Papers, Bancroft Library. This letter says nothing about Patty walking initially, but other sources generally agree that she began on foot. See also handwritten account by Patty Reed, box 8-11-308, folder 22, Reed Lewis Papers, Sutter's Fort.

Chapter 26

207   Stone and Cady: The best sources are two letters from William Graves (but dictated by Cady) to McGlashan, 5-30-79 and 6-1-79, both folder 18, McGlashan Papers, Bancroft Library. See also letter from Georgia Donner to McGlashan, 4-16-79, folder 2, McGlashan Papers, Bancroft Library; and McGlashan, *History,* 164–65. Clark out hunting: letter from Nicholas Clark to McGlashan, 11-16-79, folder 13, McGlashan Papers, Bancroft Library.

208   "I may never": letter from Georgia Donner Babcock to McGlashan, 4-16-79, folder 2, McGlashan Papers, Bancroft Library. For clothing details, see King and Steed, "Newly Discovered Documents."

Chapter 27

210   Reed and Woodworth meet: Reed Pacific Press, 199–200.

211   Eddy and Foster arrive at the lake: It isn't entirely clear if Eddy and Foster found Woodworth before Woodworth found Reed, but the difference is at most a day or two and is insignificant to the broader chronology. The best sources for the interaction of these groups are Reed's Merryman version, in Morgan, *Overland,* 300–301; and Johnson, *Unfortunate,* 102–3. See also McGlashan, *History,* 193–95. Woodworth gave an account of the whole rescue effort to the *California Star,* 4-3-47. For a general defense of Woodworth, which I find less than convincing, see King, *Winter,* 221–27.

213   "There is Mrs. Breen": Johnson, *Unfortunate,* 166.

214   partly eaten bodies at Starved Camp: There has been a lot of controversy over descriptions of Starved Camp when rescuers arrived. In my view the most reliable description comes from Woodworth's report in the *California Star,* 4-3-47.

215   "I think": letter from William Graves to McGlashan, 2-28-79, folder 16, McGlashan Papers, Bancroft Library. For other details of Stark's rescue effort, see John Breen, "Pioneer Memoirs"; letter from John Breen to McGlashan, 5-18-79, folder 11, McGlashan Papers, Bancroft Library; Johnson, *Unfortunate,* 104–10; McGlashan, *History,* 195–98.

Chapter 28

217   "I have been here": letter from Eliza P. Donner Houghton to McGlashan, 11-11-84, folder 21, McGlashan Papers, Bancroft Library.

217   Tamzene leaving her husband: We have no description of this scene from the historical record, but surely Tamzene went to George's bedside to say goodbye.

217 "They came in": letter from Frances Donner to McGlashan, 6-22-79, folder 54, McGlashan Papers, Bancroft Library. See also letter from Georgia Donner to McGlashan, 11-20-79, folder 4, McGlashan Papers, Bancroft Library.

217 Eddy and Foster ask about their sons: We have no specific account of Eddy and Foster asking about their sons upon their arrival at the cabins, but surely they must have. The account of Eddy's threat is in Johnson, *Unfortunate*, 106.

218 Tamzene Donner had reached the lake cabins: The exact chronology of the arrival of the relief party is uncertain, even by the tangled standards of Donner Party evidence. It's possible that Clark and Trudeau actually went beyond the lake and met the rescue party, or even that they were somewhere in between the lake and Alder Creek. It's also possible that Tamzene arrived just before the rescue party or just after it. The key evidence in my view is a letter from Nicholas Clark to McGlashan, 11-16-79, folder 13, McGlashan Papers, Bancroft Library.

218 "As we were ready": letter from Georgia Donner to McGlashan, 4-19-79, folder 2, McGlashan Papers, Bancroft Library. They may have been living in the Breen cabin or the Murphy cabin. For the idea they moved into the Breen cabin, see letter from James Breen to McGlashan, 5-2-79, folder 8 and letter from Georgia Donner to McGlashan, 5-2-79 (exact date difficult to read), folder 2, McGlashan Papers, Bancroft Library.

219 For both the arrival of the third relief and Tamzene's dilemma, see the following letters in the McGlashan Papers, Bancroft Library: Nicholas Clark to McGlashan, 11-16-79, folder 14; from Georgia Donner to McGlashan, 4-16-79 and 4-19-79, both folder 2, and 11-20-79, folder 4; Frances Donner to McGlashan, 6-22-79, folder 54; Eliza Poor Donner Houghton to McGlashan, 11-11-84, folder 21. See also McGlashan, *History*, 202–4.

219 "There was hardly": letter from Georgia Donner to McGlashan, 11-20-79, folder 4, McGlashan Papers, Bancroft Library.

219 Donner girls can't remember Tamzene's appearance: letter from Eliza Poor Donner Houghton to McGlashan, 4-7-79, folder 28, McGlashan Papers, Bancroft Library.

219 clothes found on the snow: letter from Georgia Donner to McGlashan, 11-20-79, folder 4, McGlashan Papers, Bancroft Library.

220 "The sugar": letter from Frances Donner to McGlashan, 5-20-79, folder 54, McGlashan Papers, Bancroft Library.

220 "crying bee" and other details of walking out: King and Steed, "Newly Discovered Documents."

220 "I do not feel": letter from Georgia Donner to McGlashan, 4-19-79, folder 2, McGlashan Papers, Bancroft Library. The only child younger than the Donner girls to escape without either parent was Naomi Pike, who was three when she was carried out by the first relief. Elizabeth Graves, who was one, also escaped, although her mother was with her for the first part of the journey, until she died at Starved Camp.

220 John Breen in wonderland: letter from John Breen to McGlashan, 4-20-79, folder 11, McGlashan Papers, Bancroft Library.

221 aborted rescue effort: Johnson, *Unfortunate*, 110–11; Woodworth letter to the editor, *California Star*, 4-3-47; letter from Reason Tucker to McGlashan, 1879, folder 53, McGlashan Papers, Bancroft Library.

Chapter 29

222 bring in property rather than persons: A copy of the agreement between Sinclair and the men is in Hall, *Donner Miscellany*, 86–87.

222 profile of Fallon: Morgan and Harris, *Rocky Mountain Journals*, 296–300.

223 Fallon's diary: This is reprinted in Morgan, *Overland*, 360–66.

224 Keseberg's version of the story: McGlashan, *History*, 205–24.

226 rumors about Keseberg killing Tamzene: *California Star*, 4-10-47, in Morgan, *Overland*, 719–21. For murder rumors: McGlashan, *History*, 216–24.

226 Fallon journal is half true: For discussions of the reliability of the Fallon journal, see King, *Winter*, 120–40; McGlashan, *History*, 216–24; and Kristin Johnson's excellent footnotes to Thornton's version, in Johnson, *Unfortunate*, 111–16.

227 "Death & Destruction": letter from Reason Tucker to McGlashan, 1879, folder 53, McGlashan Papers, Bancroft Library.

Chapter 30

228 "Tel Henriet" and other quotes from Virginia's letter: letter from Virginia Reed, 5-16-47, in Holmes, *Covered Wagon Women*, 74–82.

229 "human skeletons": Bryant, *What I Saw*, 263. This is also the source for the general scene. For the date of Kearny's departure, see DeVoto, *Year of Decision*, 476. There is no actual description of the men standing hatless at the funeral pyre, but given nineteenth-century proprieties, this seems a reasonable assumption.

230 survivor descriptions: Portraits of the survivors and rescuers are generally based on the roster pages at "New Light on the Donner Party," at www.utahcrossroads.org/donnerparty, and on summaries in King, *Winter*, 141–78. Other sources noted below.

230 Nancy Graves bursting into tears: letter from Eliza Donner to McGlashan, 8-8-79, folder 28, McGlashan Papers, Bancroft Library.

230 "I have no information": letter from Nancy Graves to McGlashan, 1879, folder 55, McGlashan Papers, Bancroft Library.

230 "The gold is still": letter from James Reed, 8-1-49, James Frazier Reed Papers, Bancroft Library.

231 Margret Reed's health: letter from Patty Reed to McGlashan, 3-13-79, folder 38, McGlashan Papers, Bancroft Library.

231 "Nothing that could": letter from James Breen to McGlashan, 7-29-80, folder 10, McGlashan Papers, Bancroft Library.

231 Graves girls marrying: Graves family roster page at "New Light on the Donner Party," at www.utahcrossroads.org/DonnerParty. For Mary Graves not wearing shoes, see letter from Mary Graves to McGlashan, 4-16-79, folder 14, McGlashan Papers, Bancroft Library.

232 "so many thousand times": letter from William Graves to McGlashan, 2-28-79, folder 16, McGlashan Papers, Bancroft Library.

232 Trudeau and his memory of the suffering: letter from Eliza Donner to McGlashan, 11-11-84, folder 21, McGlashan Papers, Bancroft Library.

232 Keseberg's fate: McGlashan, *History*, 216–24.

233 Keseberg opening a restaurant: For reasons that baffle me, some Donner Party historians have declared Keseberg's restaurant mythical. I find the evidence reasonably compelling. The restaurant is mentioned in a letter by George McKinstry, who implies that it was in a hotel or boardinghouse. We know from other sources that Keseberg ran the Lady Adams, and that it was a substantial establishment. It seems reasonable that it may well have had a restaurant. See letter from George McKinstry to Edward Kern, 12-23-51, in, Eberstadt, *Transcript,* document 122. For the Job comparison: letter from McGlashan to Eliza Donner, 4-4-79, box 2, Sherman Otis Houghton Papers, Huntington Library. For more on Keseberg, see also *Donner Party Bulletin,* no. 6, at www.utahcrossroads.org/DonnerParty.

233 Patty Reed tending Miller's grave: letter from Patty Reed to McGlashan, 4-16-79, folder 38, McGlashan Papers, Bancroft Library.

233 Fallon's death: Morgan and Harris, *Rocky Mountain Journals,* 296–300.

233 Stark's fate: McGlashan, *History,* 197.

233 Tucker's fate: letter from Reason Tucker to McGlashan, 5-16-79, folder 53, McGlashan Papers, Bancroft Library; and Neelands, "Reason P. Tucker."

234 Hastings's fate: The best summary of Hastings's life is in a historical note by Charles Henry Casey, contained in the 1932 Princeton Press edition of Hastings's *Emigrants' Guide to Oregon and California.*

234 no one traveled it twice: Strictly speaking, Hastings himself traveled it twice: eastward in 1846 to lure wagons to the route, and then westward when he turned around and led the Harlan-Young Party. But that hardly counts, in that he had little choice but to take the route he was advocating for others. Nobody voluntarily used the cut-off twice.

234 Elizabeth Graves's money: McClain, "Relics of a Historic Tragedy."

236 "It seems ages": letter from Virginia Reed to McGlashan, 8-11-92, folder 46, McGlashan Papers, Bancroft Library.

236 hikers stranded: "Storms Hinder Search for Hikers in Sierra," *San Francisco Chronicle,* 10-21-2004, 1.

237 statistical analyses of death rates: Donald K. Grayson, "Donner Party Deaths: A Demographic Assessment," *Journal of Anthropological Research* 46, no. 3 (Fall 1990): 223–42; and Stephen A. McCurdy, "Epidemiology of Disaster: The Donner Party," *Western Journal of Medicine* 160, no. 4 (April 1994): 338–42. For a more accessible version of the Grayson findings, see Jared Diamond, "Living Through the Donner Party," *Discover,* March 1992, 100–107. Some of the ages used in these studies are inaccurate, but the errors are relatively minor and do not affect the larger conclusions. For my own description of age categories in this section, I use the ages from Kristin Johnson's Web site, "New Light on the Donner Party," at www.utahcrossroads.org/DonnerParty, and I assume that approximations are accurate.

238 health effects of social networks: For a recent summary of such evidence, see Uchino, *Social Support,* especially 1–8 and 54–108. See also Putnam, *Bowling,* 326–35. For Andersonville, see Dora L. Costa and Matthew E. Kahn, "Surviving Andersonville: The Benefits of Social Networks in POW Camps," National Bureau of Economic Research Working Paper Series, at www.nber.org/papers/w11825.

238 fifteen trapped without a relative: Luis and Salvador, included in the fifteen, were murdered during the escape of the Forlorn Hope, although they probably would have died anyway.

239 "He gave up": letter from James Reed, 7-2-47, in Morgan, *Overland,* 301–5.

239 Reed children finding gold: letter from James Reed, 8-14-48, James Frazier Reed Papers, Bancroft Library.

Chapter 31

240 "A more shocking scene": *California Star,* 4-10-47.

241 Monterey paper: *Californian,* 4-24-47.

241 "In the forenoon": letter from Frances Donner to McGlashan, 4-17-79, folder 54, McGlashan Papers, Bancroft Library.

242 Donner Party as anomaly: For an excellent discussion of the overall historical context, including a discussion of death rates on the trail, see Unruh, *Plains Across,* 321–52.

242 "candid persons": *California Star,* 3-13-47.

242 "a contrary and contentious": *California Star,* 2-13-47.

243 Native Sons of the Golden West, including quotations: For a series of letters from H. W. Chapman, the head of the monument committee, to Eliza Donner, see HM 58139, HM 58142, HM 58143, and HM 58145, all in Eliza Poor Donner Houghton Papers, Huntington Library.

244 Eliza Donner at monument dedication: Her description of the events is in HM 58113, Eliza Poor Donner Houghton Papers, Huntington Library.

246 "Oh, what a pleasant": letter from Patty Reed to McGlashan, 4-16-79, folder 38, McGlashan Papers, Bancroft Library.

Selected Bibliography

Andrews, Thomas F. "The Ambitions of Lansford W. Hastings: A Study in Western Myth-Making." *Pacific Historical Review* 39, no. 4 (Nov. 1970): 473–91.
———."The Controversial Hastings Overland Guide: A Reassessment." *Pacific Historical Review* 37, no. 1 (Feb. 1968): 21–34.
Askenasy, Hans. *Cannibalism: From Sacrifice to Survival.* Amherst, N.Y.: Prometheus Books, 1994.
Bean, Walton, and James J. Rawls. *California: An Interpretive History.* New York: McGraw-Hill, 1983.
Bidwell, John. *Echoes of the Past About California.* Chicago: Lakeside Press, 1928.
———. *A Journey to California.* San Francisco: John Henry Nash, Printer, 1937.
Billington, Ray Allen, and Martin Ridge. *Westward Expansion: A History of the American Frontier.* New York: Macmillan, 1982.
Boag, Peter. "Idaho's Fort Hall as a Western Crossroads." *Overland Journal* 16, no. 1 (Spring 1998): 20–26.
Bond, Charles E. "Story of Donner Party Is Told by Member." *Pasadena Star-News,* Feb. 20, 1918.
Brands, H. W. *The Age of Gold: The California Gold Rush and the New American Dream.* New York: Doubleday, 2002.
Brayer, Herbert O. "Insurance Against the Hazards of Western Life." *Mississippi Valley Historical Review* 34, no. 2 (Sept. 1947): 221–36.
Breen, John. "Pioneer Memoirs." Statement to H. H. Bancroft, Nov. 19, 1877, CD-51, Bancroft Library.
Brock, Richard K., ed. *Emigrant Trails West: A Guide to the California Trail.* Reno, Nev.: Trails West, 2000.
Bryant, Edwin. *What I Saw in California.* Lincoln: University of Nebraska Press, 1985.
Calabro, Marian. *The Perilous Journey of the Donner Party.* New York: Clarion Books, 1999.
Camp, Charles L., ed. *James Clyman, Frontiersman.* Portland, Ore.: Champoeg Press, 1960.
Canfield, Gae Whitney. *Sarah Winnemucca of the Northern Paiutes.* Norman: University of Oklahoma Press, 1983.
Carson, Thomas, ed. *Gale Encyclopedia of U.S. Economic History.* Detroit: Gale Group, 1999.
Chaffin, Tom. *Pathfinder: John Charles Frémont and the Course of American Empire.* New York: Hill & Wang, 2002.
Crawford, Mark. *Encyclopedia of the Mexican-American War.* Santa Barbara, Calif.: ABC-CLIO, 1999.

Crawford, Medorem. *Journal of Medorem Crawford.* Eugene, Ore.: Star Job Office, 1897.

Cumming, John. "Lansford Hastings' Michigan Connection." *Overland Journal* 16, no. 3 (Fall 1998): 17–28.

Curran, Harold. *Fearful Crossing: The Central Overland Trail Through Nevada.* Las Vegas: Nevada Publications, 1982.

Del Bene, Terry. *Donner Party Cookbook.* Norman, Okla.: Horse Creek Publications, 2003.

DeVoto, Bernard. *The Year of Decision, 1846.* New York: Truman Talley Books/St. Martin's Griffin, 2000.

Donner Houghton, Eliza P. *The Expedition of the Donner Party and Its Tragic Fate.* Lincoln: University of Nebraska Press, 1997.

Eberstadt, Edward. *A Transcript of the Fort Sutter Papers, Together with the Historical Commentaries Accompanying Them.* Privately published, 1922.

Farb, Peter, and George Armelagos. *Consuming Passions: The Anthropology of Eating.* Boston: Houghton Mifflin, 1980.

Farquhar, Francis P. *History of the Sierra Nevada.* Berkeley: University of California Press, 1965.

Franzwa, Gregory M. *Maps of the California Trail.* Tucson, Ariz.: Patrice Press, 1999.

Frazier, Donald S., ed. *The United States and Mexico at War.* New York: Macmillan Reference USA, 1998.

Giffen, Helen S., ed. *The Diaries of Peter Ducker.* Georgetown, Calif.: Talisman Press, 1966.

Goldman, Laurence R., ed. *The Anthropology of Cannibalism.* Westport, Conn.: Bergin & Garvey, 1999.

Guetzkow, Harold Steere, and Paul Hoover Bowman. *Men and Hunger: A Psychological Manual for Relief Workers.* Elgin, Ill.: Brethren Publishing House, 1946.

Gzowski, Peter. *The Sacrament: A True Story of Survival.* New York: Atheneum, 1980.

Hall, Carroll D. *Donner Miscellany.* San Francisco: Book Club of California, 1947.

Hammond, George P. *The Larkin Papers: Personal, Business, and Official Correspondence of Thomas Oliver Larkin, Merchant and United States Consul in California.* Berkeley: University of California Press, 1959.

Hardcastle, Nate, ed. *Survive: Stories of Castaways and Cannibals.* New York: Thunder's Mouth Press, 2001.

Hardesty, Donald L. *The Archaeology of the Donner Party.* Reno: University of Nevada Press, 1997.

Harris, Marvin. *Cannibals and Kings: The Origins of Cultures.* New York: Random House, 1977.

Harrison, G. A., ed. *Famine.* New York: Oxford University Press, 1988.

Hasselstrom, Linda M., ed. *Journal of a Mountain Man: James Clyman.* Missoula, Mont.: Mountain Press Publishing, 1984.

Hassibe, W. R., and W. G. Keck. *The Great Salt Lake.* Reston, Va.: U.S. Department of the Interior, 1991.

Hastings, Lansford W. *The Emigrants' Guide to Oregon and California.* Facsimile ed., with a new introduction by Mary Nance Spence. New York: Da Capo Press, 1969.

———. *The Emigrants' Guide to Oregon and California.* Facsimile ed., with a historical note and bibliography by Charles Henry Carey. Princeton: Princeton University Press, 1932.

Hawkins, Bruce R., and David B. Madsen. *Excavation of the Donner-Reed Wagons: Historic Archaeology Along the Hastings Cutoff.* Salt Lake City: University of Utah Press, 1990.

Hill, Mary. *Geology of the Sierra Nevada.* Rev. ed. Berkeley: University of California Press, 2006.

Hill, William E. *The California Trail Yesterday and Today: A Pictorial Journey Along the California Trail.* Boulder, Colo.: Pruett Publishing, 1986.

Holmes, Kenneth L. *Covered Wagon Women: Diaries and Letters from the Western Trails, 1840–1849.* Lincoln: University of Nebraska Press, 1983.

Houston, James D. *Snow Mountain Passage: A Novel of the Donner Party.* New York: Knopf, 2001.

Huntress, Keith. *A Checklist of Narratives of Shipwrecks and Disasters at Sea to 1860, with Summaries, Notes, and Comments.* Ames: Iowa State University Press, 1979.

Johnson, Kristin. *Unfortunate Emigrants: Narratives of the Donner Party.* Logan: Utah State University Press, 1996.

Johnston, Verna R. *Sierra Nevada: The Naturalist's Companion.* Rev. ed. Berkeley: University of California Press, 1998.

Kamler, Kenneth. *Surviving the Extremes: A Doctor's Journey to the Limits of Human Endurance.* New York: St. Martin's Press, 2004.

Keithley, George. *The Donner Party.* New York: George Braziller, 1972.

Kelly, Charles. *Salt Desert Trails.* Salt Lake City: Western Epics, 1969.

King, Joseph A. *Winter of Entrapment: A New Look at the Donner Party.* Toronto: P. D. Meany, 1992.

———. *Winter of Entrapment: A New Look at the Donner Party.* 3rd ed. Lafayette, Calif.: K&K Publications, 1998.

King, Joseph A., and Jack Steed. "John Baptiste Trudeau of the Donner Party: Rascal or Hero?" *California History* 74, no. 2 (Summer 1995): 162–73.

———. "Newly Discovered Documents on the Donner Party: The Donner Girls Tell Their Story." *Dogtown Territorial Quarterly,* Summer 1996, 6, 16–24.

Korns, J. Roderic, Will Bagley, Dale L. Morgan, and Harold Schindler, eds. *West from Fort Bridger: The Pioneering of Immigrant Trails Across Utah, 1846–1850.* Rev. ed. Logan: Utah State University Press, 1994.

Laurgaard, Rachel K. *Patty's Reed Doll.* Davis, Calif.: Tomato Enterprises, 1989.

Lavender, David. *Westward Vision: The Story of the Oregon Trail.* New York: McGraw-Hill, 1963.

Leckie, Robert. *From Sea to Shining Sea: From the War of 1812 to the Mexican War, the Saga of America's Expansion.* New York: HarperCollins, 1993.

Leitch, Barbara A. *A Concise Dictionary of Indian Tribes of North America.* Algonac, Mich.: Reference Publications, 1979.

Leslie, Edward E. *Desperate Journeys, Abandoned Souls.* Boston: Houghton Mifflin, 1988.

Levy, JoAnn. *Unsettling the West: Eliza Farnham and Georgiana Bruce Kirby in Frontier California.* Berkeley, Calif.: Heyday Books, 2004.

Lewis, David Rich. "Argonauts and the Overland Trail Experience: Method and Theory." *Western Historical Quarterly* 16 (July 1985): 285–305.

Lienhard, Heinrich. *From St. Louis to Sutter's Fort, 1846.* Norman: University of Oklahoma Press, 1961.

————. *A Pioneer at Sutter's Fort, 1846–1850*. Los Angeles: Calafia Society, 1941.

Limburg, Peter R. *Deceived: The Story of the Donner Party*. Pacifica, Calif.: IPS Books, 1998.

Lovejoy, Asa Amos Lawrence. "Founding of Portland." Statement to H. H. Bancroft, BANC MSS P-A 45, Bancroft Library.

McClain, Jim. "Relics of a Historic Tragedy." *Overland Journal* 23, no. 1 (Spring 2005): 39–42.

McGlashan, C. F. *History of the Donner Party: A Tragedy of the Sierra*. Stanford: Stanford University Press, 1947.

McGlashan, M. Nona. *Give Me a Mountain Meadow*. Fresno, Calif.: Pioneer Publishing, 1977.

McGlashan, M. Nona, and Betty H. McGlashan, eds. *From the Desk of Truckee's C. F. McGlashan*. Truckee, Calif.: Truckee-Donner Historical Society, 1986.

MacGregor, Greg. *Overland: The California Emigrant Trail of 1841–1870*. Albuquerque: University of New Mexico Press, 1996.

McLaughlin, Mark. *The Donner Party: Weathering the Storm*. Carnelian Bay, Calif.: Mic Mac Publishing, 2007.

McLynn, Frank. *Wagons West: The Epic Story of America's Overland Trails*. New York: Grove Press, 2002.

McPhee, John. *Basin and Range*. New York: Farrar, Straus & Giroux, 1981.

McPherson, James M. *Battle Cry of Freedom: The Civil War Era*. New York: Oxford University Press, 1988.

Malinowski, Sharon, and Anna Sheets, eds. *The Gale Encyclopedia of Native American Tribes*. Detroit: Gale, 1998.

Mattes, Merrill J. *The Great Platte River Road: The Covered Wagon Mainline via Fort Kearny to Fort Laramie*. N.p.: Nebraska State Historical Society, 1969.

Merk, Frederick. *History of the Westward Movement*. New York: Knopf, 1980.

Miller, David E. "The Parting of the Ways on the Oregon Trail—the East Terminal of the Sublette Cutoff." *Annals of Wyoming* 45, no. 1 (Spring 1973): 47–52.

Mobley, Richard Scott. *"A Magic Mirror": Representations of the Donner Party, 1846–1997*. Dissertation, University of California, Santa Cruz, 1997.

Mokyr, Joel, ed. *The Oxford Encyclopedia of Economic History*, vol. 2. New York: Oxford University Press, 2003.

Morgan, Dale. *The Great Salt Lake*. Lincoln: University of Nebraska Press, 1975.

————. *Jedediah Smith and the Opening of the West*. Lincoln: University of Nebraska Press, 1953.

————, ed. *Overland in 1846: Diaries and Letters of the California-Oregon Trail*, vols. 1–2. Lincoln: University of Nebraska Press, 1963.

Morgan, Dale, and Eleanor Towles Harris. *The Rocky Mountain Journals of William Marshall Anderson*. San Marino, Calif.: Huntington Library, 1967.

Mullen, Frank, Jr. *The Donner Party Chronicles*. Reno: Nevada Humanities Committee, 1997.

Munkres, Robert L. "Independence Rock and Devil's Gate." *Annals of Wyoming* 40, no. 1 (April 1968): 23–40.

————. "The Plains Indian Threat on the Oregon Trail Before 1860." *Annals of Wyoming* 40, no. 2 (Oct. 1968): 193–221.

————. "Wives, Mothers, Daughters: Women's Life on the Road West." *Annals of Wyoming* 42, no. 2 (Oct. 1970): 191–224.

Myres, Sandra L. *Westering Women and the Frontier Experience, 1800–1915.* Albuquerque: University of New Mexico Press, 1982.

Neelands, Barbara. "Reason P. Tucker: The Quiet Pioneer." *Gleanings* 4, no. 2 (March 1989). Napa, Calif.: Napa County Historical Society.

Nelson Limerick, Patricia. *The Legacy of Conquest: The Unbroken Past of the American West.* New York: Norton, 1987.

Nevers, Jo Ann. *Wa She Shu: A Washo Tribal History.* Reno: Inter-Tribal Council of Nevada, 1976.

North, Douglass C. *The Economic Growth of the United States, 1790–1860.* Englewood Cliffs, N.J.: Prentice-Hall, 1961.

Northrup, Cynthia Clark, ed. *The American Economy: A Historical Encyclopedia,* vol. 1. Santa Barbara, Calif.: ABC-Clio, 2003.

Paden, Irene D. *Prairie Schooner Detours.* New York: Macmillan, 1949.

————. *The Wake of the Prairie Schooner.* New York: Macmillan, 1943.

Palmer, David E. *A Walking Tour of Donner Pass.* N.p.: David E. Palmer, 2002.

Parkman, Francis. *The Oregon Trail.* New York: Signet, 1978.

Petrinovich, Lewis. *The Cannibal Within.* New York: Aldine De Gruyter, 2000.

Philbrick, Nathaniel. *In the Heart of the Sea: The Tragedy of the Whaleship* Essex. New York: Viking, 2000.

Pigney, Joseph. *For Fear We Shall Perish: The Story of the Donner Party Disaster.* New York: E. P. Dutton, 1961.

Putnam, Robert D. *Bowling Alone: The Collapse and Revival of American Community.* New York: Simon & Schuster, 2000.

Rawls, James J. *New Directions in California History: A Book of Readings.* New York: McGraw-Hill, 1988.

Read, Piers Paul. *Alive: The Story of the Andes Survivors.* Philadelphia: J. B. Lippincott, 1974.

Redfern, Ron. *The Making of a Continent.* New York: Times Books, 1983.

Reed Murphy, Virginia. *Across the Plains in the Donner Party: A Personal Narrative of the Overland Trip to California.* Golden, Colo.: Outbooks, 1980.

Reid, John Phillip. *Law for the Elephant: Property and Social Behavior on the Overland Trail.* San Marino, Calif.: Huntington Library, 1980.

————. *Policing the Elephant: Crime, Punishment, and Social Behavior on the Overland Trail.* San Marino, Calif.: Huntington Library, 1997.

Rezneck, Samuel. *Business Depressions and Financial Panics: Essays in American Business and Economic History.* Westport, Conn.: Greenwood Publishing, 1968.

Roberts, David. *A Newer World: Kit Carson, John C. Frémont, and the Claiming of the American West.* New York: Simon & Schuster, 2000.

Roland, Charles G. *Courage Under Siege: Starvation, Disease, and Death in the Warsaw Ghetto.* New York: Oxford University Press, 1992.

Rose, James J. "Sierra Trailblazers: First Pioneer Wagons over the Sierra Nevada." *Pioneer* 22, no. 1 (Dec. 1999): 12–25.

Russell, Sharman Apt. *Hunger: An Unnatural History.* New York: Basic Books, 2005.

Saunders, Richard L. *Eloquence from a Silent World: A Descriptive Bibliography of the Published Writings of Dale L. Morgan*. Salt Lake City: Caramon Press, 1990.

Seguin, Marilyn W. *One Eternal Winter: The Story of What Happened at Donner Pass, Winter 1846–47*. Wellesley, Mass.: Branden Books, 2001.

Shaffer, Leslie L. D. "The Management of Organized Wagon Trains on the Overland Trail." *Missouri Historical Review* 55, no. 4 (July 1961): 355–65.

Shumway, George, Edward Durell, and Howard C. Frey. *Conestoga Wagon, 1750–1850*. York, Pa: Shumway, 1966.

Simpson, A. W. Brian. *Cannibalism and the Common Law*. Chicago: University of Chicago Press, 1984.

Smith, Genny, ed. *Sierra East: Edge of the Great Basin*. Berkeley: University of California Press, 2000.

Snow, William James. *The Great Basin Before the Coming of the Mormons*. Dissertation, University of California, Berkeley, 1923.

Solomon, Susan. *The Coldest March: Scott's Fatal Antarctic Expedition*. New Haven: Yale University Press, 2001.

Soule, Frank, John H. Gihon, and James Nisbet. *The Annals of San Francisco*. Berkeley, Calif.: Berkeley Hills Books, 1998.

Steed, Jack. *The Donner Party Rescue Site: Johnson's Ranch on Bear River*. Rev. and expanded ed. Sacramento: Jack Steed, 1999.

Stegner, Wallace. *The Gathering of Zion: The Story of the Mormon Trail*. New York: McGraw-Hill, 1964.

———. *Mormon Country*. New York: Duell, Sloan & Pearce, 1942.

Stewart, George R. *The California Trail: An Epic with Many Heroes*. New York: McGraw-Hill, 1962.

———. *Ordeal by Hunger: The Story of the Donner Party*. Boston: Houghton Mifflin, 1960.

———. "The Prairie Schooner Got Them There." *American Heritage* 13, no. 2 (Feb. 1962): 4–17, 98–102.

Stookey, Walter M. *Fatal Decision: The Tragic Story of the Donner Party*. Salt Lake City: Deseret Book Company, 1950.

Storer, Tracy I., Robert L. Usinger, and David Lukas. *Sierra Nevada Natural History*. Berkeley: University of California Press, 2004.

Tannahill, Reay. *Flesh and Blood: A History of the Cannibal Complex*. Boston: Little, Brown, 1996.

Trenholm, Virginia Cole, and Maurine Carley. *The Shoshonis: Sentinels of the Rockies*. Norman: University of Oklahoma Press, 1964.

Trigger, Bruce G., and Wilcomb E. Washburn, eds. *The Cambridge History of the Native Peoples of the Americas*, vol. 1, *North America*. New York: Cambridge University Press, 1996–2000.

Tucker, Todd. *The Great Starvation Experiment: The Heroic Men Who Starved So That Millions Could Live*. New York: Free Press, 2006.

Uchino, Bert N. *Social Support and Physical Health: Understanding the Health Consequences of Relationships*. New Haven: Yale University Press, 2004.

Unruh, John D., Jr. *The Plains Across: The Overland Emigrants and the Trans-Mississippi West, 1840–60*. Urbana: University of Illinois Press, 1982.

Vestal, Stanley. *Jim Bridger: Mountain Man*. Lincoln: University of Nebraska Press, 1946.

Waldman, Carl. *Encyclopedia of Native American Tribes*. Rev. ed. New York: Facts on File, 1999.

Ware, Joseph E. *The Emigrants' Guide to California*. Princeton: Princeton University Press, 1932.

Werner, Emmy E. *Pioneer Children of the Journey West*. Boulder, Colo.: Westview Press, 1995.

Willis, James F., and Martin L. Primack. *An Economic History of the United States*. Englewood Cliffs, N.J.: Prentice-Hall, 1989.

Winnemucca Hopkins, Sarah. *Life Among the Piutes: Their Wrongs and Claims*. Reno: University of Nevada Press, 1994.

Wise, H. A. *Los Gringos: An Inside View of Mexico and California, with Wanderings in Peru, Chile, and Polynesia*. New York: Baker & Scribner, 1850.

Archival Materials

Bancroft Library, University of California, Berkeley
C. F. McGlashan Papers
James Frazier Reed Papers
Braun Research Library, Southwest Museum of the American Indian,
Autry National Center
George Wharton James Papers
Huntington Library
Eliza Poor Donner Houghton Papers
Sherman Otis Houghton Papers
Sutter's Fort State Historic Park, California State Parks
Martha J. (Patty) Reed Lewis Papers

Index